TWENTIETH CENTURY VIEWS

The aim of this series is to present the best
in contemporary critical opinion on major
authors, providing a twentieth century perspective on their changing status in an era
of profound revaluation.

Maynard Mack, *Series Editor*
Yale University

GOETHE

A COLLECTION OF CRITICAL ESSAYS

Edited by

Victor Lange

Prentice-Hall, Inc.   *Englewood Cliffs, N. J.*

A SPECTRUM BOOK

Current printing (last number):
10 9 8 7 6 5 4 3 2 1

Contents

v

Introduction

by Victor Lange

None of the great writers of the western world has more profoundly influenced the convictions and attitudes of his own countrymen than Goethe; yet none has been more hesitantly received abroad. While he has been for the Germans an exemplary representative of a life in which extraordinary gifts of imagination and reflection were made to serve, perhaps for the last time, a unified and effective vision of man, elsewhere he has remained a remote figure of formidable scope but of peculiar national and historical limitations. Neither the man nor his role in the intellectual history of Europe has exercised quite the remarkable fascination that has been aroused at home. If to the Germans Goethe's evolving and maturing comprehension of the human purpose in an increasingly complex social setting eventually led to a classical synthesis of private and collective responsibility, his life and work have represented to foreign readers—who know little more than *Werther* or the first part of *Faust*—the very prototype of the self-centered romantic, the rebel against the clichés of religious, literary, or social orthodoxy, who turned too soon into a purveyor of generalized wisdom.

No doubt, the shadow of this statuesque Olympian has for long made it difficult or unpromising to confront Goethe's work directly and with the sort of intellectual curiosity that his singularly varied achievement requires. Too often, in the century after his death in 1832, Goethe loomed as a monolithic and peremptory figure who found allegiance mainly among those who sought a hero, a prophet, or a saint, rather than as a mind and a poet of extraordinary perception and responsibility.

To read Mr. Leppmann's account of *The German Image of Goethe* is to be shown the curious uses to which a great writer can be put by his own society. Among his French, English, and American worshipers (and detractors), the reception of Goethe's fame is no less revealing: it is a history of sometimes eloquent but seldom judicious reverence, of vigorous expressions of distaste, of often warped perspectives, and of misunderstanding. There was no doubt in Emerson's mind that "there is something gigantic about the man, measure him how you will"; and in Matthew Arnold's, that Goethe was "the greatest poet of modern times . . . because, having a considerable gift for poetry, he was, at the same time in the width, depth and richness of his criticism of life, by far our greatest modern man."

But these panegyrical flourishes have lost their ready appeal; their categorical assumption of greatness does injustice to Goethe as well as to his modern readers. Yet the doubts in the absolute validity of Goethe's work will not quite cease: T. S. Eliot was convinced that because "Goethe appears to a foreign eye limited by his age, by his language, and by his culture, and, like our own nineteenth-century authors, a little provincial, we cannot call him a universal classic." And Karl Jaspers warned in 1949 that our respect for Goethe's incomparable genius should not blind us to his shortcomings and his limited relevance for our time. Where, then, lies the indubitable living substance of Goethe's work, and which are the aspects of his achievement that our twentieth-century view has found most important?

It is an indication of the peculiarly compelling, even iridescent force of Goethe's mind that the enormous and barely surveyable canon of criticism devoted to him and his work should on the whole be more telling of the opinions of his critics than illuminating about his own intentions as an artist. To a significant degree, Goethe was the representative of a unique historical and local situation: the end of feudal Europe, the development (in Germany later than in France or Britain) of a middle-class culture, and the emergence of various modes of rebellious individualism that turned almost simultaneously against past orthodoxy and the coming economic, technical, and political revolutions. In this spectacular age Goethe participated with incomparable and unflagging intensity of judgment and an astonishing awareness of the political as well as intellectual issues of the day. As the nineteenth century in Germany contemplated its own recent past, it focused with dubious nostalgia upon the values that were asserted at that time but which now seemed irrevocably lost—upon an individualism that had flourished in a benevolently directed and coherent society, sustained by peremptory idealism and a faith not so much in uncertain opportunities as in the reassuring continuity of human endeavor.

The superficiality of this latter-day view of an age for which Goethe's life seemed the envied epitome is obvious; yet for those who came immediately after him it was easy to see in his early work the triumphant emancipation from uncongenial and foreign conventions of taste, and in his later career a paradoxical tendency to comply with decorum and tradition. In fact, it is as an altogether coherent and lucid record of a vast historical crisis that we must understand the whole of Goethe's accomplishment. For it was not merely the accident of his presence during an age of unsurpassed change, extending from the Seven Years' War to the revolutionary uprisings throughout Europe in the 1830s, from Richardson to Stendhal, Balzac, and Poe, from Handel to Mendelssohn, that makes Goethe a conspicuous figure. What distinguishes him from a host of remarkable contemporaries is his readiness, from youth to old age, to draw the world about him into his constantly receptive, unceasingly active and reflective mind. As we read through the enormous body of his more than fourteen thousand letters, or his conversations and the thousands of pages of his notebooks, it is this involvement in what goes on about him—sometimes enthusiastic, more often reserved, but always responsible—that must astonish us most. "He was alive," said William James, "at every pore of his skin, and received every impression in a sort of undistracted leisure; which makes the movement of his mental machinery one of the most extraordinary exhibitions which this planet can ever have witnessed."

Although his literary work is his central achievement, he was a man of letters in the comprehensive sense that few of his great contemporaries—Voltaire, perhaps, but no one after him—ever attained. His poetry, his plays, his novels, are for us the chief evidence of his creative intelligence. That he was, in an almost fanatical manner, interested in scientific matters no longer surprises us, though it puzzled and irritated his nineteenth-century critics; indeed, we have come to see his preoccupation with science (or "natural philosophy"), however tentative and at times wrong-headed, as the essential premise of his literary work. This scientific interest sustained his thinking and his writing and gave coherence and meaning to what might otherwise have been merely an effervescent romantic genius. As he remained attached to certain aspects of the feudal past, so he clung in his view of nature to the tradition of empirical rationality. It is obvious that his notion of science was not, in the modern sense, objective, specific, and delimiting: his purpose in dealing with natural phenomena was to discover models that would satisfy his curiosity as to the principles of functioning, of relationships, of interdependence. Moreover, scientific procedure, with its concern for cohesion and continuity, seemed for him to provide a system in analogy to which alternatives of action or moral options could be demonstrated and argued. He insisted, to the despair of his objectivist critics, upon a constant awareness of the presuppositions and perspectives of judgment, indeed, upon the indispensable element of subjectivity, for any definition of scientific data. For science, he maintained, must serve the human obligation not to impose abstractly, but to discover empirically, the forms by which life in its totality can be understood and ordered. Form and substance were, therefore, in his morphological thinking, aspects of the same phenomenon; throughout his work, whether scientific or literary, he argued this unity of substance and form and the capacity of the imagination to serve as the instrument by which we articulate the shape and structure of the world about us.

One or two of the essays in this volume suggest that the past hundred years may well have been wrong in detaching the poet Goethe from the scientist, from the administrator or the social critic. It is precisely a measure of his greatness that, as he matured, Goethe recognized the need to find forms of order and purpose for his overwhelming imaginative gifts, forms that were not merely derived from prevailing conventions, but adequate to his own intellectual curiosity and that of his liveliest contemporaries. In this search he remained an empiricist from beginning to end: no conceptual scheme—Christian, Kantian, or Hegelian—kept him from enquiring into the logic of the visible world. History, whether of individuals or civilizations, was for him the tangible sum of available forms of experience; to find and achieve form, to demonstrate it as the instrument of truth, seemed to him the natural purpose of a responsible life.

The complexity of Goethe's own personality and of his relationships to others has only recently become apparent. To several of his early biographers, his self-willed manner—sometimes extravagantly impulsive, sometimes drily pedantic—his egotism in love affairs, and his almost obsequious attachment to aristocratic society, seemed as perplexing and irreconcilable as the contrasts between his exuberant early lyrics and the discursive, mannered prose of his later years. G. H. Lewes' *Life of Goethe,* the first of innumerable biographical accounts, conveys a sense of disquiet originating in the discrepancy between the career of the inspired poet and its frustration by social preoccupations. Barker Fairley's studies superbly demonstrate the precarious balance of creative and destructive impulses as the very condition of Goethe's greatness.

But what has most significantly enlarged our view of Goethe is, beyond a more sensitive reading of his biography, the manner in which we have come to relate Goethe's life to his work. The suggestion, carefully cultivated by Goethe himself, that his writings should be taken as documents of a grand confession, has for long induced critics to assume a close, perhaps too direct, relationship between incidents of his life and their rendering in his works. That this is in some sense appropriate is undeniable: Goethe is, after all, one of the most gifted representatives of a "romantic" sensibility, in which the flow of the imagination illuminates the individual experience. But as we have enlarged our comprehension of the intricate ways of his life, his major works, though closely related to his intellectual and emotional development, have, in the light of modern literary criticism, proved to be superbly inventive and coherent works of art.

It is in his poetry that Goethe's art is most impressive. There is no European poet like him. His straightforward and definite manner and his confidence in the capacity of the object or the gesture or, indeed, the word itself to serve as the vehicle of experienced meaning may not be sufficiently radical for some poets and readers of our time, for whom the oblique and fragmentary statement offers a more plausible reaction to our dehumanized life. But if we read his poetry intelligently, we shall find it extraordinarily rewarding and valid. His imagination is inexhaustible, concrete, and disciplined; he seems to command every available formal device; he is always ready to experiment. Above all, he uses and shapes the resources of his language as no other German poet before him, and creates in his poetry and prose a manner and a style that have, for better or for worse, remained compelling to the present day. It characterizes the mobility and the scope of his artistry that he could produce, almost simultaneously, magnificent hymnic poetry, biting satirical persiflage, sustained narrative verse, and incomparably personal lyrics. Emil Staiger and Barker Fairley have shown us the range of his craftsmanship and have reminded us that, if language was for Goethe—as it was for Herder or Blake—the very shape of memory, individual and collective, then poetry was the supreme form of the imagination, of exploring the ambiguities of the human condition, the means of bridging the gulf between irrational, instinctive impulse and considered persuasion.

It has been easy, in so brilliantly gifted a poet, to underrate the degree of his critical intelligence; but the conscience of the artist was alert in him at all times, even during the early years of almost compulsive lyrical effervescence. In the several phases of his development he produced poetry of rare intellectual and emotional resonance that drew into itself the contemporary alternatives of the classical as well as the romantic perception. Even so, it was only upon Schiller's prodding that he evolved tentative formal principles of literary judgment and systematic reflections on the function of literature. The "classicism" of those ten years of one of the most remarkable friendships in literary history is based upon a faith that antiquity, seen with modern eyes, can offer evidence of that interplay of experience and reflection which Goethe valued above all. But his respect for the classical tradition and his efforts towards typological and morphological criticism owed far more to his scientific convictions of an organically developing structure of order than to Schiller's philosophical idealism.

Goethe's emphasis upon the unity and wholeness of the work of art in an age of subjective speculation led him to recognize in the "symbol"—before that term became a key concept of romantic criticism—the concrete representation of a total experience. The symbolic mode remained characteristic of his perception of the world as well as of his poetic production; it "changes the phenomenon into the idea, the idea into the image, in such a way that the idea remains always infinitely active and unapproachable in the image, and will, even though it be expressed in all languages, remain inexpressible." *

To recognize the symbolic principle, in its classical as well as modern connotations, as the unifying element of Goethe's mature thinking is to gain a fresh perspective on his purposes and procedures as a writer. His plays, less theatrical than literary (though produced with the intention of serving the didactic mission of the theater), have revealed to recent criticism, beyond any biographical relevance, their specific "poetic" structures: *Tasso, Iphigenie,* and so ambitious a fragment as *The Natural Daughter* indicate the range of Goethe's preoccupation with symbolic drama. It is, of course, his *Faust* that has received the most persistent attention. The baffling issue of the continuity or unity of its two parts has often been weighed. No doubt, in the total compass of its intellectual movement, the work advances from a desperate assertion of self in the first part to a series of increasingly skeptical confrontations of the Faustian sensibility with the forms and traditions of modern culture. But the poem is an enormous weave of symbolic statements

---

* From *Maximen und Reflexionen,* No. 1113.

rather than a dramatic biography of an individual bent upon redemption by passion or by works. Its hero is the modern mind, radical in its claims to knowledge and power, emancipated from any sustaining orthodoxy, and driven to the tragic pursuit of truth in existence itself. In Goethe's own term, *Faust* is an "incommensurable work," a grand canvas of figures and images and poetic forms that had grown slowly over half a century, sometimes turning upon the fortunes of Faust himself, more often moving across a vast territory of experience and reflection. If the colorful and romantic melodrama of the first part seemed to earlier readers the most appealing achievement of the young Goethe, the second part is for us the inexhaustible document of his old age. It is the sum of his life and of his efforts as an artist; in it the themes and intentions of all his other writings—poetry, fiction, or science—found a magnificent echo.

The works of the last twenty-five years of Goethe's life have exercised for modern readers a fascination that the nineteenth century would not have shared, and this fact indicates most strikingly the shift and extension of our critical predilections. His mind focused increasingly and with remarkable detachment on the effects of the political and social changes that the new century was about to bring. He would not abandon his conservative faith, but his conversations and his letters leave as little doubt as do his writings that he recognized the ideological challenge to the traditions on which his own moral, scientific, and aesthetic convictions were founded. Irresponsible subjectivity and economic and technological ruthlessness appeared to him equally disquieting threats to that rational humanism in which he firmly believed. His answer was not a stubborn and melancholy reiteration of his attachment to past values, but a sober and self-denying attempt to relate the experienced truths of the particularity and unity of life to the confused realities about him.

Throughout his work, from *Werther* and *Tasso* to *Wilhelm Meister's Apprenticeship,* the threatened equilibrium between the energies of the self and the collective order had been a recurring theme; now, in *Elective Affinities* or in *Wilhelm Meister's Travels,* the specific event, meticulously and fully represented, served as a symbol of the universal and typical; the large issues of communal responsibility, again demonstrated concretely and without pathos, were to indicate the limits as well as the opportunities of the resolute individual. Goethe's humanism is never more impressive, never more understanding, never more appealing than in these late works, and none represents this vision more superbly than that magic cycle of serene poetry, allusively entitled *West-Easterly Divan*. In no other work is Goethe a purer, a wiser poet; nowhere are the ingredients of great poetry more movingly combined: an intelligent view of the human condition, an unfailing receptivity of all energies of the senses, and a steady faith in man's capacity to justify himself within a universe which may, as a whole, remain beyond comprehension, but which is the setting of all our definitions and projects. It is poetry of an intensely personal kind, light to the point of casualness, kaleidoscopic and transparent in its wisdom, yet sustained by a belief in the importance of the forms and symbols of culture, whether classical or modern, western or eastern.

Wilhelm Meister's Travels, equally characteristic of the tenets and the style of the aged Goethe, is less obviously appealing. Earlier readers found this sequel to the *Apprenticeship* painfully disjointed, and were profoundly discomfited by what seemed an offensive mixture of stilted operatic behavior, of supernatural allegory, and of discursive intrusions by the narrator. "It is tiresome," said G. H. Lewes, "it is fragmentary, it is dull, and it is often ill-written." This curious novel has revealed only today, as we have become aware of the surprising technical possibilities of fiction, its intricate formal purpose. *Wilhelm Meister's Travels* is perhaps the earliest example of a large-scale narrative whose irregular shape is the result neither of whim nor of artistic indifference, but of a search for an idiom in which social and philosophical alternatives destructive to the framework of a conventional, realistic novel could be rendered intelligible. In metaphysical figures and incidents, interpolated essays and reflections, didactic and ironical at the same time, Goethe here elaborates the great issues of modern man—his relationship to the world about him, his values, pragmatic and transcendental, and the chances of his fulfillment in a society of increasing abstraction. All supposedly stable positions, Goethe argues, all ideals of individual culture and perfectability are now challenged by the forces of the "velociferous" century; and if the book ends with a vision of America, it is not in order to offer an escape to utopia, but because it was there that a new society, alert, adaptable, and above all, responsible, seemed about to emerge.

It is well to remember that in all of these late works, the *Divan* poetry, *Wilhelm Meister's Travels*, and *Faust*, the symbolic mode is not merely an artistic technique but evidence of Goethe's manner of grasping and accepting the world. In his autobiography, *Poetry and Truth*, his own life assumed the transparency and logic of a symbolic design. There are not many great poets in whose work experience and reflection, perceived form and created form, the self and his world, have so marvelously illuminated and enhanced one another.

The essays collected in this volume can only in small measure indicate the modern view of Goethe. They should, at any rate, point to our growing awareness of his extraordinary range as one of the masters of poetry, and to the pervasive consequences of his scientific and social concerns. The preeminence of German Goethe scholarship is self-evident, and no one familiar with recent Goethe studies will under-rate the remarkable stimulus which English and American criticism has provided. But the reassessment of Goethe has produced a wide-ranging critical debate, and only the exigencies of space—and of copyright—have made it impossible to include some of the significant work of French, Russian, Italian, or Japanese scholars.

The Defeat of Convention

by Barker Fairley

Nothing that Goethe has said about his poetry lends itself more readily to misinterpretation than the famous pronouncement in his autobiography that his works were "fragments of a great confession" (Bruchstükke einer grossen Konfession). Confession, taken in its usual sense, is the last word we should think of applying to him; neither absolutely nor historically can we accept it at its face value. If he had been an author of the type established in modern literature by Rousseau, if he had written with the intention of confessing, if his poetry had been prompted by the need of communicating his mind to another mind and thereby vindicating itself, his work would bear the marks of it; it would address us, it would solicit our regard, it would ask to be read. But no. What we find is the reverse of this—a poetry so rich in the opposite virtue, so unprecedented in its pervasive quality of neither seeking its reader nor avoiding him nor in any way involving him, that we lack words to describe it.

Only in a secondary sense can the word "confession" be allowed to stand. Being intimately lyrical and personal—a betrayal of himself, as Goethe put it—his poetry is the equivalent of a confession, it tells us what he would have told us if he had been minded to confess. But this is all. The so-called confession is the inevitable consequence of his creative act and has nothing to do with the act itself, which, if we are to judge by the distinctive temper of the poetry which it produces, remains strangely self-contained, self-communing. The more we read this poetry, coming to it now from this author and now from that and slowly learning to see it from many angles, the more does it impress us with its inner completeness, its rounded life, its unique self-fulfilment.

If we restore the phrase "fragments of a great confession" to its

"The Defeat of Convention." From *Goethe as Revealed in His Poetry*, by Barker Fairley (New York: Frederick Ungar Publishing Co., Inc., 1963), pp. 141–61. Copyright © 1963 by Frederick Ungar Publishing Co., Inc. Reprinted by permission of the author and the publisher.

context—it is usually quoted out of context—there is no difficulty. "And so," he writes, "there began that tendency, which I could never deviate from all my life, to turn what delighted or tortured or otherwise occupied me into an image or a poem and be done with it, both in order to correct my notions of outer things, and to compose myself inwardly. No one needed this gift more than I, because my nature flung me continually from one extreme to the other. Thus, all my works are fragments of a great confession. . . ."

It is clear from this passage—and the larger context makes it clearer still—that Goethe did not intend to stamp his poetry as confessional, and that he gives us no real authority for doing so. What he says, if we read him closely, is that he wrote it as a reckoning with himself, and that its confessional aspect follows from this. It is the reckoning with himself that is characteristic, not the confession. For while the impulse to write for oneself, to free oneself by writing, far from being unknown to others, is perhaps the primary poetic impulse, and there is no poet great or small who has not felt it and acted on it; in Goethe this impulse operates with a cogency and a persistence which puts him in a class apart. Instead of turning into an accomplishment, a vocation, a faculty separate and circumscribed, as poetry usually does, Goethe's poetry retains from first to last its crucial importance—functional more than cathartic—for his mental and bodily health. It is as deeply rooted in him as the instinct for food and the instinct for sleep; it is equally necessary to him; and it operates with the same infallibility. Given the required crisis in his life, the poetry will come of itself. It is regulative, preservative. When he needs to sleep he sleeps, and when he needs to write poetry he writes poetry. No sooner does the stress of joy or sorrow, the turmoil of doubt, the tension of deep insight become acute than the poetic instinct awakens in him and helps to correct disturbance.

The most famous example is that of *Werther* which, by giving expression to the suicide mood incidental to his early emotionalism, liberated him and restored him to a more normal state of mind. But what it is less easy to believe, though he says it himself, is that this controlling function is at the bottom of all his poetry and is as vital to him at the end of his life as it was at the beginning. There is conclusive evidence of this in the last of his love-poems. The "Trilogie der Leidenschaft," written in his seventy-fourth and seventy-fifth years at the time of his fantastically hopeless passion for Ulrike von Levetzow, is, if anything, more necessary to him, more a matter of life and death, than the *Werther* which he wrote at twenty-four.

Here, in his waning life, we can say more confidently than in his youth that if he had lacked the power "to say what he suffered" he would have gone to pieces.

There is this interesting difference between *Werther* and the "Trilogie der Leidenschaft"—the earliest and the latest of the greater emotional crises recorded in Goethe's poetry—that the recording of the latter crisis frankly recognizes and expresses its vital function and shapes itself accordingly, while in *Werther* the function is implicit and not immediately discoverable. It is only by reading the commentaries to *Werther* that we can arrive at anything more than conjecture as to its private relation to Goethe, and it is only because we have his express word for it that we know for certain that he healed the sickness of his spirit by writing it down.

This is true of the poetic works as a whole. They do not tell us in so many words why they came into existence. It is only in the "Trilogie der Leidenschaft" that the poetry lets out its secret at a crucial moment, though there was a hint of it at the close of *Torquato Tasso*. Here at last, in obedience to that growing explicitness of his poetic life manifested in the final stages in the writing of *Faust,* Goethe states in his own verses and in the midst of his anguish—the words occur at the end of the first of the three poems —that he sings to save himself and that, like his own Tasso, he must look to his power of self-expression to free him from his present torment. "How touching it is when the poet sings to escape the death that comes at parting! A prey to these torments, and not free from blame, may he be given the power to say what he endures":

> Wie klingt es rührend, wenn der Dichter singt,
> Den Tod zu meiden, den das Scheiden bringt!
> Verstrickt in solche Qualen, halbverschuldet,
> Geb' ihm ein Gott, zu sagen, was er duldet.

And it is part of the same explicitness when he arranges the three poems so as to express both the crisis and the recovery from it, reversing the order which they take in date of composition and giving them as a connected whole the spiritual movement and consummation which his poetry had enabled him to achieve in his person a hundred times, but which he had never before so lucidly conveyed in the poetry itself. First we read the announcement of the passion, couched in the form of an address to the ghost of Werther, who comes from the grave to commune with his progenitor, the dead facing the living across the deep gulf of years; next the Elegy, the Marienbad Elegy, rehearsing the last meeting of the lovers—the anticipation, the fulfillment, the parting, the misery—and then deliberately seeking the means of recovery—in the splendor of the outer world, "Is not the world left? Are not the rocks still crowned with sacred shadows? Is there not the harvest?"

> Ist denn die Welt nicht übrig?   Felsenwände,
> Sind sie nicht mehr gekrönt von heiligen Schatten?
> Die Ernte, reift sie nicht?

in illusory dreams of her whom he has lost, in the deeper truth of his abiding recollection of her as she was, in the ultimate values which he can extract from this great memory. Yet all in vain, the experience crushes him as it crushed Werther, and the Elegy ends on a note of despair, leaving it to the concluding poem to resolve the despair, and with healing music to lead the sufferer back to life and the acceptance of life.

What Goethe's poetry does for him here at the nadir of tribulation we must imagine it doing also at the zenith of happiness. He tells us that "everything on earth can be endured, except a succession of happy days":

> Alles in der Welt lässt sich ertragen,
> Nur nicht eine Reihe von schönen Tagen,

and we can see from this and from other indications that the inner necessity would be as great at this extreme as at the extreme of suffering. Among the happiest days which Goethe has recorded are those which produced the *West-östlicher Divan,* and here, more than in any other extensive body of his verse, we can feel its tonic quality as we read it. There is something inimitable about it at this stage. Marianne von Willemer—the inspirer of the *Divan*—was more nearly his spiritual mate, more nearly a woman of genius, than any other woman he had known intimately, and she was pledged to one who was both her benefactor and his friend. It was the old Werther triangle again, and just as precarious. Yet this time all passes off serenely and even joyfully with no aftertaste of bitterness, no frustration. And while this comfortable issue must be ascribed in part to niceties of temperament and affinity which we are not in a position to investigate, something must also be due to the restorative virtue of the poetic life, which in this case operated with surprising ease and felicity. It so happened that Marianne had poetic gifts as well as he, and this quickly opened the poetic vein in him and made it a part of their intercourse, so that day by day the wings of poetry lifted them and made the hard ground light beneath their feet. There are moments of tragedy here, but they are quickly expressed and mastered, while the prevailing mood is one of exhilaration, rising now and then to sublimer flights, but for the most part disporting itself adroitly in unambitious situations. There is a perennial fascination in these verses, transcending somehow their intrinsic merits; nowhere else shall we find the game of poetry lending itself to such delicate mastery of life. Only because he can be Hatem and she Suleika can they venture so nimbly where others would fear to tread, and it is this secret knowledge, this expert connivance in wisdom, which gives the *Divan* verses their special flavour, making them sometimes playful, sometimes cryptic, but always bracing and cordial like the wines they celebrate.

We can see now why Goethe's poems should affect us so differently from the general run of poems, good and bad. Being so vital an exercise of his nature they habitually spend themselves in their relation to him, and are able to ignore, if not to dispense with, the communicative elements which so readily associate themselves with the poetic art. If Goethe's verses seem to be strangely independent of any recipient, and to make us feel again and again that he would have written them just the same if he had been suddenly alone in the world, it is because Goethe, the producer of them, is his own recipient. Writing because he must—in obedience to an organic law stronger and more persistent in him than in any other human being we know—he establishes a kind of creative life which returns upon itself and comes to rest or to fulfilment at or near the point at which it started. This is a poetry which turns on its own axis, it is like the forest which fertilizes itself with its own leaves, it is the mysterious and emblematic snake which circles itself tail to mouth, knowing good and evil.

It is natural that a poet so constituted should take his poetry for granted. Goethe does this. He is at heart the most nonchalant of authors, writing his verses as a matter of course when he is impelled to write them, and remaining unperplexed when the impulse deserts him. He is as little concerned in his inner mind with the worth and the prestige of his poetry after he has made it as he is reluctant to woo it, force it, organize it, before he has made it. The poet's pride, the poet's ambition, scarcely touches him in all his long lifetime. We shall look in vain in his writings for the note of Horace's "aere perennius," or of Shakespeare's

> Not marble nor the gilded monuments
> Of princes shall outlive this powerful rhyme,

or Ronsard's "Quand tu seras bien vieille . . ." or Hölderlin's "Grant me a summer and an autumn, you mighty ones, for my ripe song":

> Nur einen Sommer gönnt, ihr Gewaltigen,
> Und einen Herbst zu reifem Gesange mir.

It would be as unnatural in Goethe to sound this note as to pray that his life might be prolonged in order that he might sleep. When he imagines himself entering the Mohammedan paradise and the houri at the gate demands his credentials, he submits his common humanity and asks for no favours as a poet. "Stop this fussing and let me in, for I was a man, and that means a fighter":

> Nicht so vieles Federlesen!
> Lass mich immer nur herein:
> Denn ich bin ein Mensch gewesen,
> Und das heisst ein Kämpfer sein.

And if we go back forty years to the days when he was burgeoning with promise and might be expected to display his consciousness of it, we shall find that this indifferent and unprofessional attitude must have been his from the beginning. In the only poem of these years in which he expresses the desire to create—he never expresses it again—he does so merely in the interests of a fuller life and with little thought of artistic achievement. His mind passes quickly from thoughts of art to thoughts of nature, insight, experience, and he ends, "O Nature, how I long for you, long to feel you truly! For me you will be a merry fountain, playing from a thousand jets. You will make all your powers bright in my mind and extend my narrow existence into an eternity":

> Wie sehn' ich mich, Natur, nach dir,
> Dich treu und lieb zu fühlen!
> Ein lust'ger Springbrunn wirst du mir
> Aus tausend Röhren spielen.
>
> Wirst alle deine Kräfte hier
> In meinem Sinn erheitern
> Und dieses enge Dasein mir
> Zur Ewigkeit erweitern.

And so it is everywhere. Tasso's concern is with the problem of living, and his pride as a poet only awakens under the deliberate taunts of Antonio or under pangs of suffering which compel him to remember that he has the poet's resources to fall back on.

This suggests a certain subordination of poetry to other interests. Goethe, it is sometimes argued, put life first and poetry second and is therefore less completely a poet than those who reversed the order and wrote poetry at all costs. But this does not follow. It is true that he subordinated his poetry, but he did not subordinate it to anything extraneous—as, it might be claimed, all poets do who in any way professionalize themselves and write to earn money, or to instil patriotism, or to teach morals, or to propound an idea. By referring it to its proper fount and origin he simply emphasized a subordination which already existed in the nature of poetry, and in this sense it could be held that he made his poetry more fundamental and was therefore the truer poet. For that matter, it is as impossible to imagine Goethe renouncing the writing of poetry, or losing the power to write it, as to imagine him contemplating the loss of it or fearing lest it should fail him in any ambition. There were periods when he wrote little, and there were periods when he wrote nothing, yet the faculty was latent in him all the time and was not less powerful at the end of his life, though the crises were fewer, than it had been at the beginning. The picture of Goethe writing a Farewell to Poesy or breaking his staff and drowning his book for good and all is one which we cannot visualize. It was not in his power to say at any moment that he would write—except perfunctorily, as he sometimes did—and it was still less in his power to say that he would not write, since the compelling need might arise at any moment. The poetic art is wholly natural to him, more natural to him probably than to any other poet, and he treats it accordingly.

Any study of Goethe's management of poetic convention must begin at this point. Having by sheer naturalness avoided, outwitted, defeated the most elementary form of conventionality in poetry— that conscious or half-conscious recognition of a potential hearer which establishes at the outset a change of mood in the poet corresponding to the very similar change in real life—Goethe proceeds to do the same with the more elaborate forms of it. The unselfconsciousness which enabled him spontaneously to execute "Um Mitternacht" or "Harzreise im Winter"—or, if further examples are needed, "Versunken" from the *Divan,* or "Tagebuch (1810)," the latter an almost unbelievably natural treatment of an erotic theme—underlies all his workmanship, and can be discovered in it, no matter what phase or aspect of it we explore.

Consider his use of meter. Only the most perfunctory examination is needed to establish Goethe among the richest and happiest of metrists. Give him time and he will entertain you with the freest of free verse, the severest of unfree; the extremes of the colloquial and the formal; German doggerel, Latin elegiac, Italian sonnet, or Persian ghazal. There is no end to it. *Faust* itself is a treasure-house of metrical adventure; on this score alone Goethe is a supreme master of verse-forms. Yet it is only by an effort that we bring ourselves to say it, and in reading the poetry we become conscious of it at one moment only to forget it the next. Far from drawing our attention to this aspect of itself—as Milton's or Victor Hugo's poetry does—this poetry consistently distracts us from it. Just as there are people whose unusual bearing and vitality prevents us from studying their features in the act of talking to them, so these verses by their very character prevent us from merely looking at them and make us unconscious of their appearance as we read them.

There can only be one explanation. The creative reader duplicates the act of the creative poet and finds in the effect the poems have on him the key to the state of mind which made them. Goethe, we must infer, came naturally by this metrical flexibility and was not studious of it. The poetry seems to tell us this, and we have ample proof besides. This master of verse-forms, we find, is a tiro in prosody; as soon as he becomes conscious of the technique of his verses he is a child and must manage to forget the technique if he is to recover his mastery of it. His words to Herder in a letter accompanying the manuscript of *Iphigenie auf Tauris,* now ready for publication, are such as no academic prosodist and few poets of any sort could have written. He tells Herder that there are lines which still dissatisfy him, and he gives him a free hand to make such changes in them as he thinks desirable. This was a work upon which Goethe had brought himself metrically to a standstill. The problem of converting it from its iambic prose into regular blank verse was one that he had waited most of ten years to solve, so incapable was he of playing the technician and coolly polishing his lines. And when in the end he studies the theory of prosody and learns the rules of the game, he brings himself to a deadlock and is willing at the last moment to surrender his text—or parts of it— to the tender mercies of another.

The meaning of this is clear. The rules had to be in his bones if they were to be of use to him, the book-knowledge paralyzed him. We shall find in *Iphigenie auf Tauris* effects of meter, rhythm, word-music fit to stand with the best in poetry, yet they are essentially un-studied, they came of themselves; he forgot the rules in order to write them. Orestes' line which says that the fresh faces about him soon "betray the marks of a creeping death,"

> Den Schmerzenszug langsamen Tods verraten,

with its pained sibilants, its transposed and retarding middle foot, and its ominous closing vowels, has all the merits the prosodist could give it, yet we cannot take it as an example of Goethe's virtu-osity, because he wrote it as iambic prose and lifted it bodily into his blank verse without altering a syllable.

If we ask why he chooses blank verse at this point the answer is all of a piece with the rest; it is not an arbitrary choice, such as Lessing made when he adopted blank verse as the suitable dramatic meter for Germans, or such as Schiller made when he decided that Lessing was right and followed suit; it is an instinctive choice prompted by deeper motives. For while it is true that Goethe first toyed with blank verse as an alternative to alexandrines, and we possess a few lines about an early tragedy, *Belsazer,* in evidence of it, he was young and precocious then, and had not found himself. When he came seriously to this meter it was with the spirit of Char-lotte von Stein upon him. To express that spirit it was as natural for him to hit upon blank verse as to hit upon the story of Tasso, not because it was a useful meter for elevated drama, but because in a European perspective it was a Renaissance meter, and appro-priate to the mood of Renaissance idealism with which she had filled him. When this mood has spent itself Goethe drops the meter and rarely writes it again; without the emotional justification he cannot use it.

This analysis holds good for all Goethe's meters, even the folk-meters which he came upon so early. If he adopts the forms of folk-poetry it is not because they are an attractive convention which promises to be fashionable, but because he is filled full of folk-poetry. Herder talks to him about it by the hour, he roams the villages around Strassburg and copies it down from the lips of the peasantry, and with all this vivid actuality behind him he writes or refashions the "Heidenröslein," he writes the "König in Thule" and a few other pieces—a handful in all—returning to folk-poetry at rare moments in later life to write a "Blümlein Wunderschön," and show that the spirit of it is in him all the time, even when he seems farthest from it, but never writing it as a habit, never in all his long life repeating himself in it. In this he stands in vivid contrast with the younger German poets of his day, and especially with Heine, who so brilliantly adapted the folk-song to the purposes of his sophisticated lyricism, and then used it and used it till it wearied him, and he dropped it from utter satiety.

This natural use of meter is not uncommon in poets who, like Shakespeare, stick chiefly to one meter and use it as a matter of routine. Goethe—and this is what makes his case unique—uses all imaginable meters, and is incapable of routine; look where we may we shall fail to find either mere routine or mere experiment in his changes of form. If he touches the sonnet, he has been drawn to it by a tentative love-affair and intimacy with a sonnet-loving circle; it is more than literary adventuring with him, his heart is in it. The elegiacs of his middle years, permanently rooted though they seem, fall away from him in due course; and lighter, looser meters replace them, more attuned to the growing exhilaration of his late sixties. He evolves a new meter to suit a new theme, and having used it once with consummate appropriateness he has done with it for good; his two most noble ballads, "Die Braut von Korinth" and "Der Gott und die Bajadere," both exemplify this. The consequence is that we never accept what may seem to be an arbitrary choice of meter, as we would unhesitatingly in another, without asking ourselves what deeper motives may account for it. Twice Goethe uses *terza rima*—once to convey the monologue on the Alpine rainbow in *Faust,* and again to convey his aged thoughts at the sight of Schiller's skull. In the first case he may have remembered the dazzling close of the "Paradiso," he may have felt the need and the fitness of an Italian meter to express the southward movement of his poem; in the second case he may have preferred an exacting and unpracticed meter to give him artificial steadiness in face of the visible signs of corruption which confronted his poetic mind, and which—as we know from other occasions—he involuntarily shrank from with an almost animal fear. None of these explanations may suffice, yet we are compelled to inquire in this spirit, because we can be nearly certain that Goethe was incapable of making a purely conventional choice of meter, and of fitting his thoughts to it. But for this the remarks of Simmel on the discrepancy between the content of the Marienbad Elegy and its meter would have little meaning. At first sight the meter—a plain six-line stanza, with alternate rhymes and then a couplet—is acceptable enough, and it is only when we realize that it lacks the

Goethean inevitability that we are in a position to understand Simmel's explanation. This meter, he says, is as the comparative impotence of old age coping with the spring-floods of love, the youth and the senility of this tragic episode being reflected in the clash of form and mood. Thus the very inadequacy of the meter gives it its deeper expressiveness and truth.

There is only one signal and sustained instance of prosodic self-consciousness in Goethe, and it is a most welcome one, because it is an exception which not only proves the rule, but requires it. In the Helena act of *Faust* the meters are so profound in significance that it is they rather than the *dramatis personæ* which express and carry on the action. The Greek trimeter, in which Helena addresses us—it is anticipated by Erichtho's speech at the beginning of the Classical Walpurgisnacht and remembered in Faust's words at the beginning of Act IV—is as indispensable as Helena herself. Without this meter of hers we should not experience the actuality which Goethe intends, we should not recognize her for the very thing of beauty that Hellas knew. It is only through the trimeter and the choric rhythms that alternate with it that Goethe is able to bring back the Athenian drama with any sense of its poetic reality. Put this passage into prose, and its meaning evaporates. And in the later passage where Faust teaches Helena to speak in rhyme the meaning passes wholly into the metrical form, and a prose rendering would destroy it outright. Here, we might say, is meter used more consciously and with a completer sophistication than ever before by any poet. But we can also say with equal truth that it is meter elevated into a symbol of the changing spirit of man and purged as never before of all mere externality. It is only because Goethe's apprehension of meter is so much more than conventional that he is able thus to dramatize it, and to invest trimeter and couplet and stanza with a speaking force greater at moments than that of the characters who use them.

It is the same everywhere, in plot structure as in metrical structure. Goethe rarely complies with the conventional standards of dramatic and narrative literature, and he never complies in longer works without forfeiting something of his power. The mastery which he achieves with superb ease in short poems, lyrical and narrative, he cannot attempt with impunity on a larger scale. He shows in his early drama, *Clavigo*, that he has all Schiller's knack of stage dialogue; the conversation between Carlos and Clavigo, in which the vacillating lover is masterfully swayed by the subtle rhetoric and the stronger will of his unscrupulous friend, is as well handled as any in *Kabale und Liebe,* and the whole play is the-atrically effective. Yet we cannot say that the real Goethe is in it. It has neither the vernal freshness of *Götz von Berlichingen,* nor the felicity of his early lyrics, nor the mysterious power of *Werther* and the *Urfaust*; and it has no qualities of its own to compare with these for a moment. *Clavigo* impresses us rather as a good and promising work by some other author that has strayed by accident into Goethe's pages than as an authentic and unmistakable piece of himself; it will be best appreciated by those who wish Goethe had been otherwise, and who deplore the possible frustra-tion in him of a talent for drama; but in the end it will be found to contribute little or nothing to his true stature. Thus the cleverest of Goethe's early writings is his least worthy.

In the one other notable instance in which he makes a drama conform satisfactorily to the accepted standards, he also pays a price. When Iphigenie tells the truth to Thoas and precipitates the final crisis of the play, we have to admit that the inevitability of great drama is lacking, that this crisis is not necessitated as the strangling of Desdemona is necessitated, because Iphigenie's rela-tions with Thoas are such that she might have told him quietly and obtained her wish. Remembering Thoas's given word that she was free to return to Greece when the opportunity came, we might say that this less dramatic solution would have been more convincing. But in order to drive home a moral idea, and to round off his play —each of these intentions is foreign to him at other times—Goethe forces upon the situation a tension and uncertainty which it hardly warrants and thereby falls short of the highest that is in him.

His narrative art is like his dramatic; it succeeds in proportion as it is not careful to conform. *Hermann und Dorothea,* by far his outstanding achievement in the art of sustained story-telling, does not hold us to-day as the amorphous *Werther* holds us or the philosophically overloaded *Wahlverwandtschaften.* The failure of this beautifully conducted idyll of German life to endear itself as it should, even to those who are native to it, is not so much the fault of its somewhat alien hexameters as of its comparative lack of depth. Its formal mastery—slightly marred by the intrusion of the theme of the French Revolution, which, instead of underlying the poem, seems to be superimposed upon it here and there, but never-theless a real and incontestable mastery—cannot blind us to the fact that the poem sees no deeper into life than it is given to lesser poets to see, and that here, as before, Goethe loses more than he gains when he sets out to compose as others do, be it never so skilfully. *Werther*, we may admit, cannot compare with *Hermann und Dorothea* in narrative technique; its concluding pages are its least convincing pages, they remind us that the poet had finished before the story-teller and that the poet was the stronger of the two. Yet if we are to choose whom we shall sit with at the well it must be the melancholy Werther, not the estimable Hermann and Dorothea, for he sees more than they, and his words are undying.

Everything goes to show that Goethe excels when he defeats the conventions, whether by breaking with them as he does in the best of his longer works, or by fulfilling them unawares as he almost invariably does in short poems. When he is complying with the conventions expressly he is seldom or never at his best. The virtue of his poetry is in the pure organic impulse which sets it going, and if he has a technique it is the technique of guarding this impulse, of carrying it up into the working-out of the poems, and, as far as possible, of letting it write them. This does not mean that in the final result he dispenses with convention; that is beyond the power of any poet, and Goethe, as his work shows, would be the last to desire it. It means that a convention has to be second nature with him before he can use it to advantage; he must assimilate and digest it, and wait for it to come as part of the initial impulse, flowing with it and strengthening its flow, rather than as some improvised dam or filter which erects itself against the impulse and deprives it of its momentum.

Incredible as it may sound when we consider Goethe's range and variety, this is the technique, the inner technique, of all his work, no matter how cultured, deliberate, and sophisticated it becomes. The technique may be less perfect in one case than another; the longer the poem the less capable it is of dispensing with inorganic elements. Yet the truth remains that Goethe practised this technique from first to last, and that it is the essential technique of every piece of his verse, long or short, that we value for its own sake.

This technique, this way of dealing with himself, was forced upon him by his literary environment. There was no easy tradition for him to drop into as there was for Shakespeare, no obvious and excellent themes for him to treat, no ready mould to pour them into. The only alternative to the kind of poetry he elected was a highly artificial, arbitrary poetry, such as Schiller produced when by sheer will and intellect he established a tradition of verse-drama in Germany which owed nothing to the world about it and was entirely based on moral and literary judgments. This was possible for Schiller, and it was commendable in him; but for Goethe it was not to be thought of. His nature precluded it and left him no choice but to grow everything within himself, to create in himself the environment which failed him in the literary world. He sometimes deplored this condition—as well he might when we consider the immense spiritual endeavor which it entailed—and regretted that he was not born into a more poetic age, in which the stage was set and the audience ready. Yet we can only rejoice that it was not so, and that Goethe was compelled by the world about him to be the poet he was.

If he had only known it he was fortunate in his disadvantages. A nature poet, if ever there was one, he had no exhausting problem of poetic diction to wrestle with, as Wordsworth had. The conventional language and the literary fashion which he had followed in his early Leipzig poetry was the shallowest imaginable; it trafficked in the emptiest of conceits, the most tenuous of pastoral superficialities. It was the negation of the Goethean ideal, as we now see it. Goethe acquired it all in a flash and even turned out a little masterpiece or two of precocious virtuosity. His "Brautnacht" beats the withered old poetasters at their own game. Yet when the moment came to break with it, it might never have existed. He turned his back on it and wrote as if he had never known it; he never echoes it involuntarily, he never reacts against it, he is completely free from it. And, what is more, he finds the poetic resources of the language virtually untapped. Born, as he was, into the later eighteenth century, he found waiting for his magic touch a poetic vocabulary with all the bloom and dew of an unspoilt world upon it. When he writes of love blessing "the fresh fields and the teeming world, asmoke with flowers,"

> Du segnest herrlich
> Das frische Feld,
> Im Blütendampfe
> Die volle Welt,

he enters into a verbal inheritance as little worn by usage as Walther von der Vogelweide's six hundred years before him. It is as fresh as Chaucer's; there seems to be no conventional verbiage to reckon with. Klopstock and others who were true poets before him seem rather to have loosened the soil about the poetic resources of modern German than to have quite unearthed them, and it was left to Goethe to discover them as if none had done it before him. The Klopstockian reminiscences here and there in his early poetic speech are as nothing beside its freshly germinating, sprouting life; the words came breaking through the mould like the spring grass and flowers. There was something in the language when he picked it up which relieved him of all dilemma; he could write with no thought of what was poetic or not poetic, and with no fear of recalling others unconsciously and finding what many modern poets have found—that the return to nature was blocked by the sophistication of the speech-medium they were compelled to use, that the echoes of other poets lay too thickly about the words they had heard in their cradles for them ever to succeed in liberating themselves from the dead hand of the past.

We see then that Goethe—though he was perhaps the only poet who was capable of despising the language he wrote in—was ideally situated for the task he was born to fulfil, because his almost miraculous defeating of convention would have been itself defeated if he had not had a clean palette and a clean canvas to work with. For this reason alone a French Goethe, or even an English Goethe, could never have been; their better opportunities would have robbed them of the great opportunity. It was only the peculiar retarding of German culture and the consequent paucity of literary tradition that made it possible for Goethe to exist in the modern world as the unprecedented poet we now know him to be. To an extent which we should have thought impossible his work is at once highly cultured and wholly natural; it contains all the conventions of the past; all the forms, meters, and literary devices of all the ages find their way into it sooner or later; but never a conventional way, for everything is re-experienced and re-made. The whole of his poetry from the simple to the elaborate, and from the raw experience in life to its highest formal refinement in art, is organic in one and the same sense, and the inorganic or less perfectly organic elements which we find in other poetry are negligible or non-existent.

Thus Goethe's poetic mind was marvellously true to its kindred points—true to the self which speaks and to the nature which prompts. He sanctioned nothing that was not his by more than intellectual right, and he sanctioned nothing that was not also natural. And by satisfying the one standard he satisfied the other. By seeing to it that all he expressed was a part of himself he put nature's stamp on it; and by seeing to it that all he expressed was natural he made it his own. The poetic instrument which he discovered and perfected was the ideal instrument for the recording of himself and, through himself, of nature. Of the three items—

nature, his art, himself—the first had to be taken as it was; the second was as good as he could make it; everything hung upon the third item, which was Goethe. And in the Herculean task of getting the last ounce out of himself he had the secret thought to sustain him that whatever he truly experienced he could set down in poetry with less loss in the telling than any man before or since.

La Maladie du Siècle

by Karl Viëtor

"I am weary of bewailing the fate of our generation of human beings, but I will so depict them that they may understand themselves, if that is possible, as I have understood them." [1] It is the state of his generation's soul which Goethe sets forth in *Werther*; the extreme character of the case affords a complete diagnosis. "Look you, the end of this disease is death! The goal of such sentimental enthusiasm is suicide!" [2] The disease of which Goethe speaks threatened the young intelligentsia everywhere in Europe, but nowhere more than in Germany. It was the softening and the excess of emotion which we call sentimentality. A tense and idealistic youth found itself cut off from the world of great action, worthy achievement, and lofty striving by an antiquated social order. In all cultural matters, in science, art, philosophy, the bourgeoisie had assumed leadership and justly felt that it possessed the highest moral cultivation. But in politics and society the middle class was still under constraint, still subject to the domination of princely absolutism and feudal caste. The storm clouds of revolutionary change had just begun to appear on the horizon. In the sultry calm which preceded the great storm shortly to break in France, there developed a state in which spiritual energies were pent up within and active striving was flung back upon itself. Idealistic feeling and will languished ineffectually. "Here we have to do with men living in the most peaceful of circumstances whose

"La Maladie du Siècle." From *Goethe the Poet*, by Karl Viëtor (Cambridge, Mass.: Harvard University Press, 1949), pp. 28–34. Copyright 1949 by Harvard University Press. Reprinted by permission of the publisher.

[1] Ich bin müde, über das Schicksal *unsres Geschlechts* von Menschen zu klagen; aber ich will sie darstellen, sie sollen sich erkennen, wo möglich, wie ich sie erkannt habe.

[2] Siehe, das Ende dieser Krankheit ist Tod! Solcher Schwärmereien Ziel ist Selbstmord!

lives have been spoiled for them by want of deeds and by their exaggerated demands upon themselves." [3] Where the inner life was intensified to such a pitch, any accidental passion that arose must lead to a crisis which could only be resolved by the most fatal means. "Look you, the end of this disease is death!"

In the spring of 1772 Goethe went for several months to Wetzlar, a small town not far from Frankfort, where the supreme judiciary of the German realm had its seat. Here he came to know a young girl called Charlotte Buff. She entranced him by her gay kindliness and the healthy naturalness of her character. When Goethe met her, Lotte was the fiancée of a young man who was Goethe's friend, but passion did not inquire what was permissible or possible. Unattainable as she was in her steady loyalty to her fiancé and to her husband later, Goethe loved Lotte with an intensity which was only increased by his tortured vacillation between hope and despair. Finally he summoned strength "himself to desire what was necessary" and to flee before he was enmeshed by inextricable complications.

He had escaped the grimmest fate only by a hair's breadth. When he was again in Frankfort, alone and suffering, he heard from his Wetzlar friends that a young man called Jerusalem had taken his own life. He had been in the same situation as Goethe, but had not been able to bring himself to escape in time. "The poor lad! When I came back from my walk and he met me out in the moonlight, I said to myself the man was in love. Lotte must still remember that I smiled over it. God knows, loneliness undermined his heart . . ." [4] Goethe's own experience was associated with the melancholy history of young Jerusalem. For a year and a half the elements were assembled until the composition crystallized into a whole. Goethe must have written down Werther's story quickly, in the space of a few weeks during the spring of 1774 ("almost unconsciously, like a sleepwalker"), so completely formed was the story in his mind. Only now did he feel himself fully healed, and

---

[3] Wir haben es hier mit solchen zu tun, denen eigentlich aus Mangel von Taten, in dem friedlichsten Zustande von der Welt, durch übertriebene Forderungen an sich selbst das Leben verleidet. (*Dichtung und Wahrheit,* Part III, Book XIII.)

[4] Der arme Junge! Wenn ich zurückkam vom Spaziergang und er mir begegnete hinaus im Mondschein, sagt ich, er ist verliebt. Lotte muss sich noch erinnern, dass ich drüber lächelte. Gott weiss, die Einsamkeit hat sein Herz untergraben . . . (Letter to Kestner, November 1772.)

"as after a general confession, again happy and free and justified for a new life." But the past was still so immediately present to him that his composition exhibits the colors of living reality throughout. Rich as the age was in autobiographical sketches and documents of personal confession, no other writing is capable of communicating reality with such masterly art. Goethe's book went straight to the heart of a generation devoted to the cult of nature. Its success was unprecedented.

Die Leiden des jungen Werthers ("The Sorrows of Young Werther"), as the title of the anonymously published first version of 1774 reads, is a romance in letters. The author poses as an editor of private papers. Such fictions were popular in the eighteenth century. The role assumed by the author, looked at from the point of view of his audience, amounted to a concession to the mass of readers that the truth of reality is superior to the higher truth of poetry; such a concession was no artistic deprivation to the author. At the same time he was able to swathe the autobiographic content in a veil and withdraw it from importunate curiosity. What was highly personal and intimate appeared as something objective and documentary. The epistolary novel was a new species, a creation of the century which had shown great interest in the secrets of the individual and "the immediacy of existence." The most important models were Richardson's novels and Rousseau's *La Nouvelle Héloïse*. Both involve correspondence between several persons. Goethe does not dispense with the dialogue form but transforms it to a "conversation in spirit" which the writer conducts with a hidden interlocutor.

In their origin as in their effect these are no true letters but highly intimate confessions which a lone man makes to himself, monologues of a suffering soul. Only Werther's voice is heard; the friend to whom he writes appears only in the reactions which his replies evoke. This new form gave psychological depth to the epistolary novel and at the same time supreme artistic simplicity. Nowhere and at no time has it been surpassed. The models for the descriptive parts, with their objectively faithful portrayal of rural life, idyllic and patriarchal conditions, and simple folk, were the new novels of the English—those of Sterne, and above all the books of Oliver Goldsmith. Goethe gratefully calls them his teachers, and says that they are "as interesting, as affectionate," as their own domestic life. In them Goethe found confirmation for the realistic tendency of his own narrative style: "Proceed from the domestic, and spread yourself, if you can, over the whole world." [5]

Among European novels *Werther* is the first in which an inward life, a spiritual process and nothing else, is represented, and hence it is the first psychological novel—though naturally not the first in which the inner life in general is seriously dealt with. The conflict between an immoderately burgeoning passion and the ordered world of society is here described, as it were, "from within." The scene is the soul of the hero. All events and figures are regarded only in the light of the significance they have for Werther's emotion. All that happens serves but to nourish the absolutism of Werther's emotion—a fatal propensity which swells to a demonic possession and engulfs all other inward forces and possibilities.

The germ of the disease is already present in Werther before he is attacked by his passion; his passion only serves to aggravate it. As Werther describes himself at the beginning of the book, he is already a lonely man who seeks refuge from life in the bosom of nature because nothing will satisfy his insatiable heart. He speaks of nothing as frequently as of this heart, which he spoils like an ailing child. For him it is the epitome of his worth, the source of his personal life. "Ah, what I know, anyone may know. My heart is mine alone." His inner being appears capable of satisfaction only by an emotional realization of the infinity of the universal. But this is an experience which increasingly alienates him from life. Only idyllic landscapes give him inward peace; only with children and simple folk can he associate on terms of friendship; the patriarchal world of the *Odyssey* is to him a "lullaby." But his soul is filled with dark premonitions and yearning, and he sinks into his twilight dreams. This man could be healed, could be saved only by a transformation which would force him to move among the realities of life, to expend his pent-up inner riches in plans and deeds. But this transition from the sentimental state of youth to the sphere of adult activity does not come about.

The encounter with Lotte gives his searching emotion an object to which it can fasten. Now begins the spiritual event constituting the inner action of this book, which, by the standards of literary composition, is rather a lyrical drama than a novel. Goethe himself has referred to this psychic process as an illness, since every great passion is a sort of disease. As we look on, the passion of love

[5] Geh vom Häuslichen aus, und verbreite dich, so du kannst, über alle Welt.

tightens its grip upon the unresisting sufferer; we see how its effect
is the more disruptive because it draws to itself all the forces which
constitute Werther's greatness: his gifts of unqualified feeling, his
demands for the fullness of existence, his readiness to devote himself wholly to the great thing which has seized upon him. The hero
is destroyed by what is noble and good in him. Later Goethe once
said: "Man's longing for the ideal, when deprived of its objectives,
or when these are spoiled, turns back on itself, becomes refined
and intensified until it seems to outdo itself." [6] Werther is ruined
because of and in spite of his possession of a great heart, an ideal
soul. He suffocates by the abundance of his inward life. Qualities
which might have raised his being to a pinnacle in friendlier
times and under more favorable circumstances become his doom.

Goethe's expressions leave no doubt as to what he considers the
cause of Werther's ruin in the outer world. The cause lies in the
fatal conditions under which the intellectual young men of the
age had to live. Since the age denied them opportunity to act
greatly, they were left with no other satisfaction than to dream
and to feel greatly. The fulfillment which they could not find in
active life they were forced to seek in inward existence. Mme de
Staël has described this situation excellently:

> Since the form of their governments afforded them no possibility to
> win fame and serve their country, they devoted themselves to every sort
> of philosophic speculation and sought in heaven a field for the activity
> which narrow limitations denied them on earth. They found satisfac-
> tion in ideals because reality offered them nothing to occupy their im-
> agination.

Because the world had no room for them, they wished to expand
their egos to infinity. "I turn back into myself and discover a
world" (Ich kehre in mich selbst zurück und finde eine Welt).
To the motive of inward passion grown rank there was added
another, which explained why the pent-up dynamism could not
unburden itself outwardly. Even the modest activity which was
permitted to bourgeois officials was made impossible for Werther
by the painful scandal which thrust him out of a society composed
of the gentry. Now every path to the sphere of action was barred
to him; after a vain attempt at flight he submitted without resis-
tance to his "endless sorrow through which any vital force that

[6] Das Ideale im Menschen, wenn diesem die Objekte genommen oder ver-
kümmert werden, zieht sich in sich, feinert und steigert sich, dass es sich
gleichsam übertrumpft. (To F. W. Riemer, August 1808.)

letter 10 oh 5.

was in him must eventually be extinguished." Could a man be more lonely than he now was? Things went so far that he lost even his communion with nature. The pantheistic feeling for the "unmeasured sea," the ever-creating abundance of the universal spirit in which his ego, suffering in its limitations, sought self-forgetfulness, was now displaced by the picture of an "ever-devouring, ever-regurgitating monster," an unfeeling destructive power with no concern for the survival of the individual. In the composition of the book the alternation of seasons corresponds to the transformation of inward mood. The month is May when Werther's love begins; it is December when his end comes. So, too, in the first portion his companion is the vital and energetic Homer; in the second the melancholy, unbelieving Ossian, whose gloomy pathos introduces the fateful moment when Werther locks the unattainable in his arms for a single time and so loses her forever.

Nothing in this book, not even its truth of expression unparalleled at the time, so deeply stirred Goethe's contemporaries as the self-destruction of the hero. Without charity, but also without reproach (as is appropriate to "true representation"), the suicide is here presented as the necessary consequence of a passion whose power transcended the "bounds of humanity." Christians found it immoral; rationalist skeptics and libertines thought it ridiculous to take passion so seriously. But among young men who themselves suffered from Werther's malaise there were many to whom his example gave courage to put a period to their suffering as he had done. The poet found it necessary to admonish such readers, who did not understand that the book was to be read, so to speak, against the grain, in a motto affixed to the second edition in Werther's name: "Be a man, do *not* follow me."

Then and later Goethe was accused of having provoked the "Werther fever" by his "dangerous book." He replied quite justly that he had not originated the disease but had only uncovered the evil which was latent in the young men of his time. The nature of such an epidemic of soul sickness Goethe could report correctly, inasmuch as he had with difficulty succeeded in saving himself from a similar crisis. Outbreaks of world-weariness, he says, recur in the history of civilized nations periodically. Byronism was a somewhat analogous phenomenon. In the life history of the individual something of the same sort occurs. In all ages *taedium vitae* is a problem in the development of high-spirited young people. "Frustrated fortune, hampered activity, unsatisfied wishes are not the lesions of a specific age but of every individual man. It would

Weltschmerz

be too bad if everyone did not go through a period when *Werther* struck him as if it were written for him alone." [7] Otherwise, for all of its artistic excellence, *Werther* would be nothing more than a document in the spiritual history of Europe and not the great work it is—the exemplary representation of a tragic conflict arising out of the situation of the modern individualist. Idealism of feeling, which demands complete realization, founders here on the reef of social usage as it is established by the formal order of civilization and by fate. . . .

[7] Gehindertes Glück, gehemmte Tätigkeit, unbefriedigte Wünsche sind nicht Gebrechen einer besonderen Zeit, sondern jedes einzelnen Menschen, und es müsste schlimm sein, wenn nicht jeder einmal in seinem Leben eine Epoche haben sollte, wo ihm der "Werther" käme, als wäre er bloss für ihn geschrieben. (Eckermann, January 2, 1824.)

Goethe's Version
of Poetic Drama

by Ronald Peacock

Drama, and particularly verse drama, has had a very checkered course since its great days in the sixteenth and seventeenth centuries. It would be difficult to give reasons; what makes an art flourish at a particular time and not at others is one of the thornier questions that criticism has to face. Two things can be said about drama, however, with some degree of certainty. It flourished most when printed books were not numerous, and few people learnt to read. It came therefore by quite natural means to hold a high place in the entertainment world; and though this of course does not explain poetic quality, it is reasonable to think that it helped the poets to get their poetry across. And that leads us to the second point. The audience that was thus secured easily for the theatre exerted influence on the entertainment itself. Some features of Elizabethan plays, such as the accumulation of horrors and the partiality for scenes of broad comedy, even in tragic plays, can be attributed to the demands of the spectators. Later, the audience of the French classical theatre, with a leaven of learning and a more disciplined taste, influenced the choice of subject and the conventions. When these conditions are absent, good poetic drama survives only as an act of literary assertion. If competition from another sort of entertainment is strong, as was to be the case with the novel, and if the audience lacks cohesion, or purpose, or a trained taste, then the form loses its unity of entertainment and poetry, and takes two directions for two levels of taste, a popular one and a refined one, with the latter playing the losing game. Attempts to revive poetic drama have in these circumstances the character of conscious literary judgment imposing itself on the theatre; and even if great genius achieves some success, its products seem curiously detached and have an air of literary and social homelessness.

It was in such a situation that Goethe and Schiller entered the theatre. Their plays show very little give-and-take with an audience. They are composed on an ideal plan, developed solely by themselves from distant literary models—Shakespeare, the Greeks, Racine—and imposed on an institution in which very ordinary sentimental plays and chivalrous romances never for a moment ceased to flourish. Goethe's first important play, *Götz von Berlichingen,* owed more to literary and lyrical enthusiasms of the *Sturm und Drang* than to impulses from a living theatre. In his succeeding plays, the extreme degree of personal choice in the subjects is a symptom of the position. Shakespeare, by and large, did write the same sort of play that his contemporaries wrote. But where, in Goethe's case, is there amongst contemporary writing a play that by its nature is like *Egmont,* or *Iphigenie auf Tauris,* or *Torquato Tasso,* or *Die Natürliche Tochter,* or *Faust?* There is a single reasonable example, *Nathan der Weise,* a drama in verse, with a didactic aim; a play in which Lessing attempted to convey a general idea current at the time in the literary form that he thought had a greater prestige than any other. Goethe's position is not dissimilar; the link with the contemporary theatre is weak, but the relation with the field of ideas clear and direct. I said a moment ago that Goethe's subjects betray a very personal choice. But if we consider his themes rather than the plots he used we see plainly that he was working in a given atmosphere. The eighteenth century searched devotedly for a new conception of the good life, inquiring into reason and nature for its ideals, and restlessly pursuing a vision of civilization. Goethe's greatest and most characteristic plays, *Iphigenie auf Tauris, Torquato Tasso, Faust,* are variations on this theme of *Bildung,* of progress towards a culture that should embrace the individual and society.

The point is important for several reasons. It helps us to remember that Goethe's plays have a context; have a relationship to the age, and not only to him. And that leads us to the broader problem we mentioned: what determined at the time the relations between the subject and the form of drama? Was there a subject that required dramatic expression and moreover *verse* as well? The general histories of drama are shy of the plays we have just named. They don't fit in. The historian hurries past, from Lillo and Lessing, Diderot and sentimental drama, to *Götz von Berlichingen* and *Egmont*, then quickly to the *Sturm und Drang* group and Schiller, and the Ritterdrama; that is the scheme of things. How many, with the great traditions of drama in mind, have stopped to inquire why some of the finest poetry of the age appeared in two or three dramas that "don't fit in"? It is not very illuminating to tie yourself to the history of a form at the second and third level, when you ought to be asking how it stood in relation to the principal poetic inspiration. The more so, since the greatest poet was in fact using the form. That is the challenge both to history and to criticism.

Ontogenetic interpretation, powerfully reinforced by Dilthey's psychological method, has not made things easier by emphasizing Goethe's personality and underestimating the influence of literary traditions. One might be led to think sometimes that the purpose of reading him was merely to observe how rich and varied an inner life he had, and how skilfully he disembarrassed himself of his sufferings at every stage. Presented as documents of this inward process, his works cease to be more than advertisements of a spiritual heroism, or perhaps egotism. It is not to be denied that Goethe often worked closely to his own actual experiences, making a direct use of them for his poems. But it is possible to exaggerate their "personal" quality. I feel that many of Goethe's experiences, whether personal or social, were in fact stimulated by ideas of the time, because his imagination responded to them, and thus molded his actual emotions as well as his poems. It would be difficult to say with confidence whether the humanitarian feeling of *Iphigenie auf Tauris* flowed from his love for Charlotte von Stein, or whether the character of that love was not itself determined partly by the humanitarianism of the century.

We are here at grips with a subtle interplay of forces, in which Goethe's sense of values responds to certain ideas and ideals of the time, and he dramatizes that response. He uses characters and a plot, because you can't write a play without them; but they themselves do not contain the real drama. They point to an impersonal mental drama that is really the thing Goethe wants to express. The germ of the conception is to be found as early as *Götz von Berlichingen*, which is superficially an imitation of Shakespeare, but in essence an enthusiastic portrayal of a champion of freedom and "natural" justice. *Egmont* appears to be a study in character; yet Egmont, however brilliantly portrayed as a person, is still more an idea. The mainspring of his nature is a splendour of vitality and

spontaneous genius that at its best is heroic, and for Goethe and
his time constituted a precious value. But Egmont's assurance can
also degenerate into insouciance; he lacks prudence, reason, and
the disciplined statesmanship that enable William of Orange to
meet the crafty calculation of the Spanish tyrants. William wins,
Egmont is a victim. Yet Goethe is not satisfied with placing Egmont
in a situation which because it ends tragically seems to put him
in the wrong and give the palm to the wisdom of Orange. Through
the peculiar and much-discussed allegorical vision at the close of
the work, he justifies Egmont and restores the balance between the
two men and their differing genius. Except for this close, the appearances of the play are orthodox; it seems a straightforward historical drama. But the exception is significant as the most obvious
symptom of an inherent tendency in the play which was of the
greatest importance for what was happening in Goethe's handling
of dramatic form. We see in fact the true Goethe emerging, using a
historical subject to portray something that he feels about ideals of
life. It is not simply a question of how human character produces
tragedy or comedy, or how life drives us into a trap, or of evil
opposed to good. The play tests ideals of conduct and expresses a
sense of conflicting kinds of virtue, of how different kinds of good
seem to be mutually exclusive.

What is embryonic here comes to a first stage of fruition in
Iphigenie auf Tauris and is completed in *Torquato Tasso*. In the
former, Goethe's new drama of ethical sensibility receives a clear
form, though in this case we do see good and evil opposed. Its basis
is the existence of a sphere of innocence and purity, and on the
opposing side one of passion, deceit, barbarity, and brutal action.
Iphigenie is the guiltless member of a guilty race, saved by Diana
from being sacrificed at Aulis, and now serving as her priestess in
Taurica. She is protected and even loved by King Thoas. She lives
within the sanctuary, severed from the grossness of life, kept un-
defiled by her office, and though she makes no claim to be more
than a simple human being, she acts by a virtue that removes her
from baseness and vice, and shrouds her person in sanctity and
nobility. On the other side there is her family and ancestry: Tantalus and his race, with a history of presumption and crime, of
tyranny and selfishness, a horrible succession of patricide, fratricide,
infanticide, reaching down to the latest excesses, the adultery of
Clytemnestra, the murder of Agamemnon, Orestes' revenge on his
mother, the persecution of Orestes by the Furies. The tension between these two spheres gives the moral atmosphere of the piece.

It crystallizes, as you know, in a conflict in the main character, when Orestes, seeking liberation from the Furies, arrives in Taurica, and falls under the law that requires strangers to be sacrificed to the gods. Iphigenie must either recognize the gods and the barbarous ritual they demand; or defy them, and save her brother by an impious act and a cruel deception of Thoas her protector. At this point Goethe detaches his Iphigenie from the mythical material and Greek religious conceptions and makes her evolve an ethical ideal consonant with the rational and humane aspirations of the eighteenth century. She reveals the position to Thoas and stakes everything on his humanity. In a closing scene made splendid by its optimistic assertion of faith, Thoas responds to her feeling and allows the sister and brother to go back to Greece.

In this setting Iphigenie and Orestes are symbols. I mean by that something more than a reference to a so-called "experience" of Goethe's. Traditional interpretations of the work have made great play with the idea that Orestes is purified by the spiritual force of Iphigenie, and it is customary to see in this a poetic expression of Goethe's own ethical development, partly under the influence of Frau von Stein. Even Gundolf, whilst holding off the meaner sort of biographical commentary, and keying up the matter to a pitch of heroic magnificence, adheres substantially to this conception. It is a pity such readings are pressed so far, because they create confusion about the aims and value of poetry, and of Goethe's poetry. I have just now indicated how a chain of wickedness and guilt of indescribable horror lies behind Orestes' own murder of his mother, and all of it essential to the idea of the play. I do not know what Goethe had personally to put at the side of this. The natural excesses of exuberant youthful emotion, and a sequence of love affairs, do not seem to me to be a sufficient parallel. He may have got hints from his own lapses; but until evil in some violent form breaks out in our lives, that is all most of us have to go on to help us to understand great wickedness. Orestes is not Goethe; he is imagined. When, in the remarkable third act, we see him overcome by suffering and remorse, the scene evokes profound compassion not because of Goethe's guilt, and not only because of Orestes', but because of the guilt and evil of the whole world, here deliberately gathered together by the poetic imagination into a single symbol of trenchant force.

Similarly Iphigenie is not merely a girl who doesn't tell lies. If we take truth and deceit in this play in a literal sense, the effect is flat, and certainly so ordinary an ethical notion contrasts oddly with the munificence of ethical response which makes the triumph of the work. Truthfulness here is conceived in the absolute sense of spiritual integrity, of which adherence to the truth is but the most obvious and most easily perceived aspect. It is the consistency with oneself and one's faith which gives us our defense against chaos and protects human relations against the caprice and malevolence that disrupt them. It is this that Iphigenie is concerned about when she utters her challenge to the gods: "Rettet mich, und rettet euer Bild in meiner Seele." The conventional notion of telling the truth is inadequate to describe her situation. She has to save her soul by constancy and innocence, and the choice facing her, quite beyond anything that is covered by the word convention, is that which confronts everyone who wishes to be civilized.

Following such a line of thought we escape from a certain pettiness that clings to personal interpretations and begin to apprehend a greater imaginative dimension in the play. It is impossible to think in terms of Goethe or particular characters but only of voices which echo opposing worlds and forces. Iphigenie and Orestes, in a remarkable poetic process, are each absorbed as individuals into the one ruling idea of the play, until they lose particularity as persons and exist with an intensity which is that of poetic symbol alone, all their personal being transcending itself in the impersonal spirituality of the theme. If it seems that Orestes is "purified" by his sister, that simply means here that the world in which he moves is engulfed by the light of Iphigenie's world and its potency destroyed.

Torquato Tasso amplifies and intensifies this process of poetic composition. Again we have to run counter to accepted ways of looking at Goethe's work. In the first place, the vividness of the portrayal of Tasso is to some extent misleading; though the fact that a quite pitiless censure is mingled with the pathos is enough to make one suspect that more is involved than the person of Tasso. It would be a very unsatisfactory drama if it were merely a near-tragedy about a sensitive and morbid genius. To read it in literal terms would call for a standard of judgment from the traditional dramatic form of the sixteenth and seventeenth centuries, and by that standard it is extremely faulty.[1] Secondly, it would not be

---

[1] I think it could be argued that Goethe's interest in the psychology of a certain type of genius tended to run away with him, and I would maintain that it led to a fault of execution without altering the fundamental conception that I am here trying to expound and believe to be the most important aspect of the work.

quite so great a work as it is, were it simply about a Goethe conflict, objectified partly in Tasso and partly in Antonio. If, on the other hand, we go behind the persons of its surface, we see unfolding a drama remarkable for the range of its implications concerning the conflicts of our mental life and social situation. The plot, flimsy and totally inadequate as orthodox drama, is the merest pretext to suggest these conflicts. The imagination responds to the idea of freedom and creativeness, of spontaneous joys and natural happiness; social and political living, on the other hand, make imperative the different but equally justified values of disciplined manners, of propriety, of discreet wise conduct. Any ideal of the social whole requires all these values; but any reality shows them continually in conflict. This is the theme of *Torquato Tasso;* and the idea of the two souls in Goethe's breast is not the end of the piece, but the beginning. Goethe felt the division in himself, but its importance for the play is that it gave him the knowledge of the larger conflict that goes on in human society. Either side without the other falls short of completeness, whether you look at it from the individual or the social point of view. Goethe shows a poet at cross-purposes not only with a man of action, but with a world of the utmost refinement. Tasso is opposed to no Machiavelli, but to Alfons and the Princess, to the human civilization that permeates their court and their lives, of which Antonio is but one part. All this cultivated Ferrara atmosphere is wonderfully portrayed; it is the essence of the play's spirit; it gives us the very image in the poise of language, manners, and conduct, of what is meant by being civilized. It is the real pivot of the drama, the point to which we refer both Tasso and Antonio, the ideal picture of a way of living that is compounded of taste and reason, of what Tasso has to give, combined with what Antonio has to give. That is why Goethe's Ferrara demands the friendship of the two men, as a symbol that disparate elements of civilization have been brought into harmonious relationship. This reconciliation is one to which we aspire, because it would in fact be integrated life. Goethe's work expresses this simple human aspiration that two sets of values should be harmonized; and at the same time a shadow falls over the scene from the sense that they might be irreconcilable, or at least that to be civilized costs you something personal, the too private world and too private joy. Hence the peculiar blend in the tones of the piece; of delicate idealizing fancy, of something that passionately suggests idyllic aims, and on the other hand a tragic sense of opportunities missed, of human imperfections not to be overcome, of prices to be paid in suffering and renunciation.

The phenomenon we observed in Iphigenie repeats itself. As the play proceeds we become more and more aware that a wholly mental world is being evolved and abstracted from a world of persons. These persons have often been criticized as unreal, and so they are if we judge by the standards of ordinary life which are here irrelevant. It is not the Princess and Alfons and Leonore that matter, finally, but the culture they incorporate; not Tasso, but the idea of imagination, liberty, spontaneity, and individual happiness; not Antonio, but the idea of discretion, political wisdom, statesmanship, right conduct. Consider what happens when we hear a passage like this:

> *Prinzessin.* Auf diesem Wege werden wir wohl nie
> Gesellschaft finden, Tasso! Dieser Pfad
> Verleitet uns, durch einsames Gebüsch,
> Durch stille Täler fortzuwandern; mehr
> Und mehr verwöhnt sich das Gemüt und strebt,
> Die goldne Zeit, die ihm von aussen mangelt,
> In seinem Innern wieder herzustellen,
> So wenig der Versuch gelingen will.

> *Tasso.* O welches Wort spricht meine Fürstin aus!
> Die goldne Zeit, wohin ist sie geflohn,
> Nach der sich sich jedes Herz vergebens sehnt?
> Da auf der freien Erde Menschen sich
> Wie frohe Herden im Genuss verbreiteten;
> Da ein uralter Baum auf bunter Wiese
> Dem Hirten und der Hirtin Schatten gab,
> Ein jüngeres Gebüsch die zarten Zweige
> Um sehnsuchtsvolle Liebe traulich schlang;
> Wo klar und still auf immer reinem Sande
> Der weiche Fluss die Nymphe sanft umfing;
> Wo in dem Grase die gescheuchte Schlange
> Unschädlich sich verlor, der kühne Faun,
> Vom tapfern Jüngling bald bestraft, entfloh;
> Wo jeder Vogel in der freien Luft
> Und jedes Tier, durch Berg und Täler schweifend,
> Zum Menschen sprach: Erlaubt ist, was gefällt.

> *Prinzessin.* Mein Freund, die goldne Zeit ist wohl vorbei;
> Allein die Guten bringen sie zurück.
> Und soll ich dir gestehen, wie ich denke:

Die goldne Zeit, womit der Dichter uns
Zu schmeicheln pflegt, die schöne Zeit, sie war,
So scheint es mir, so wenig, als sie ist;
Und war sie je, so war sie nur gewiss,
Wie sie uns immer wieder werden kann.
Noch treffen sich verwandte Herzen an
Und teilen den Genuss der schönen Welt;
Nur in dem Wahlspruch ändert sich, mein Freund,
Ein einzig Wort: Erlaubt ist, was sich ziemt.

Tasso. O wenn aus guten, edlen Menschen nur
Ein allgemein Gericht bestellt entschiede,
Was sich denn ziemt! anstatt dass jeder glaubt,
Es sei auch schicklich, was ihm nützlich ist.
Wir sehn ja, dem Gewaltigen, dem Klugen
Steht alles wohl, und er erlaubt sich alles.

Prinzessin. Willst du genau erfahren, was sich ziemt,
So frage nur bei edlen Frauen an.
Denn ihnen ist am meisten dran gelegen,
Dass alles wohl sich zieme, was geschieht.
Die Schicklichkeit umgibt mit einer Mauer
Das zarte, leicht verletzliche Geschlecht.
Wo Sittlichkeit regiert, regieren sie,
Und wo die Frechheit herrscht, da sind sie nichts.
Und wirst du die Geschlechter beide fragen:
Nach Freiheit strebt der Mann, das Weib nach Sitte.

When I hear this I begin to lose touch with Tasso and the Princess as persons, however vivid they are, and to feel that there is something still more important than they. I see Goethe's mind responding first to one value, and then to another, and sensible of a dilemma. But then behind Goethe's mind I become aware of the general human consciousness involved in a conflict within itself, and Goethe's mind is simply the medium that clarifies it. So it is constantly throughout this play, and it is not difficult to see that we are very close to the technique of *Faust*. First we observe persons in an exchange of sentiments, then the play of ideas and evaluations of experience gets the upper hand, and we forget the persons, to find ourselves spectators of the human mind staging an intimate drama of its own dilemmas. Conversations that seem at first to be perfect pieces of meditation, epigrams that succeed each other so naturally and yet with such startling abundance, passages that might seem to be an inappropriate irruption of didacticism into a drama of personalities, appear before long as the result of an underlying motive with a well-defined effect: they create the mental perspectives, outside time and space and particular individuals, where the real conflict, the permanent crisis, is staged. The dramatic propriety that normally rests in the relation of character and action is less important here than the sense of contrasting ideals; it is a drama that goes on behind the drama of persons. Everywhere the poetic voice transcends the limits of a scene in a plot, creating a new dramatic order. And the superb vocal style, the wonderfully sensitive thought and rhythms of the verse, which it would be easy to admire as a supernumerary effort, are seen to spring from the heart of the subject.

The essential nature of a Goethe play is a drama of symbols illustrating a drama of the search for values; and the method of *Iphigenie* and *Tasso* is the same as that of *Faust*. Nothing has been more unfortunate than the application of Shakespeare's standards to Goethe's work, suggested, as ill-luck would have it, by Goethe's own early enthusiasm for him, and by the general imitation of Shakespeare on the incentive of Lessing. Shakespeare's dramatic image of life adheres to the time-and-space reality of human relations, and his foundation is a coherent personal destiny. It is, of course, true that his plays are also "symbolic," and that over and above the story we become aware of a philosophic or lyrical meditation; for no great works of poetry are without an idea, they are never simply "human stories." But even so the lyrical meditation and the objective drama in Shakespeare are correlated at all points, the meditation growing out of the very fullness and vividness of the picture of life. Goethe's picture of life in this sense is fragmentary. It is characteristic that his interest in the action-and-character kind of plot is subordinate, and compared with the greatest dramatists he is uninventive and relatively unskilled in handling dramatic material of that kind. In reading any of his plays we constantly have to overcome irritations. But the important thing is that Goethe starts from possible ideals of behavior and finds the dramatic conflict between them; and so his image of the mental drama of values is complete. He has broken with the conception of drama that was the legacy of the sixteenth and seventeenth centuries, and we should be careful not to make the mistake of criticizing his plays by the standards of Shakespeare and Racine alone. It is a new kind of drama, and in deciding whether it is a good one, we have to bear in mind that there is room for variety in the theatre. The puzzling thing about Goethe's plays is that they are neither dramas of personal destiny nor plays of ideas; yet they contain persons who are very living, and they deal with ideas all the time. Iphigenie, Tasso, Faust, are intensely vital conceptions, but the actual "plot" they are involved in is faulty and incomplete. And on the other hand the "ideas" in these plays do not mean debate, ideology, and argument, of which the persons are mere mouthpieces. The clue to the riddle lies in the kind of thought that Goethe is preoccupied with. It is thought about how to live, about what is valuable in living, about the quality of experience. Such thought is inseparably interwoven with life and decisions about life; with our emotions and our senses, with our character as well as with our intellect, and it can only be apprehended with complete clarity in visual images of how people behave. This is the secret of Goethe's poetic subtlety; for he has created these visual images. Hence it is that though he doesn't start from character in making his plays, his persons nevertheless have an intense life. They are unindividual; they are governed by generalized conceptions; they always throw light in some way on a pattern of behavior, on an ideal, or a typical aspect of experience; but they are vivid because it is living that is involved. The conflict in Goethe's drama appears projected in different persons because that is the only way to secure the dramatic picture; but behind that it lies, as I have suggested, in the mind of everyone who is at all sensitive to these things. It lay in the mind of Goethe, and all the passion and emotion with which he himself experienced moral conflict he has poured into his characters. The elements of his own actual experiences that we see reflected in his persons, and on which he certainly drew liberally and to great advantage, are parts of his dramatic method, the tools he uses to fill his symbolic persons with life, and to communicate the whole mental experience as one that takes place in the conditions of life. His essential subject is the sensitiveness of the mind to ideals, the drama of how sensibility comes to grips with values, and it is presented by a method of remarkable originality.

From this point of vantage it is easier to meet criticism of Goethe's drama, because it is clear that with his delicate inward creation Goethe also creates his own canon and makes obsolete the standards previously applicable. Iphigenie has of course been called before now, rather apologetically, a *Seelendrama*. But I think that was meant to convey the notion of a play of psychological conflict in one person, whereas Goethe's plays generalize explicitly beyond the single individual. When we have perceived his originality, the faults that orthodoxy stigmatizes matter less. All the trouble about the Iphigeneia subject from the Greek is a striking example. For the modern writer that material is very intractable. Even Racine had great difficulty in handling a subject that involved human sacrifice and the miraculous intervention of a goddess. His problem was to make a tragedy that would fit Aristotle's rule and be acceptable to reason; but in shifting the tragic emphasis from Iphigenie to another character he loses unity and his piece breaks down, leaving us with the feeling that this great master of technique is not at his best. Goethe, using the later history of Iphigeneia, has also to face the problem of the religious framework with its gods and their commands and rites, which are so unacceptable to modern thought. He deals very cavalierly with them, and his arrangements are makeshift. But it doesn't matter finally, because the whole point is that his Iphigenie should incorporate an ethical attitude superior to barbarous cults. In the total result, therefore, we feel that he has achieved more than Racine, because he has achieved his purpose, a unity of idea. Though we have to overcome a sense of irritation, we do so in the end, not only because we see that it is important that we should do so, but because Goethe is in fact succeeding.

When we view the succession of Goethe's dramas we see the evolution of a consistent method. *Torquato Tasso* seems to me to be the pivot of the development. Under the surface orthodoxy of *Götz von Berlichingen* and *Egmont* we have observed anticipations of the method. In both those plays there is something Goethean that doesn't square with the framework Goethe took over, and looking back at them from *Torquato Tasso,* we see how they contain an embryo of his true subject. The incipient iambic verse in the close of *Egmont,* and the recasting of *Iphigenie,* take on a particular significance from this new point of view; for the convention of verse supported his imagination in its direction towards an original subject and a subtle form. The technique appears increasingly in the revisions of *Faust,* that is to say, after the writing of *Tasso.* It becomes, indeed, plain for all to see, the symbolism and allegory growing more and more obvious and elaborate. We are all perhaps in danger of reading *Tasso* literally, but no one can make that mistake with *Faust.* This work, of course, has a long history, and its various stages show the evolution of Goethe's dramatic method, and almost every degree of success and failure. The

fragmentary *Urfaust* is the nearest Goethe came to a straightforward human tragedy of passion, and it is unique in his plays. The
conception of the extended *Faust* is from the start a drama dealing
with the awareness of values; it actually begins with Faust abandoning the intellectual sciences as one-sided and inadequate, and
dreaming of an experience that would telescope the sum of life
into an instant and make him see all value in a single moment.
Faust himself is not a person; he is personality used by poetry to
image a mental arena. Mephistopheles, Helena, Gretchen, are all
saturated with symbolism. But they are living poetic figures because what they symbolize has always a reference to a way of life.
They are without the particular individuality that we associate
with character in real life; to that extent they are abstractions,
stylizations. But what they represent are always forms of living and
experiencing, to be perceived not in ideas that they might talk
about but in what they are and how that is expressed in human
behavior. They are therefore parallel figures to those of *Iphigenie
auf Tauris* and *Torquato Tasso*. They are, of course, much more
complex in their symbolism than the earlier creations; but in that
we observe not a difference, but the elaboration of the same poetic
method. *Faust,* moreover, insists as little on a conventional "plot"
as the earlier plays, and for the same reasons: a conflict of passion,
or will, or character, or fate, gives way to the conflict of values
that is present everywhere in the nature and structure of human
life, and in our consciousness of it.

A point is reached, of course, at which Goethe overshoots the
mark and allows allegory to develop at the expense of that sense of
life to which we have referred, and his work then becomes pro-
gressively more abstract and literary, and less vital as dramatic
poetry. The decline is noticeable in *Die Natürliche Tochter* which
satisfies neither as a human drama nor as a mental one. The method
is the same, and it is outwardly emphasized by abandoning individual names and using the stereotyped "König," "Baron," and
so on. But it has become abstract and schematic, just as the style,
wonderful as a technical effort, has sacrificed its true foundation
and become virtuosity. As time went on Goethe lost the intense
personal feeling and the vivid sympathetic imagination that give
the persons of the great plays, however ideally conceived, their life.
His later essays in dramatic poetry, *Pandora,* most of *Faust II,*
have some fine qualities; but they show the fundamental method
developed without sufficient dramatic substance to justify the link

with the theatre. They are often beautiful in their formal outline and provide many examples of Goethe's power of fusing philosophical and lyric statement. They tend, however, to be diagrammatic illustrations of didactic ideas, the dialogue contains more reflection than action, and the verse is too diffuse. Hofmannsthal was attracted by the "operatic" qualities of these later parts of Goethe's work; and such a suggestive analogy would imply a different relationship with the theatre which would raise interesting speculations. From the point of view of poetic drama, however, they are remote from the theatre. In his best period Goethe's generalizations were in immediate contact with experience; in the decline they easily become detached and wear too often the look of knowledge supported only by faint memories of life.

We set out with the question in our minds, what place does Goethe's drama occupy in the history of the form, and what relationship does it establish between poetry and drama in his time? We mentioned one or two factors of significance: the lack of a proper theatrical setting, or a live theatre with an audience sensitive to poetry and itself helping to shape drama, like the Elizabethans, or the aristocracy of the Grand Siècle. Then we noticed the presence of a decided background of ideas, mainly ethical and educative in tendency, and far more important, when Goethe started to write, than any form of imaginative literature.

The arresting feature of this situation is that the most refined poetic sensibility of that time seized on what was most vital in its intellectual consciousness and made that the new subject of drama, or, to put it another way, extracted from it its *dramatic* aspect. Herder and Schiller could teach and preach; say what was true, what was beautiful, as a matter of intellectual judgment. Goethe absorbed their climate of ideas; you can't read his plays without recollecting Lessing, Herder, Voltaire, Rousseau, and Winckelmann, all devoted to the search for civilized living. But his distinguishing mark is that he never thinks without feeling; the apprehension of ideas is connected at every point with sensibility; thought and ethics are always impregnated with imagination and transformed into the kind of experience that calls for poetry as its natural expression. He effected a subtle alliance between ethical ideas and the contexts in life through which they are perceived and felt; and drawing on this he was able to portray in drama the general consciousness in the act of being invaded by ideas and ideals; the sense of values evolving; the mind in the very process of being sensitized to truth, poetry, civilization, and subjected to all the difficulties and conflicts the process brings with it. His plays are full of the dramatic tensions of our minds trying to shape our lives.

This distinguishes him from Schiller, for whom it can be claimed that he put across ideas, but not that he created poetic images like Tasso and Faust. Goethe has suffered from the fact that Schiller has always been a popular success in the theatre, and I feel that my argument lays upon me an obligation to make at least a short comment on their comparative merits as dramatists. I do not want to disparage Schiller; we know well enough why he should be respected. But in judging his work there are at least as many qualifications to be made as in the case of Goethe. The fact is, of course, that there is no German dramatist without spikes; none whom we can admire with abandon as we admire Shakespeare and Racine for their wonderful fusion of acting, drama, and poetry. But no dramatist anywhere in Europe after Racine has reached their level. The most we get is an interesting development of single features. Grillparzer and Ibsen succeeded more than anyone else in preserving a tense action whilst exploiting something new in the form. Goethe added a new poetic intensity at the expense of the plot of incident. Schiller maintained a strictly theatrical effectiveness within a framework derived from Shakespeare. In the broad sense that he associated drama with the ideas of the time, he worked on similar lines to Goethe. But his method was to pick out a few of the grand ideas that interested him and elaborate them in a rhetoric both of language and of theatre, frankly enthusiastic and tendentious, and penetrating successfully to a wide public. Goethe found the poetic form not for this or that idea, but for the whole ethical response of the time; not for slogans and precepts but for the actual spiritual process. From Schiller's plays we deduce ethical sensibility; in Goethe's we see it imaged. When it comes to a stirring action in the theatre, Schiller has it, obviously. But on the formal side he is without interest; his plays are orthodox, that is to say, imitative, both as program pieces, and as tragedies. *Wallenstein* is always judged to be his best play because it is the least tendentious, and comes nearest in fact to what a generalized notion of Shakespearian history and tragedy lead you to expect. Technically speaking, Schiller looked backwards, and therefore his popular success in the theatre can scarcely be urged against Goethe's originality. Schiller's drama is defective by the standards it tries to conform to, and for our finer judgment it is saved principally by our sense of a noble personality behind it. Goethe's plays, on the other hand, deliberately abandon orthodox standards because they have a new poetic purpose.

If his conception made it inevitable that he should deviate from well-established notions about stage drama, it restored vitality to a great form, added something new, and preserved the unity of poetry and drama. The *Rührstück* and the *Ritterdrama* were popular entertainments; at the most the former was associated with the moral explorations of the age at a debased level. The *Sturm und Drang*, dramatizing with a great deal of fuss, was no more than a minor German eddy in the spiritual life of a European age. Goethe's verse plays, pushed aside as curiosities by historians of drama, are in fact central, because they show poetic and dramatic genius applied to the main stream of thought, and incidentally give to German poetry a European status. Their heterodoxy is the consequence of a vital subject-matter, the adaptation that a traditional form, handled by genius, always makes to meet the demands of a new outlook.

We do not wish to claim too much for Goethe's drama; but not too little either, and in the past it has been appreciated abundantly as the work of Goethe, not enough as a contribution to poetic drama. The new subject was not so easy to treat for the theatre as the old drama of will, passion, and fate. It is inward, admittedly less productive of external incident and theatrical effects, it is delicate and sensitive. But it is tense and exciting, and extends the possibilities of the form. These plays are often said to be for reading and not for acting. Yet their language urges as irresistibly to speech as that of Shakespeare and Racine. We observe, moreover, that Goethe anticipates one of the great developments of modern thought and poetry. We no longer think of art in simple naïve ways, having become much more self-conscious about our psychological processes. We think, and we observe how we are thinking; see, and observe how we are seeing. We look for forms of experience as well as for contents, for images of mental movement as well as for external nature. The simple drama of character and plot no longer compels innocent attention, as modern dramatists know. Something of this complexity is present in Goethe. His drama shows an early stage in the development of self-consciousness, and his genius is apparent both in the anticipation and in the bold exploration of a new form for it. Surveying the course of dramatic poetry in Europe, we see that he transformed drama in order to attune it to a new major phase of experience. At its best, the form he found, based, like all great drama, on the poet's voice, is one of the subtlest the dramatic imagination has yet evolved.

Goethe's *Iphigenia* and the Humane Ideal

by Oskar Seidlin

Early in 1802, fully fifteen years after the completion of Goethe's *Iphigenia in Tauris,* the theater of Weimar prepared the play's first performance in the city which, since 1775, had been Goethe's home and, by being Goethe's home, was to become a shrine to the human urge for veneration. Goethe, at that time the artistic head of the ducal theater, showed himself rather uncoöperative and diffident during the preparation of this, one of his greatest plays, for the stage. He left the whole business of scene arrangements, of cutting, and revising in the hands of his trusted friend Schiller, and displayed the attitude of a more or less bored bystander. Indeed, it is quite understandable that, after his long and burdensome experience as the manager of the ducal theater, he was loathe to become too deeply involved in the mechanical matters of play production when one of his own works was placed on the repertoire. Indeed, we know how reluctant he was all through his life to face a past manifestation of his development, a skin which he had shed, to relive the agonies from which an earlier work had sprung; and agonies, the fearful pains of a tormented heart, are the subsoil from which his *Iphigenia* had grown, as they are so often the subsoil of his works which he himself, in his autobiography, called "but fragments of one great confession." Yet in his correspondence with Schiller in which he discusses the forthcoming stage production, he makes hardly any mention of either the technical or the emotionally personal considerations which may have prevented him from playing a more active part in revising his drama for the theater. However, in one of his letters to Schiller (January 19, 1802)

"Goethe's *Iphigenia* and the Humane Ideal." From *Essays in German and Comparative Literature,* by Oskar Seidlin (Chapel Hill: University of North Carolina Press, 1961), pp. 30–44. Copyright © 1961 by University of North Carolina Press. Reprinted by permission of the publisher. This essay was originally a public address delivered at the University of Washington, Seattle, within the series of Goethe lectures in 1949.

we are struck by a rather curious remark. It is here that Goethe calls his *Iphigenia* "ganz verteufelt human" ("quite damnably humane.")

"Quite damnably humane"—what does he mean by that? We can hardly believe that he wanted to repudiate the very basis upon which his *Iphigenia* was built: the extremely noble conception of a humane idealism which nowhere in German letters has found so stirring and so magnificent an expression as in this play. Yet it might be possible that, when using these strange words, he was anticipating the criticism of a new era leveled against his great play, leveled against the man Goethe altogether, a criticism directed against the loftiness of an ideal which was considered superhuman in its purity, a criticism against an all too easy belief in man's perfection, in his ability to assume the stature of a god, a criticism against the benign serenity and the unshakable optimism of the eighteenth century; in short, a criticism brought against Goethe by some of his detractors of the nineteenth century, against Goethe, the Olympian, the imperturbable one, unmovable and unmoved by doubts, unassailed by the horror of man's smallness and frailty, so smugly satisfied with what he had reached, and what he had proclaimed to be within the reach of man.[1] Needless to say that there never was a Goethe of this sort. But he must have felt how easy it would be to twist him into the pat picture of a glacial loftiness, to make him a lifeless model of Sunday-school idealism, a preacher of a textbook perfectionism, of starry-eyed goodness; and in the Mephistophelean whimsicality which was so much a part of his being he tagged the words "damnably humane" onto his Iphigenia, as a warning to those who would raise his heroine to the superhuman heights of sanctity, and as a warning to those who would turn away from his heroine because she had been raised so dizzily high.

And indeed to dizzy heights Iphigenia seems to rise. Although Goethe followed rather closely the external course of events of the old Greek legend, he had changed the emphasis, the inner organism of the fable so radically that Schiller was quite right in calling Goethe's Greek drama "astonishingly modern and un-Greek."

---

[1] It is, of course, this self-reliant and self-assured "humanism" against which so much of twentieth century Goethe criticism (e.g. Ortega y Gasset's and T. S. Eliot's) has reacted more or less violently. About the image of man in German classicism as a noble but dangerous delusion cf. Heinrich Weinstock, *Die Tragödie des Humanismus: Wahrheit und Trug in abendländischen Menschenbild* (Heidelberg, 1953).

What Euripides, in his *Iphigenia among the Taurians,* had presented was, as all of Greek tragedy, a ritual festival: man cruelly enmeshed in the inhuman schemes of the gods, thrown at their mercy, driven to crimes because it was so ordained, punished with labors by which alone he can free himself of the curse with which the gods have afflicted him, and finally rescued, not by his own power, but by the interference of the gods who, while lifting man from his desperate plight, lift themselves to everlasting glory.

So Orestes, who has killed his murderous mother upon Apollo's order, and is from the day of this hideous crime on pursued by the Furies, the goddesses of vengeance, arrives with his friend Pylades on the shores of Tauris. According to Apollo's decree he can rid himself from the frightful pursuers only by bringing back to Greece the statue of Apollo's sister Artemis which, without Orestes' knowing, had for many years been attended to by his own sister, the Artemis priestess Iphigenia. It is a dangerous venture that Orestes is embarking upon, dangerous to carry away the statue, almost impossible to elude the death which awaits every captured foreigner at the hands of the priestess Iphigenia in accordance with the law of the barbarian land. Yet the three Greeks, Iphigenia, Orestes, and Pylades, after recognizing their identities, conspire in a clever plot by which they not only deceive the stupidly credulous barbarian King Thoas and snatch from under his very eyes the holy statue, but make their escapes with Iphigenia in the bargain, who for so many years had been kept an exile in the land of the Taurians. However, to make it quite plain that man's redemption is not man-made, the waves toss the three fugitives back onto the shores of Tauris, deliver them again into the hands of the infuriated King Thoas. Their doom would be sealed if, at the last moment, Pallas Athena were not to descend *ex machina,* impress upon the king the will of the gods and order him to let the three Greeks go free. What a frightful picture of man's forlornness of his moving under the curse to murder, under the curse to die, under the curse to live, a dark spectacle only dimly lit by the hope that one day the gods may relent their cruel play, only proudly lit by the national feeling of Greek superiority over the uncouth and sluggish slow-wittedness of the barbarians.

Such is the story and the factual material which Goethe, while following it in its outline, actually lifted out of its hinges. The strings that guided the destiny of man from the heights of Mount

Olympus have been cut; and the scene is no longer the twilit in-between of the above and the below, but the familiar ground of our earth, the strange and familiar ground of the human heart. No longer a ritual incantation, but a song of man, of his personal plight, his personal hopes, his personal atonement. It is still the matricide Orestes who arrives at the shores of Tauris, but the crime he has committed is his own crime for which no god but he himself is responsible and answerable: the rashness and the wildness of his blood which drove him to the outrage. His terrible fall is man-made, self-made: and therefore his punishment is man-made, and self-made, too. It is no longer the concrete goddesses of revenge that pursue him; he is pursued by the voices of his own heart, by a feeling of guilt and a remorse so bitter that he is actually driven to the verge of madness. Instead of Orestes, the cursed one, the man over whom a terrible fate is suspended, we meet Orestes, the diseased one, the man whose very blood is poisoned. And what is his particular disease? Remorse, feeling of guilt? To be sure, re-morse and feeling of guilt torture Orestes most powerfully, but they do not actually represent a disease. His illness is a more frightening one: the will to live is extinguished in Orestes. And perhaps we must reinterpret Orestes' horrible misdeed in terms of modern psy-chology. Is Goethe really telling the story of the mythological hero Orestes who killed his mother Clytemnestra, or is he not rather telling the story of a sick human heart, of his own sick heart, the story of a man who, in the image of his mother, has killed the source of life, who has lacerated with his own hands the womb which gave him birth, and is now longing for extinction? For it is extinction that Orestes is pining for, deliverance from what he calls "life's fitful fever," the great forgetfulness, the eternal dark-ness, the realm of the shadows over which the sun, star of the day, never rises. This indeed is the extreme and blissful vision of his diseased mind: the underworld into which he sees himself trans-ported, the nothingness in which the unbearable conflicts of exist-ing, the burden of living have fallen away. This scene, Orestes in the Inferno, which so mistakenly has always been taken only as a poetic hyperbole for his madness, finds at the end of the play an exact counterpart: Orestes, sword in hand, willing and ready to fight against the king who, as he thinks, blocks to him and to his beloved ones the return into life. To be sure, he is mistaken; there is no need for this fight; but that he who once addressed the one who seemed to bring him death with the words

> Ja, schwinge deinen Stahl, verschone nicht,
> Zerreisse diesen Busen und eröffne
> Den Strömen, die hier sieden, einen Weg—

that he can now raise his sword in defense proves that he has been
healed, that he has found his way back into the upperworld.

Since man's affliction comes from within, his salvation must come
from within, too. The center of the Greek legend, that an external
deed, the carrying away of the holy statue, could lift the agony
which racks Orestes, was bound to become irrelevant to Goethe.
He had to reinterpret this part of the myth, and his reinterpreta-
tion makes the humanization of an ancient ritual ceremony complete. In the most magnificent scene of recognition Orestes realizes
what Apollo really wanted him to bring home: not the image of
the god's sister Artemis, but his own sister Iphigenia, not the object of a religious rite, but the living embodiment of man's salvation, Iphigenia the great healer of man's wounds and ills.

Iphigenia the healer, man's great sister, his own flesh and blood
and yet an independent self, as a woman the object of love and yet
beyond all possessive desires, involved in our fate and yet free to
rise above it. In Goethe's Iphigenia the conception of sisterhood
seems to have found its tenderest impersonation, as much as, to
the emotional consciousness of Occidental man, the Virgin Mary
has become the impersonation of the conception of motherhood.
Iphigenia is indeed not *a* man's sister, but *the* sister of man. It is
surely not by chance that through Goethe's story of the human
brother and sister, Orestes and Iphigenia, shines the image of
higher brother and sister relationships, of the mythological relationship of Apollo and Artemis, and finally of the cosmic relationship of sun and moon. Goethe's Iphigenia is not by chance the
chaste priestess of the moon-goddess Artemis; for the magic power
of the moonlight, its soft victory over the frightening darkness of
night, its soothing calm that resolves all tensions, its cool and melancholy aloofness from the strain of our daily burdens—all this
seems to have taken on human shape in Iphigenia. Of the healing
magic of the moon, of the great balm which it sends into man's
heart ridden with fear and pain, Goethe has sung again and again,
as early as in the first monologue of Faust:

> Ach könnt ich doch auf Berges Höhn
> In deinem lieben Lichte gehn,
> Um Bergeshöhl mit Geistern schweben

> Auf Wiesen in deinem Dämmer weben,
> Von all dem Wissensqualm entladen
> In deinem Tau gesund mich baden—

and never more beautifully than in the first stanzas of his poem "An den Mond":

> Füllest wieder Busch und Tal
> Still mit Nebelglanz,
> Lösest endlich auch einmal
> Meine Seele ganz;
>
> Breitest über mein Gefild
> Lindernd deinen Blick,
> Wie des Freundes Auge mild
> Über mein Geschick.

Unless we see Iphigenia as the embodiment of an intimate human relationship, indeed as the human embodiment of well-meaning cosmic forces, we run the risk which the nineteenth century was unable to avoid: to take her as the mouthpiece of a lofty moral gospel. Yet Iphigenia is entirely free of any dogmatic doctrine, no matter from which religious or ethical realm this doctrine may be derived. To be sure, Goethe's *Iphigenia* is the loftiest symbol of the German humane idealism, yet it is an idealism of a specific brand which tries to do away with the nefarious dualism of body and soul, of nature and spirit. The image of man which Goethe has created in his Iphigenia is "the beautiful soul," a conception so dear to his heart because here and here alone the dichotomy of an animalistic and a spiritual part of man is resolved. The law which Iphigenia lives and which triumphs through her is neither the natural law "Thou must," nor the ethical law "Thou shalt," but a miraculous reconciliation in which the "must" and "shall" are one and the same. Following Shaftesbury, Goethe has taken the attribute of such a human attitude, the adjective "beautiful," from the aesthetic sphere; because it is in the work of art that form, the stamp of the spirit, has merged so completely with the material, the given flesh, that an insoluble whole has resulted.

Iphigenia's greatness is exactly this: that she is constitutionally unable to do the ignoble, even if all practical reasoning, even if a specific order of the gods would seem to force upon her the wicked deed. It is not a moral law that prevents her from deceiving the king and from carrying out the plot by which the statue of the goddess Artemis could be spirited away: quite the contrary, the spe-

cific order of Apollo would require her collaboration in the dubious scheme. It is her heart which says "no"; not virtue, but
instinct, not a noble ethical decision, but her incapability to do
wrong. She does not have to weigh the pros and cons; in fact, she
is quite unable to do so as she herself states: "I cannot argue, I can
only feel." There is in her an immediacy of moral awareness that
is in no need of a moral code. The law is not suspended above her
but has grown into her, is actually part of her. A heart so unfail-
ingly sure does not need a higher authority to give it direction, and
again, as with every aspect of the legend, Goethe has transformed
the external into an internal element. For Iphigenia the gods are
not external agencies which impose their commands upon man;
they exist only in man, in the voice of his heart. This indeed is an
utterly un-Greek conception, but it is an un-Christian conception
as well, and nothing seems to me more awkward than to make a
Christian saint out of Iphigenia. For Goethe the unerring heart is
the only guarantor of the existence of God, as he himself has expressed it in one of his most beautiful poems, "Das Göttliche":

> Heil den unbekannten
> Höhern Wesen,
> Die wir ahnen!
> Ihnen gleiche der Mensch;
> Sein Beispiel lehr' uns
> Jene glauben.

For a Christian such lines may verge on the blasphemous: God's
existence, our belief in Him made dependent upon the example
that man sets. And it is exactly the same sentiment which Iphigenia
voices. In the moment of her extreme crisis, when faced with the
horrible alternative of shedding her brother's blood on the altar or
of plotting against the king, who for so many years has proved generous and kind to her, she cries out to the gods, "Save me, and save
your image in my soul!" It is she, man, who sets the standards, the
image to which the gods have to live up; by letting her down, by
destroying her, the gods would let themselves down, would destroy
themselves. In fact, she goes so far as to defy the gods openly.
Apollo had ordered Orestes to bring back the statue of Artemis:
this is the unmistakable will of the god. Yet what does Iphigenia
do? While all the plans are set to spirit way the holy image, she
informs the king of the plot which she herself had helped to prepare; she acts to prevent the execution of Apollo's will, because to
her it is inconceivable that the gods want a deed carried out which

involves deceit, theft, and trickery. And there is almost divine irony in the fact that Apollo seems to endorse, *ex post facto,* Iphigenia's decision, that he, so to speak, takes his cue from her; for what he really wanted, so we hear now, is not the homecoming of an image, the glorification of a holy statue, but the glorification of a human soul which cannot be corrupted even by what may have presented itself as a divine command.

Well, so one may ask at this point, was not Goethe quite right, was not the more realistic nineteenth century quite right in calling this Iphigenia "damnably humane"? Does not this sheer goodness, this infallible righteousness smack of the angelic which we may coolly admire but which cannot really mean anything to us, because it is blind to all the pitfalls, all the gnawing doubts, all the painful anxieties of man's existence? But to argue thus means, so it seems to me, to overlook the orbit in which this Iphigenia moves, the function which she fulfills in this world. As we said before, her greatness is not actually of a moral nature; what she embodies are vital forces in the human heart, the force of light, the force of regeneration, the force of hopefulness. We cannot and should not isolate her, but we must see her in her close relationship to her brother, a relationship so intimate that she herself can say to him, "My fate is bound insolubly to thine." Orestes *and* Iphigenia, the broken heart *and* the unbreakable one, the despair at existing *and* the hope for redemption, the involvement in sin and cruel deeds which life imposes upon us every day *and* the aloofness of a priestly purity: they together constitute man's condition. Neither Orestes nor Iphigenia is a behavioristic human model; rather they represent in polar juxtaposition vital forces in man, the force of self-destruction and the force of regeneration. Exactly as inexplicable as is the working of an energy is the effect which Iphigenia has upon all who surround her. What she works seems magic; she does not manifest herself by action or by preaching, she is, so to speak, an impulse by which the withered and the dead forces in those whom she touches are revitalized. This is true not only in the case of her healing of Orestes who, upon mere contact with her, turns to the road of recovery. It is equally true in the case of King Thoas who, by the mere fact of her being, of her being near him, has developed from a barbarian tyrant into a civilized king. Iphigenia does not stand for values; she *is* the value. She does not set an example for her fellow men, but becomes a part of them, a part that overcomes the sinister forces in man's breast. This indeed may be called magic, or perhaps better, a mystery, the profoundest mystery in which Goethe believed, the inscrutable and irrational power of what he called "die Persönlichkeit," a power against which there is only one means of defense: acceptance. In his novel, *The Elective Affinities,* he has epitomized it in the words: "In the face of the great superiority of another person there is no means of safety but love."

Yet it is not only through association that Iphigenia is involved in the sufferings of man. Her words to Orestes, "My fate is bound insolubly to thine," must be taken quite literally. She lives and she moves under the same frightful shadow which darkens the mind of her brother. It is quite characteristic that Goethe put into her mouth the long recital of crimes and outrages which have exacted their bloody toll from the house of Tantalus, from her house. After she has told the king the grisly story of treachery, rape, and murder, she sees herself as a link in an endless chain of sin and cursedness:

> Dies sind die Ahnherrn deiner Priesterin;
> Und viel unseliges Geschick der Männer,
> Viel Taten des verworrnen Sinnes deckt
> Die Nacht mit schweren Fittichen und lässt
> Uns nur in grauenvolle Dämmrung sehn.

"The slings and arrows of outrageous fortune" which harass Orestes to the point where it seems to him impossible to live on, harass Iphigenia no less. In fact, the events she has to go through during the course of the play seem like a diabolically cruel trap from which there is no escape at all. Surely, man's position can hardly be viewed in a more tragic light than the one Goethe spread around Iphigenia. Everything seems to conspire against her, even the tender emotions which she awakens in the hearts of others seem to cause and accelerate her doom. Not only the wrath of the gods, but even the love of men work towards her destruction. For Goethe has added a motif which is completely lacking in the old tradition of the myth, Thoas' love for Iphigenia, the tenderest human feeling which, however, seems to close the trap around her completely. Because she has rejected the wooing of the king, he has, in his resentful anger, revived the barbarian law, already abated by Iphigenia's influence, that every foreigner captured on the shores of Tauris must be sacrificed to the goddess. And the reintroduction of this inhuman rite will now force Iphigenia to kill her own brother and, by doing so, exterminate the house of Tantalus, so sorely tried and pursued by the gods. The ring is closed around her so neatly that there is indeed nothing left but a "peering into frightful gloom."

Can man live? This is the question, not only of Orestes, but of Iphigenia as well, when the cards are so inexorably stacked against him. Is "to be or not to be" really still a question when we are driven, step by step, into deeper entanglement with nowhere a door left into freedom and liberation? Is not complete loss of consciousness indeed the "consummation devoutly to be wished," since our whole life is nothing but a painful sickness unto death, spared to no one, the innocent one no less than the evil-doer? Are we not lost before we have started? Is Iphigenia not lost? Indeed, is she not dead before she is even put to the test of living?

At this point, it seems to me, Goethe's play takes on its deepest meaning. The land of the shadows to which Orestes turns as the last hope since life has so cruelly beaten him,—Iphigenia has lived in it for years. Once, in Aulis, she was marked to die in order to appease the angry goddess. But before the sword fell upon her neck, the goddess carried her away to a distant and remote country. It is an island, which means it is separated from the rest of the world, not only isolated by the waters, but isolated by the cruel law that everyone who sets foot on these shores must die. It is the underworld, the place beyond space, the place beyond time. For time stood still when Iphigenia arrived, and no messenger ever brought her news of the world, of her world. Both Orestes and Iphigenia are moving under the shadow of death; Orestes sees the underworld in his most exalted vision, Iphigenia has for many years lived in the kingdom of death. Yet the direction of their desires is opposite: Iphigenia, her spirits undaunted by the lure of death, wants to return, return home, return to life. Orestes, his spirits broken by the onslaught of life, wants to cross the border whence no traveler returns. Iphigenia remembers and wants to make her memories reality again. Orestes does not want to remember, but wants to flee into eternal forgetfulness. It seems quite significant to me that Iphigenia's first word, indeed the first word of the whole play, is "heraus" (out of); while Orestes' first words at the beginning of the second act are: "It is the path of death that now we tread"—both of them indicating motion, but motion in opposite directions: Iphigenia's direction—the road out of deadness, Orestes' direction—the road into the night.

Indeed, "frightful gloom" envelops Iphigenia no less than Orestes. But the word that counts in the quotation above is the word "to peer." Iphigenia's eyes are open, and they remain open although nothing that can be seen seems to present itself. She is willing to face even utter darkness, and this willingness to face it makes her great, not superhumanly great, but humanly great. That she does not turn away when Pylades unlocks before her eyes the horrible deed which her own mother perpetrated against her father, that she does not turn away when Orestes unlocks before her eyes the horror which is raging in his breast, that she keeps on "peering" even though there is nothing to be seen but "frightful gloom"—this is the final test of her humaneness. There is none of the righteous shudder of the angel, there is none of the benign aloofness of the saint; this is simply a human heart not willing to shut itself even if the most abominable sins, the vipers of the abyss are arrayed against it. In the words of T. S. Eliot's "Gerontion" Iphigenia could well call out: "After such knowledge, what forgiveness?" But Iphigenia knows the answer that Gerontion does not know: the forgiveness is hope.

Goethe's *Iphigenia* is not an easy message of hope, and not a message of easy hope. It is hope wrung from the deepest despair. Even the noble and brave heart trembles lest all be in vain. The moment comes when she, too, has reached the bottom of the pit, when the word "heraus" seems to her a pious and mocking delusion. At the end of the fourth act, in the poem which we usually refer to as "Das Parzenlied," it dawns upon Iphigenia that everything may be futile, that no hope and no faith can exact a friendly answer from the gods, that only silence or Olympian laughter answers the cries of the human heart:

> Sie aber, sie bleiben
> In ewigen Festen
> An goldenen Tischen.
> Sie schreiten vom Berge
> Zu Bergen hinüber;
> Aus Schlünden der Tiefe
> Dampft ihnen der Atem
> Erstickter Titanen
> Gleich Opfergerüchen,
> Ein leichtes Gewölke.
>
> Es wenden die Herrscher
> Ihr segnendes Auge

> Von ganzen Geschlechtern
> Und meiden, im Enkel
> Die ehmals geliebten,
> Still redenden Züge
> Des Ahnherrn zu sehn.

Even Iphigenia, the hopeful one, the hope of man, is not spared the most heart-rending doubts. Yet it seems that this very doubt, the journey through the hell of despair, gives her the strength to do the liberating deed. That man could be forever lost, that all his fortitude and striving should end with the triumphant laughter of the forces of evil, this was indeed inconceivable to Goethe. Man may be entangled, may entangle himself in error, sin, and crime, he may have to travel through a dark world and the darkness of his own heart, but that he was meant to perish without any chance of resurrection, this was simply unthinkable to Goethe. He could not deliver his Faust into the hands of the devil, he could not leave Iphigenia in the "fathomless chasms," because the admittance of such a possibility would undo the Creation, would make life itself a farcical game, utterly meaningless and shallow.

A message of hope, and yet no message of easy hope. Bound to a fate which we cannot escape, forced by practical necessities, driven by our own selfish desires, living in a world in which goodness is by no means a guarantee for survival—how can we do the free deed which alone can extricate us from the entanglements in which life involves us daily? This exactly is Iphigenia's question. How can she act as a free agent, obedient only to the voice of her heart, when she is assailed from all sides by forces of necessity which allow no room for a free decision? It is almost a test case with which we are confronted here: is action at all possible to a creature so thoroughly conditioned, confined, and bound as man is? Subject to the immutable laws of nature, subject to the inscrutable will of higher forces, is man not indeed doomed forever, reduced to the level of animal existence? Is reason, the gift by which he thinks he can lift himself above the dictates of his own confinement and temporality, not a senseless mirage which makes him only more miserable since it teases him with a conception of freedom which he cannot possibly attain? Is not Mephistopheles right when, talking to the Lord about man, he characterizes him with these contemptuous words:

Ich sehe nur, wie sich die Menschen plagen.

Der kleine Gott der Welt bleibt stets vom gleichen Schlag,
Und ist so wunderlich als wie am ersten Tag.
Ein wenig besser würd' er leben,
Hättst du ihm nicht den Schein des Himmelslichts gegeben;
Er nennt's Vernunft und braucht's allein,
Nur tierischer als jedes Tier zu sein.
Er scheint mir, mit Verlaub von Euer Gnaden,
Wie eine der langbeinigen Zikaden,
Die immer fliegt und fliegend springt
Und gleich im Gras ihr altes Liedchen singt;
Und läg er nur noch immer in dem Grasel
In jeden Quark begräbt er seine Nase.

Can man ever avoid the hopping and flitting and dancing, can he
ever stand upright? Is not Iphigenia caught in a dilemma to which
there is no solution? Conditions are such that in order to save her
brother, in order to save herself, she can do either of two things.
She can appease the king and accept his wooing and, by doing so,
become unfaithful to herself, to her mission in life which, she
knows, awaits her in Greece. Or she can carry out the scheme, col-
laborate in the theft of the statue and, by doing so, become unfaithful to the king who has trusted her as he has trusted no one else.
The trap is so neatly set that only one of these two decisions is
possible. Yet Iphigenia decides—for the impossible, for the thing
that, in a determined and conditioned world, cannot be done, for
a free, a gratuitous deed. Against necessity, against everything and
everyone, including the command of the gods, she pits what her
heart tells her is the right thing to do. There is nothing reckless
and nothing superhuman in Iphigenia's action when she faces the
king and tells him the truth, when she gives away the plot which
is already successfully under way. She is shaken by doubts, she is
shaken by fear because she knows very well what an enormous risk
she is taking. If she fails, and fail she may very easily, everything
is lost, her brother, herself, and with her man's faith in the
victory of life over death, of light over darkness. Yet the challenge
must be met, because only by the free deed, by rising above his own
condition, by thrusting himself into absolute insecurity, can man
prove that he is man, the paradoxical being, immersed in the
flux of temporality and yet capable of penetrating to the eternal
by apprehending timeless existence within time and above it. And
only this free deed can be a liberating deed, can break the chain
from which we all are smarting, can, in the midst of misery, help-

lessness, and forlornness which, indeed, are our share, reëstablish the dignity of man.

Man, the paradoxical being who in Goethe's own words "can do the impossible," mercilessly bound by an unalterable fate and yet capable of a free decision, of the gratuitous deed by which he can shape his own destiny. But paradoxical in a still higher sense. For the deed born from the most intimately personal crisis, from man's need for his own personal redemption, is at the same time the deed that can shape the destiny of all mankind, alter the face of the world. For this indeed is Iphigenia's greatest glory: by saving her soul she not only decides her own future and that of her house, but blasts a path into a vast and unknown future. Out of her deed rises a new millenium. It is in her farewell to Thoas that the full meaning of her act of liberation becomes evident:

> Nicht so, mein König! Ohne Segen,
> In Widerwillen scheid' ich nicht von dir.
> Verbann' uns nicht! Ein freundlich Gastrecht walte
> Von dir zu uns . . .

Through Iphigenia, a world, separated by hatred and suspicion, has become united. The horror of man's loneliness is overcome in her last vision: Tauris, the island, separated from the inhabited world by the unsafe element, the water, and isolated by the cruel law against all foreigners, Tauris has been joined to the continent of the living, has become part of the *oikumene*. There is now no longer a Greek world and a barbarian world set against each other in atavistic and eternal enmity. There is, from now on, *one* world held together by love and understanding. The last words of Iphigenia, some of the most beautiful poetry in the German language, sound like a complete revocation of Iphigenia's first monologue. At the beginning there was the atmosphere of the prison: man caught by a merciless fate, banished to the deadly island where no messenger ever appears. Now the walls have fallen. It is not by chance that in Iphigenia's last speech the messenger plays such an important part, the man who goes back and forth to relate and to keep alive interrelationships:

> Bringt der Geringste deines Volkes je
> Den Ton der Stimme mir ins Ohr zurück,
> Den ich an euch gewöhnt zu hören bin,
> Und seh ich an dem Ärmsten eure Tracht:

Empfangen will ich ihn wie einen Gott,
Ich will ihm selbst ein Lager zubereiten,
Auf einen Stuhl ihn an das Feuer laden
Und nur nach dir und deinem Schicksal fragen.

This indeed is man's paradoxical condition that the deed done for the sake of his own personal redemption harbors in its folds the future destiny of the whole world.

This then is Goethe's humane idealism. It has nothing whatsoever to do with an easy belief in man's perfection, with shutting one's eyes to the smallness and the frailty of man's existence. It takes full stock of the destructive forces that act upon man from within and without, of the cruel necessities of life, of the doubts, the despair, the murderous passions in our heart. In Goethe's *Iphigenia* there are, muffled by a deceptive serenity, the cries from the Inferno, the sighs from the Purgatorio, but there is, at the same time, the conviction that the gates to the Paradiso cannot be forever closed.

In an American author, Nathaniel Hawthorne, I recently found a phrase which could fittingly stand as a motto over Goethe's *Iphigenia*, as a pithy condensation of Goethe's view of man's fate. It reads: "at once all shadow and all splendor." Indeed, *Iphigenia* is not "all splendor," not "damnably humane," but it is not all shadow, either. A gulf separates it from the easy optimism of the eighteenth century, and a gulf separates it from the philosophy of despair which has taken hold of so many a contemporary thinker and poet. One of them, one of the greatest German writers of the twentieth century, Franz Kafka, who at this point comes to mind because he loved Goethe more dearly than any other writer he knew—Franz Kafka once wrote the aphorism: "There is hope, perhaps plenty of hope, but not for us." Goethe, had he heard this statement, would have angrily shaken his head. He might have pointed to his *Iphigenia* and to Iphigenia's message: there is hope, perhaps very little hope. But the little there is, is for us.

Goethe's Craft of Fiction

by Victor Lange

Amid the incomparable variety of impulse and purpose that is offered in Goethe's work, there is no segment so coherent and so characteristic of his evolving poetic practices as his fiction, none, certainly, that is so palpably related to the development of his personality. To Goethe himself, in the process of writing and in retrospect, his novels assumed a seriousness of concern which, apart from *Faust*, not many of his plays, nor much of his poetry could claim, and which, as efforts both at broad intellectual summaries and at persuasion, are matched only by his scientific writings. There is no need to recall in any detail the importance of *Werther* in rendering the explosive unrest which dominated his youth; or the evidence, in *Wilhelm Meister*, of that remarkable conquest of actuality and self-discipline that reflects his maturing in Weimar. We are aware of the source of *Wahlverwandtschaften* in his deepening understanding of the incongruities and paradoxes that relate the human being to his surrounding world; and we have come to respect the prophetic wisdom of age that places the *Wanderjahre*, however curiously composed, in the immediate neighbourhood of the second part of *Faust*.

I do not wish to elaborate upon these more general aspects of Goethe's fiction. They have justly been the object of much critical effort; and whatever varieties of interpretation may yet be achieved from this point of view, we can add little to the established lines of relationship between Goethe's philosophical convictions and their reflection in his novels.

What I propose to do is at once less ambitious than the larger purpose, and more, perhaps, in keeping with our contemporary interest in the special properties of fiction. I should like to examine some of the reasons that led Goethe from time to time and at critical points in his career, to the medium of fiction, and to elaborate upon certain characteristic qualities of his narrative art.

It is well to remember that the term fiction is a broad and elusive one that should not be restricted to Goethe's five novels, *Werther, Theatralische Sendung, Lehrjahre, Wahlverwandtschaften,* and *Wanderjahre.* It must be applied to a substantial number of shorter tales, among them, of course, the superb *Novelle,* and, indeed, to aspects of works and pieces of work that contain, if only indirectly, elements of narrative purpose, such as parts of *Dichtung und Wahrheit, Italienische Reise,* the *Kampagne in Frankreich* or *Der Sammler und die Seinigen.* This considerable body of fiction has a distinct personal character. It is in many respects different from contemporary narrative practices, though not altogether independent of them: if we realize that the main stream of fiction in which Goethe himself shared extends from Boccaccio and Cervantes to Fénelon and Prévost, from Richardson and Sterne to Rousseau and Marmontel, from Cooper and Irving to Scott, Stendhal and Balzac, we cannot expect him to have remained untouched by the varying conventions of that tradition. He read all these authors eagerly and with a feeling for their special intentions, and commented intelligently upon them. Yet he was not, in an emphatic or exclusive sense, attached to the form of the novel: he never instinctively seized upon it as the inevitable, congenial medium. We must not think of him as one of that dedicated company to which Melville or Balzac, Henry James or Conrad belong, but rather as the eighteenth century man of letters who, like Voltaire or Rousseau before him, used the devices of fiction where they seemed most appealing and whenever they offered a particularly telling form of discourse.

At the same time this more conventional regard for fiction would hardly have come to life in Goethe if he had not possessed a ready anecdotal talent and a feeling for the effects of story-telling that struck even his early listeners as irresistible and that later gave not only to his talk but to his historical and aesthetic writings an admirably concrete quality. But the two, the available forms and the natural bent, became in his case closely interrelated and, as they were brought into mutual play, remarkably modified one another. Whenever Goethe turned to the writing of fiction, his storyteller's imagination was subordinated to a sense of formal responsibility, which compelled him to scrutinize the available devices of fiction and to exploit or modify them as it seemed necessary. We must certainly not underrate the element of decision and of artistic calculation that persuaded him, at certain periods of particular inner disturbance, to prefer the medium of fiction to the modes of lyrical expression which appear to be so much more congenial to him. There is no great poet in whom these two ways of writing seem so far apart as they are in Goethe: his novels, with the possible exception of *Werther*, have none of the urgent brilliance of imagination, none of the radiance of speech or rhythm that distinguish his lyrics. Instead, they are in design and language urbane, reflected, disciplined to the point of transparency. The central aim that produced them was a remarkable measure not, as in his poetry, of self-representation but of self-denial. In his fiction he did not wish, ultimately, to represent himself or the intensity of his perception but rather, with the novelist's paradoxical impulse toward involvement and objectivity, to give an account of the human being in a particular situation of time and place. It is with the varying manner of this accounting that we should be mainly concerned.

In his reflections on the writing of *Werther*, Goethe stresses the historical perspectives from which the mood and climate of the book can best be understood. He offers in *Dichtung und Wahrheit* an extraordinarily detailed picture of that spiritual dilemma in which the sentimental mind found itself—to live in an obsolescent and confined society in which yet here and there new and revolutionary energies of feeling and speculation emerged—energies, however, which with all their intensity remained inarticulate because suitable and generally intelligible terms for them had not yet evolved. In the social as well as the literary realm the persistent presence of empty forms demanded a constant testing of the available modes of life and art, and an effort at the creation of a fresh and usable idiom. We know that the experience of this discrepancy between a new substance of feeling and a painful sense of the inadequacy of current attitudes was unusually lively in Goethe; the letters of the years 1772–1773 reveal it as one of his central themes. But what distinguishes him from his contemporaries was his concern with turning this experience into poetic form. It may seem as we compare *Werther* to what we know of Goethe himself, that the line between life and art is remarkably thin; there is little in *Werther* that is not experienced, little indeed, that we cannot verify and document in its original biographical context. But in a work of art life, whether as motivating impulse or incident of experience, is never merely reported: it is subordinated to a com-

pelling central intention. There can be no doubt that the manner
in which Goethe here turns life into art, the achievement, for the
first time in his career, of a closely motivated narrative, and the
poetic demonstration of an intricate spiritual process was the result
of unmistakable artistic deliberation; and we shall not do justice
to the kind or the degree of this deliberation if we overemphasize
Goethe's reference to the lack of any preliminary scheme, or if we
take literally his own hint as to the "somnambulist" state in which
the book was written, "ziemlich unbewusst, einem Nachtwandler
ähnlich . . ."

For several months in 1773 Goethe had experimented most effectively with the powerfully personal idiom of the hymn, a form
peculiarly suited to that ambiguous state of mind in which elegiac
and aggressive attitudes were inextricably mixed. In so far as this
mood of heroic exultation is appropriate to *Werther* the hymnic
technique is effectively carried over into the novel: the similarity
between *Ganymed* and several of Werther's letters is familiar
enough. Yet, now, early in 1774, he decided—and it was no casual
decision—to experiment in an altogether different medium, the
medium of fiction. Fiction, we must remember, was, in spite of its
enormous popular appeal, a form of dubious critical respectability,
even though it had, for various reasons, recently attracted a number of distinguished minds: Wieland had turned to it, Herder was
an avid consumer of novels, and what drew Goethe to Sophie La
Roche was, beyond a passing and somewhat amused interest in her
rôle as "sentimental" confidante (and in the pretty eyes of her
daughter Maximiliane), above all her acknowledged success as a
writer of effusive tales. He must have felt that only fiction of one
sort or another could provide the kind of vehicle, the objectivity
that was needed to make a nearly incomprehensible state of inner
disturbance tangible and credible. For it was certainly not only his
love for Lotte Buff in Wetzlar that caused the imbalance of his
mind that we have come to accept as characteristic of this period.
Yet from this love, brief and strangely artificial as in many respects
it actually was, he now drew the symbols of his first exercise in sustained imagination.

When, "nach so langen und vielen geheimen Vorbereitungen,"
he began writing, he cannot have been sure precisely what form
the narrative would take. His choice of letters was a fairly obvious
one, though they were not to be, they could not be, of the dramatic
kind that Richardson and the vogue of epistolary novels had made
familiar. Werther's correspondence is one-sided, a monologue that

only at first seems eager for an echo and gradually ceases to pretend that anyone can share in what is said. At the same time these letters suggest whatever attachment to the world of concrete yet increasingly insufficient reality this radically introspective mind could possibly maintain. If we read the first two or three of them carefully, we come to realize Goethe's reliance upon the devices of the contemporary novel—especially as he attempts to lay out, somewhat tentatively, the suitable elements of plot and motivation. But in spite of his initial dependence on the figures and incidents of the European sentimental novel—Werther's separation from his friend, his memories of a curiously unreal love, a contested will, etc.—Goethe moves forward almost at once to his real poetic purpose: to describe, without resorting to the shopworn tricks of satire or caricature, the inadequacies of a world in which, not the mere sentimental "man of feeling," but the man of irresistible if irrational emotional energies, cannot find his way. He develops, step by step and with a prodigious sensitiveness for poetic rhythm the portrait of an eccentric in a world that has itself lost its center. He provides examples of those current and accepted modes of life into which Werther, if he had been more obtuse, might have translated his spiritual energies; but he dismisses them all: the community of village and family, the aristocratic society, politics, organized religion, even the pattern of love as a satisfying human relationship—none of these is adequate for him. The insufficiency of all props, the discovery of an inevitable sense of loneliness, the recognition of the void which he must bring himself to accept—these are motives which beyond any mere unhappy involvement in love Goethe wanted to convey.

I do not here wish to enter into this astonishingly rich web of meaning. It is important only to insist upon the immense difficulties, the technical difficulties, that must have faced Goethe as he wrote. Far from having to deal with recognized and clearly pointed social conflict such as he might have remembered from Rousseau's *Nouvelle Héloïse,* he was confronted by a situation that was incomparably more elusive and complex. He was not a purveyor of argument such as Rousseau or Lavater, and he knew that this barely definable situation had to be rendered not only with the fullest awareness of the underlying sense of the ambiguity of life, but with an array of the sharpest possible detail. Where could he go among contemporary masters to find the kind of imagery, the poetic gestures, that would be familiar to his readers? The language of his poetry and that of his generation had derived its freshness and strength from Klopstock, and Goethe acknowledges his immeasurable debt to him in that famous scene where the name of the venerated poet takes on the force of a poetic symbol.

But for the more particular ingredients of fiction he had to turn to the English novelists, and among these to the one congenial mind and craftsman that was constantly before him as he wrote: Lawrence Sterne. Herder had in Strasbourg praised him, and long after Goethe had disavowed the facetious rituals of sentimental worship in Darmstadt, Sterne remained for him the most memorable among the English novelists. In Sterne he recognized the same Wertherian experience of a dissolving universe, held together only by the intensity of a restless mind, clinging, not to dubious reality, but to remembered, filtered, and reassociated fragments of feeling, observation, and learning. There are striking differences, of course, between Sterne's manner and Goethe's, and their fiction is related to different historical and social conditions. But there is, surely, in *Werther* as well as in *Tristram Shandy,* that predominant element of abysmal loneliness from which only torrential speech offers relief: broken bits of monologue, endlessly insisting, garrulous and Irish in Sterne, impassioned, lyrical, and at times a little ponderous, in Goethe.

Above all, even here in this seemingly impulsive account of Werther's sufferings the carefully established element of irony must not be missed: no one could be a more incongruous recipient of Werther's letters than the sober friend Wilhelm; how often do we not feel amused rather than moved by Werther's solemnity as aggravating in its way as the pedantry of Albert; does he not at times seem to display an exasperating preoccupation with his own eccentricity, aware, so to speak, of the mirrors at both ends of the room? The others, Werther complains again and again, waste their time; the others take themselves too seriously; they, not he, are indifferent to the troubles of their fellow-men. "Sometimes I could implore them on bended knees not to be so furiously determined to destroy themselves." The narrator's irony alone could make the telling of Werther's incredible experience tolerable, and it was precisely by this quality so seldom fully recognized in the critical discussion of the novel, that Goethe hoped to save the book from being as maudlin and self-indulgent as many a hasty reader was later to think. This ironic attitude enabled him to transpose the experienced reality from a mere confession to a symbolic design; it permitted him, not only in the transparent figure of the editor but in the narrative itself, to maintain himself as a trustworthy story-teller and allowed him to preserve in this account of a crumbling world a perception, a perspective, that remains steady and credible.

It is not minimizing Goethe's achievement if we say that for this first work on a large scale he invented little and borrowed nearly every detail, if not from his own experiences—either remembered, or recorded in letters to his friend Merck—then from the stock of contemporary fiction. He took many of the figures and situations, motifs and scenes from Richardson, from Goldsmith, from Rousseau and others; he used the familiar device of interpolated references to sermons and literary reminiscences; he marshalled Homer and Ossian, Shakespeare, Klopstock, and Lessing as poetic representatives of states of mind that could not be more tellingly elaborated. He employed his lively sense for the revealing scene, the anecdote, the episode, that remained so characteristic of all his later work. His portraiture, it is true, is not specific, he builds his figures by circumstantial evidence: in their physical features nearly all the characters remain indistinct. But it was not Goethe's way, certainly not, as a rule, in his fiction, to produce creatures of fresh and topical authenticity. Even in 1774 he experienced life with the preconceptions of a literary mind; and artistic notions and forms tended, here and later, to determine, sometimes even to anticipate, his observations. It seems to me clear from all we know of his stay in Wetzlar that he there superimposed a set of literary costumes upon reality; now, many months later, he could recall and use them in a poetic design almost without further inspection.

We must not forget that the often described creative unrest which inspired *Werther* was only one of its sources; the other and the more tangible was Goethe's desire to prove himself, as at that time he often confesses, in the rôle of an author; and as the author of a successful piece of fiction he remained famous for the rest of his life. Yet, how little *Werther* was a work of merely professional practicality must be apparent to anyone who turns in comparison to *Wilhelm Meisters Theatralische Sendung* begun three years after the appearance of *Werther*. It is the only large project which occupied him throughout the first twelve years in Weimar, and it shows his eagerness to speak in the terms of the society in which he now moved. It reveals little of the perturbation of the previous years but remains instead, certainly in its initial chapters, palpably close to the fashionable fiction of the time. It begins, not auspiciously, like a family novel, and its early plot promises neither a figure of much interest nor any uncommon involvements. Although it pretends to be a piece of psychological fiction, it is interlarded in the fashion of the time, to whatever purpose, with elaborately argued passages of literary criticism. Where it has warmth and immediacy we recognize the elements of autobiographical reality; but we shall notice an extraordinary difference between Goethe's use of experienced life here and in *Werther:* while the verifiable incident is there interwoven in a context warranted by the poetic design, it seems in *Theatralische Sendung* often to insist upon its own importance. The accounts of Wilhelm's early life and the celebrated episodes of the puppet theater spring, not entirely, but primarily, from the delight in autobiographical recollection, and from Goethe's impulse at self-portraiture and self-explanation which, wholly unlike that leading to *Werther,* was later to produce *Dichtung und Wahrheit.*

This element of authenticity is the reason for the impression of directness which we gain, at least in the first half of the book, quite in contrast to the oblique manner of *Werther.* For the joining of these experienced incidents Goethe relies at first union upon a palpably antithetical manner: each sentence, each scene, each sequence of events, each group of characters and set of arguments is developed with that deliberate balance which Goethe admired in Goldsmith but which remains here somewhat mechanical. There are only moments of resonance in the language which moves along with unaccented regularity; even in the more emotional scenes we feel none of the fire of Werther's speech.

What I have said is most obviously so in that earlier part of *Theatralische Sendung* where Goethe remains within the conventions of the middle-class novel. Yet to a careful reader it must be clear from the beginning that the theme of disappointment, of frustration and disillusionment which Goethe seems to have had in mind for this new novel (see *Tag- und Jahreshefte,* "Bis 1786") could hardly have been fully represented within the framework of its first design. The world of the theater to which Goethe almost at once leads Wilhelm, was to supply the symbols, not, by any means, of challenge and artistic promise, but of disturbance and jeopardy. And to develop this world of the theatre with all its seductive appeal became, in the last four books, Goethe's main purpose. From the beginning Wilhelm was not intended to be an "active" character; he was to be manipulated by the author not for his own sake but for the sake of the world he was to reflect: "Wilhelm ist . . . ein armer Hund, aber nur an solchen lassen sich das Wechselspiel des Lebens und die tausend verschiedenen

Lebensaufgaben recht deutlich zeigen . . ." (to Kanzler Müller, 22 January 1821). He could not possibly have said this of Werther, whose independence, whose almost heroic, if tragic assertion *vis-à-vis* a world of ever decreasing vitality constituted, in contrast to Wilhelm's career, the very theme of the earlier work. If we formulate the relationship between life and its projection into a fictional character in an emphatic way we must say that Wilhelm, not Werther was Goethe himself. But as Goethe now identified Wilhelm with himself, as long as the narrator appeared, in fact, to relate his own life, he could not hope to transcend, even in the extended sphere of the theatre, the narrow world in which the story had begun. This was the point of technical difficulty which for years made it impossible for Goethe to proceed; and when he sought a solution to this critical dilemma he chose not to change the point of view of the narrator, not to emancipate him from his own experiences, but to elaborate the world of ambiguity and to symbolize it in Mignon, who would lead the reader from the firm yet unpromising reality of the first book into an unreal but resolutely poetic dimension.

It is in the *Lehrjahre* that Goethe reconsiders the scope and usefulness of the autobiographical incident. There is distinct significance in the phrase with which in 1782 he referred to *Theatralische Sendung* as "mein geliebtes dramatisches Ebenbild." Later, in 1794, as he recomposed the matter of the earlier novel, he spoke of the *Lehrjahre* as a "pseudo-confession." We must not miss the positive note of detachment that lies in the qualifying prefix "pseudo." For, what had blocked the satisfactory evolution of *Theatralische Sendung* was not, in the last analysis, a matter of substance, not any change in his attitude toward the validity of the theater or of art as media of education; it was, rather, the unpromising attempt to write an autobiographical account in terms of conventional fiction, or, to put it differently, to use the properties of the middle-class novel to describe a career, his own career, that was in nearly every respect in open conflict with them. This conflict between sensibility and the social order was similar to that in *Werther*, but there Goethe had represented it impressively by transcending conventional literary forms and thereby had been able to give poetic plausibility to its radical implications and consequences. *Wilhelm Meister* was begun, and heistantly continued, as little more than a satirical account of Goethe himself.

The preliminary notes for a revision of the novel (1793) indicate that Goethe was aware of its shortcomings; he knew that what was needed was a change in the perspectives from which this aesthetic and pedagogical utopia might gain its coherence. "Nun ward das Werk, überrascht von der Tendenz seiner Gattung, plötzlich viel grösser als seine erste Absicht." No one has described more brilliantly than Friedrich Schlegel the masterly balance of relationships between ideas, figures, and poetic devices and between compassion and irony, that were to make the *Lehrjahre* the central work in the history of German fiction. "Wer Goethes 'Meister' gehörig charakterisierte, der hätte damit wohl eigentlich gesagt, was es jetzt an der Zeit ist in der Poesie." Not many subsequent critics have been so sensitive to the poetic values of the novel. Since it contains so much of Goethe's cultural philosophy at the height of his life, the kind of attention it has received has been unduly focused upon the impressive element of intellectual purpose. Seldom and only recently have sufficient attempts been made at discovering how that wisdom created its own appropriate narrative form.

We gain little for our appraisal of the book as a work of art if we merely reiterate the familiar epithet of *Bildungsroman*. What Goethe here intended to achieve was the education, not of Wilhelm, but of the reader, and instead of representing a body of society, he hoped, by this novel, to create one. The ideal upon which this society was to rest is not in any clear sense prescriptive; it aims, rather, at a state of "grenzenlose Bildsamkeit," which is, in the sense of Goethe's own humanism, infinitely receptive and open. This range of perceptiveness, this sensitiveness to the nuance becomes the measure of the novel as a whole. Reality and appearance, life and the stage, design and accident may seem forever intermingled, and the plot even in the final version, is far from offering that clearly profiled sequence of events which ordinarily creates narrative suspense. The characters are all keyed to Wilhelm, they exist only for his sake, and, with few conspicuous exceptions, have little independent life, little vitality of their own, and no clear-cut disposition for goodness or evil. "Diese Menschen, die man lieber Figuren als Menschen nennen dürfte . . ." (Schlegel), are, as Goethe himself, in 1821, put it, merely foreground props, "vorgeschobene Personen, [hinter denen] durchaus etwas Allgemeines, Höheres verborgen liege . . ." But instead of the literal presence or the allegorical character which some of them offered in the earlier version, they have now taken on a genuinely symbolical force. "Es mache ihm Freude und Beruhigung," Goethe confessed in 1821, "dass der ganze Roman durchaus symbolisch sei."

It was Friedrich Schlegel who first emphasized the central importance of Mignon—"das heilige Kind, mit dessen Erscheinung die innerste Springfeder des sonderbaren Werkes plötzlich frei zu werden scheint"—as a poetic image peculiarly adequate to the ambivalent climate of the novel. It was he, also, who recognized the elaboration of Mignon's world as a means of asserting the narrator's right, indeed his compulsion, to draw almost simultaneously upon several kinds, several dimensions of reality, "jenes magische Schweben zwischen vorwärts und rückwärts." What Goethe meant by displaying this mobility of the narrator (not merely his detachment, as in *Werther,* but his privilege of assuming the function of the central poetic intelligence) did not, perhaps, quite as much spring from that "romantic irony" which Schlegel thought he could detect. Its true character can best be understood if we recall the critical debate on this point between Goethe and Schiller.

Schiller was altogether sceptical of the legitimacy of fiction and, certainly, attached to a most conventional view of it. He had only a limited understanding of the poetic aims by which Goethe here and elsewhere hoped to extend the effectiveness of the narrative. We know that Schiller urged upon Goethe a more closely considered demonstration of the rôle of philosophy in Wilhelm's development; but this was precisely what Goethe did not wish to do. He knew and had read with little enthusiasm Klinger's philosophical novels, he was not much interested in Jacobi's *Allwill,* and he had barely commented upon Wieland's *Agathon*—all works with an explicit philosophical purpose and little poetic resonance. In so far as Schiller now urged this modification upon him, he fought energetically and stubbornly against it: "Ich hatte nur immer zu tun, dass ich feststand," Goethe admits as late as 1829 to Eckermann. But he was interested, though not uncritically, in Schiller's insistence upon a certain kind of detachment in the rôle of the narrator—a rôle which Schiller, in the spirit of contemporary æsthetics, equated with that of the wholly objective epic poet. By this definition the perspicacity of the narrator was to be kept within the strictest limits of social convention and experience; Goethe on the other hand wished to extend his own narrative range to include non-realistic realms of imaginative experience that were bound to exceed the scope of Schiller's notion. If Goethe defines the novelist's objective as a rendering of "Leben als Gegenstand der gemeinsamen Betrachtung," he assumes for the narrator a degree of independence and mobility that went far beyond Schiller's empirical conception of the epic poet's function.

The correspondence between Goethe and Schiller reveals another difference of poetic principle: had Goethe merely wished to draw upon the picturesque resources of the supernatural, he would not have transgressed the common practice of the day or, indeed, gone beyond Schiller's own understanding of fiction. But it was his peculiar *use* of this suprarational area, and his joining of the real and the unreal as equivalent realms of meaning that appeared to Schiller at times to violate the limits of the epic convention. As early as 8 July 1796 Schiller had expressed his uneasiness, "dass bei dem grossen und tiefen Ernste, der in allem Einzelnen herrscht, und durch den es so mächtig wirkt, die Einbildungskraft zu frei mit dem Ganzen zu spielen scheint." More than a year later, in a letter of 20 October 1797, he is still more explicit and, with extraordinary critical perception, touches upon one of the cardinal difficulties confronting the novelist: "Die Form des *Meisters,* wie überhaupt jede Romanform, ist schlechterdings nicht poetisch, sie liegt ganz nur im Gebiete des Verstandes, steht unter allen seinen Forderungen und partizipiert auch von allen seinen Grenzen. Weil es aber ein echt poetischer Geist ist, der sich dieser Form bediente und in dieser Form die poetischsten Zustände ausdrückte, so entsteht ein sonderbares Schwanken zwischen einer prosaischen und poetischen Stimmung, für das ich keinen rechten Namen weiss." Goethe's reply suggests his respect for Schiller's considerations, and his awareness of the almost crippling difficulties offered by the "impure" form of fiction: "Eine reine Form hilft und trägt, da eine unreine überall hindert und zerrt." Yet, he remained convinced that the narrator's freedom of movement, the blending of seemingly discrepant imaginative elements, offered advantages that he was not willing to sacrifice to any traditional view of epic consistency. Something of the same independence had given special poetic force to *Werther,* its cautious avoidance had made *Theatralische Sendung* a specimen of satirical portraiture.

It may seem curious that this turn in *Wilhelm Meister* to the multiple technique, to the refraction of meaning on several levels, the telescoping of events and incidents, should have occurred at a time when his attachment to the classical ideal of formal purity and distinctness was most emphatic. We shall not go wrong if we assume that it was in fiction, in this form of doubtful authenticity but of considerable flexibility that he recognized a promising and perhaps a necessary modern extension of the classical pattern. His initial interest in the formal derivation of the novel from the ancestral epic soon gave way in his literary criticism of that time, and, indeed, in his actual practice of fiction, to the belief that modern prose fiction, "die moderne Erzählung und der Roman," must convey some of the philosophical purposes that once sustained the classical tragedy: "novel" and "tragedy" are two terms that he uses henceforth almost synonymously. And what, in the same conversation with Eckermann, he felt most to have been Schiller's mistake in judging *Wilhelm Meister* was his unwillingness to permit the element of tragedy in the novel. "Schiller tadelte vor allem die Einflechtung des Tragischen, als welches nicht in den Roman gehöre." By 1829—with a considerable body of modern fiction before him that had since justified his view—he could add: "Er hatte jedoch Unrecht, wie wir alle wissen."

In the essay "Über epische und dramatische Dichtung," it is "der nach innen geführte Mensch," the increasing insight of the human being, that is to be the subject of the novel, and from Mme. de Stael's *Essai sur les Fictions,* which Goethe translated with obvious sympathy for its tenor, he quotes as the main purpose of modern fiction: "die Abstufungen, die Entwicklungen, die Inkonsequenzen des menschlichen Herzens zu regen." This now was the recurring theme in the stories that were to make up the *Unterhaltungen der deutschen Ausgewanderten.* There he accepted, without intending to offer more than an instance of civilized and civilizing story-telling, the common and, to him always, congenial form of the didactic anecdote. But as if troubled by the regularity of these pragmatic tales, he attached to them a piece of most irregular, yet brilliant, narrative in which, more to Schiller's amusement than satisfaction, he abandoned nearly all discursive logic in favor of a series of poetic images that derive their effect almost entirely from the relationship in which, as images, they are placed. *Das Märchen* has been much interpreted. It is not so much a "fairy-tale," in the conventional sense of the word, as a parable in which the radiance of the imaginative impulse and the accretion of poetic detail appear to obliterate any distinctly recognizable structure of meaning. From the first line we move in an element of strangeness, even of confusion and disorder; yet the details of this suspended order are observed with the eye of the mineralogist and of the author of the *Science of Color,* and recorded with the utmost precision. What matters from our present point of view is Goethe's attempt to supersede the previously employed form of the didactic anecdote, with its limited allegorical overtones, by a more complicated type of narrative to which he himself now refers as symbolic. No critical term, especially in Goethe's use of it, is more treacherous. But if we take a passage which occurs in a letter to Schiller of 16 August 1797, we have a sufficiently reliable definition of the meaning which he now attaches to the symbol in narrative practice. "Symbolisch," he says there, "sind eminente Fälle, die, in einer charakteristischen Mannigfaltigkeit, als Repräsentanten von vielen andern dastehen, eine gewisse Totalität in sich schliessen, eine gewisse Reihe fordern, Ähnliches und Fremdes in meinem Geiste aufregen und so von aussen wie von innen an eine gewisse Einheit und Allheit Anspruch machen." We should note the cautiously repeated word "gewisse," by which he modifies, significantly, three qualities of the symbol: the poetic symbol suggests a "certain" totality, continuity, and unity—a turn of speech which points unmistakably to the sense of complexity and ambiguity which he is now convinced the contemporary artist must represent. And when he wrote the notes on *Rameaus Neffe,* he felt convinced that the ingredients of the classical forms had been differentiated by the critical experiences of the moderns, and that the demarcation lines of the traditional literary genres must therefore be kept fluid. "Wohl findet sich," he writes in a famous passage ("Geschmack"), "bei den Griechen, sowie bei manchen Römern, eine sehr geschmackvolle Sonderung und Läuterung der verschiedenen Dichtarten, aber uns Nordländer kann man auf jene Muster nicht ausschliesslich hinweisen. Wir haben uns andrer Voreltern zu rühmen und haben manch anderes Vorbild im Auge. Wäre nicht durch die romantische Wendung ungebildeter Jahrhunderte das Ungeheure mit dem Abgeschmackten in Berührung gekommen, woher hätten wir einen *Hamlet,* einen *Lear,* eine *Anbetung des Kreuzes,* einen *Standhaften Prinzen?* Uns auf der Höhe dieser barbarischen Avantagen, da wir die antiken Vorteile wohl niemals erreichen werden, mit Mut zu erhalten, ist unser Pflicht . . ."

One way in which these "barbarian advantages" were to be represented was in that modern form of symbolic fiction which Goethe henceforth regarded as the most important medium for conveying the tragic view of life. It is hardly a coincidence that his increasing interest in prose fiction between 1800 and 1809 was accompanied and supported by his reading of the ancient tragedians. In his letters and essays of that time and later we find numerous references to a quality in Greek tragedy of moral ambiguity and suspense which strikes him as comparable to the sensibility that produces the modern novel. There is a passage in *Nachlese zu Aristoteles Poetik* which points, somewhat uneasily, to this disturbing insight: "Wer auf dem Wege einer wahrhaft sittlichen inneren Ausbildung fortschreitet, wird empfinden und gestehen, dass Tragödien und tragische Romane den Geist keineswegs beschwichtigen sondern das Gemüt und das was wir Herz nennen, in Unruhe versetzen und einem vagen, unbestimmten Zustande entgegenführen." And in a series of reflections on Johanna Schopenhauer's novel *Gabriele*, he formulates as late as 1823 the inescapably tragic implications of modern fiction: "Der Roman . . . stellt das Unbedingte als das Interessanteste vor, gerade das grenzenlose Streben, was uns aus der menschlichen Gesellschaft, was uns aus der Welt treibt, unbedingte Leidenschaft, für die dann bei unübersteiglichen Hindernissen nur Befriedigung im Verzweifeln bleibt, Ruhe nur im Tod."

It is with these two issues in mind, with Goethe's understanding of the symbolic narrative and the specific function of the novel as a conveyer of tragic discrepancies, that we can best judge the character of *Die Wahlverwandtschaften*. In some respects the novel seems to have much in common with the climate of the *Unterhaltungen*. Its aristocratic society, the same civilized manner, the restrained gesture, the formalized speech are unmistakable; and the cool, clear flow of the narrative recalls the urbane scepticism of the cleric. But, as we read along, we become aware of an extraordinary extension of the familiar perspectives. The figures and involvements that were in the earlier tale deliberately opaque now assume a strange luminosity; the human relationships that were before clear-cut matters of sympathetic interest now ramify to the point of incalculable complexity. All assumptions of order are now questioned and are threatened by forces which spring from depths of experience that lie beyond rational calculation. What Goethe wished to elaborate in this work is the theme of an interplay of fundamentally irreconcilable energies. To represent these in plausible figures and involvements was his first task, to make intelligible the extraordinary element in which these figures and involvements share—an element of jeopardy, of multiple meanings, of the intermixing of creative and destructive impulses—was the other.

This demonstration of the tragic condition of life is, in varying settings, the central motif of all of Goethe's fiction. Here, in *Die Wahlverwandtschaften*, it is set forth most movingly and most convincingly, with completely consistent poetic logic and with a meticulous, even pedantic, skill that interweaves the tangible and the suprarational. The pressure upon the aristocratic world of this

book from forces which are comprehended only in so far as they
seem scientifically—or pseudo-scientifically—intelligible, is exercised, gauged, and controlled for us, the readers, by a narrator who
is absolutely impartial. He alone makes that seemingly normal, all
too formalized world transparent, he illuminates it by an astonishing number of concealed and at first sight barely relevant lights.
We must insist on the curious character of the story-teller—at once
absolutely detached and deeply involved—in order to find the key
to the story. We must remember his utter self-control before figures,
activities, opinions, that are to him, with all their polish and propriety, painfully, even absurdly, inadequate to the unsettling but
inescapable natural forces that undermine and destroy the sensible
and the hectic alike.

If we read *Wahlverwandtschaften* naïvely, without being quite
aware of the enormous achievement of self-possession in the narrator, we are bound at times to think it a strangely antiquated, sometimes even absurd tale. But there is nothing in the book that is not
related to this central function of the narrator: to share, concretely
but without partiality or visible emotion, the inanity of a society
which is, in all apparent respects coherent and effective, yet, because it remains insensitive to the overwhelming reality of elemental emotions, is condemned to sterility. Nothing could be more
telling than the pretentious puttering that passes for work, the long
drawn-out business of building Charlotte's house, or the polite but
usually inconclusive conversations, notably those on marriage and
on the scientific principle that gives the novel its title. What is
more characteristic of the weaknesses in that society than Eduard's
erratic and inconsequential fits of resolution, or Mittler's pompous
platitudes? This society—from which Ottilie gradually emancipates
herself at the cost of her life—operates within a setting of nature
which Goethe carefully, insistently unfolds, but which is of real
importance only to Ottilie (and, perhaps, to the minor, yet revealing, figure of the gardener).

It was not easy—especially for one as deeply committed as was
the mature Goethe to an indubitable respect for all forms of order
—to represent this world, to illuminate it at once in all its tempting elegance and its insufficiency, without snobbism or without resorting to caricature. But he succeeds, and only here and there,
possibly in the portrait of Luciane, loses a little of his patience.
Wherever he can he uses indirect devices, such as the figure of the
English aristocrat who has nothing immediately to do with the
plot as such, but who serves as a symbol of the sort of life that the

society which Goethe here describes, is, or will be condemned to lead: a life of perpetual commotion and change, similar in many respects to that which *Wanderjahre* later exemplifies. Although he is the owner of one of the magnificent estates in England, he has forced himself, deprived of all genuine ties, to roam about the world. And it is indicative of the irony that underlies the whole novel, that this "uninvolved" character tells the story *Die wunder-lichen Nachbarskinder,* a brilliant, fairy-tale like, almost operatic inset which reflects, twice removed and on a parabolic level, the central theme of the novel, or one important element of it: the confusing, the unsettling, the destructive force of passion. This force, Goethe seems here to say, is ineluctable, and its consequences can be represented only in a poetic mode that offers its own logic and provides its own resolutions.

It is something of the realm of the fairy-tale into which Ottilie herself seems gradually to merge. In her—the only character of whom Goethe speaks with deep emotion—we find, of course, the counterpart of Mignon, the same gauche and yet transfigured crea-ture who learns, as she is forced into the paralyzing orbits of pas-sion and obtuseness, that she must withdraw from that society, re-nounce it and only thereby achieve the integrity of contemplation that may give her peace. She will not use the confusing instrument of speech: increasingly she is attracted to pictures, images, and sym-bols, and her one wish, more and more insistently expressed, is to be respected in her isolation—"mein Inneres überlasset mir."

I must not dwell upon any more aspects of this inexhaustible novel. What matters most for our understanding of its perplexities is the attitude of the narrator, and the wholly discreet, measured, and judicious manner of his speech by which he hides and circum-scribes a barely tolerable knowledge of fearful and unspeakable tensions. We must also be struck by Goethe's preference not for color and plasticity, but for the non-sensual, abstracted outline, the careful yet never lifeless or merely academic architectural sym-metry, and his choice, always, of the indirect light. It is doubtful whether Goethe was ever, as we are sometimes told, an "objective" observer of physical reality, or whether he ever recorded his obser-vations without first filtering them through his essentially intellec-tual sensibility. There is, at any rate, nothing direct in *Wahlver-wandtschaften.* Goethe's language does not reveal (as in *Werther* and his poetry at that time) the depths of spiritual anguish, but rather conceals them; and with the same intention of mirroring or refracting reality, he uses interpolated anecdotes, charades, and portfolios of prints that invite speculation. Ottilie's diaries point to the same end: they do not so much explain or justify her inner motives as, through coincidental reflection, cast them into sharper relief.

Goethe, we know, was at all times averse to abstract definition of spiritual reality, and ever since the early days of his study of Spinoza had found comfort, not in speculation, but only in the immediacy of concrete experience. He had described himself often enough as dedicated to the tangible world, and, as late as 1831, confessed that the "direct contemplation of things" was everything to him: "words mean less to me than ever before." He could not have been more to the point if he had spoken about *Wahlverwandtschaften*. It is his most symbolic work in the sense that the insights which his contemplation, his *Anschauung,* of the natural phenomena offered him, are here stated in a coherent world of images which refer to what must remain inexpressible in discursive speech. All life, we remember him saying, is symbolic; and where it is fully represented, "indem es vollkommen sich selbst darstellt," it reveals its unity. In the *Versuch einer Witterungslehre. 1825* he gives to this conviction its most succinct expression: "Das Wahre, mit dem Göttlichen identisch, lässt sich niemals von uns direkt erkennen, wir schauen es nur im Abglanz, im Beispiel, Symbol, in einzelnen und verwandten Erscheinungen; wir werden es gewahr als unbegreifliches Leben und können dem Wunsch nicht entsagen, es dennoch zu begreifen."

Throughout his life, then Goethe's perception, his thinking, his speech, his writing, is attached to images; and even where in his fiction the symbolic density of *Wahlverwandtschaften* is not attained, this tendency is, nevertheless, apparent in the anecdotal and episodic manner to which I have earlier referred. After the completion of *Wahlverwandtschaften* he comments upon his fondness for illustrating a given point by the use of several stories: "Ich liebe mir sehr Parallelgeschichten. Eine deutet auf die andere hin, und erklärt ihren Sinn besser als viele trockene Worte." This utterance will help us explain the shape of his last novel, *Wilhelm Meisters Wanderjahre,* a work which has for long been looked upon as a remarkably clumsy catch-all for a miscellany of wisdom, and in which we are only now beginning to suspect distinct poetic purposes. The scope of the novel is considerable: it was to offer, not so much the further adventures of Wilhelm Meister, as the portrait of a society in transition. This portrait was to have the fea-

tures of Goethe's own times; but its motives and the consequences
of its intellectual assumptions, were to be rendered poetically so
articulate as to give it in effect the character of a utopia. Yet, this
term we should apply only to the prophetic range of Goethe's social analysis and not, strictly speaking, to the form of the novel.
Its characters are not projected into a future setting; they display,
rather, an astonishing mobility in time and place, they are com-
pounds of classical, medieval, and modern attitudes, their faces,
their functions, their destinies are not fixed nor at any time fully
and distinctly revealed. The world through which Wilhelm and
his son are led is pieced together from a multiplicity of details,
each in itself important, but deriving its full force only from the
light which they all, in turn, cast upon each other. What results,
or what, at any rate, Goethe meant to produce, was an interlocking
system of archetypal forms which would suggest as he put it, "in
einer Art von Unendlichkeit," something of their infinite symbolic
range. As he hoped to represent the volatile, the relativistic, yet in
its way challenging character of the emerging century, he transcended this social theme, at the same time, by elaborating the
more general symbolism of mobility in permanence and recurring
patterns in the flux. He rejected any temptation to resort to the
lyrical or the fanciful; as a reporter he is reliable to the point of
factitiousness: the novel is, not to everybody's taste, interlaced with
discursive passages of dry sociological, scientific, and technical detail. But Goethe's use of these "unpoetic" pieces of analytical, even
statistical, information reflects a considered view of their function
within a new type of fiction: they are more carefully integrated
than may at first sight be apparent, and they serve to indicate
Goethe's advance from the psychological novel with a central hero
to a synthetic panorama of contemporary experience. To convey
this experience in its compelling actuality he represented certain
aspects of it, not in a symbolic key, not transposed, but through
the sober description of technical and scientific processes. Taking
the novel as a whole, it cannot be said that this resolute rendering
of the raw materials of reality is adequately blended with the symbolical or allegorical elements that surround it in the various parts
of the narrative; but the intention behind it foreshadows something
of the experimental and philosophical fiction of our own time.
Even more unmistakably than in *Wahlverwandtschaften* the narrator functions in *Wanderjahre* as the ever-present organizing intelligence: his knowledge, his intellectual mobility is nearly absolute, he can and must bring his special understanding and his

command of the diverse realms of modern experience freely into play. In some sense this rôle was compatible with Schiller's view of the epic poet who was to "do his business openly, publicly, in the market place"; and Goethe does not hesitate in the course of the novel to speak explicitly of the duties and privileges of the narrator who, being well informed can and must speak publicly of what he knows. As a wise guide, he presents the multiple aspects of the world, not artfully interlocked, but in strict factual succession, *nebeneinander,* as Goethe reflects, not *ineinander verschlungen.*

All this gives to the *Wanderjahre* a curiously rhetorical character, and it was part of Goethe's plan that the version of 1821 should end in a public address on the subject of that readiness to rove and journey which, he felt, would determine the thinking of the coming century. This consistently rhetorical form of fiction which Goethe here developed, was in no sense in conflict with his lyrical production, but could maintain itself in clear and deliberate contrast to it. In his Notes to the *Divan,* in the section "Verwahrung," he reiterates the inevitable contrast between the imaginative immediacy of the lyric poem and the public, and therefore rhetorical, character of fiction: "Poesie is rein und echt betrachtet, weder Rede noch Kunst; keine Rede, weil sie zu ihrer Vollendung Takt, Gesang, Körperbewegung und Mimik bedarf; sie ist keine Kunst, weil alles auf dem Naturell beruht, welches zwar geregelt aber nicht künstlerisch geängstigt werden darf; auch bleibt sie immer wahrhafter Ausdruck eines aufgeregten, erhöhten Geistes, ohne Ziel und Zweck. Die Redekunst aber, im eigentlichen Sinne, ist eine Rede und eine Kunst; sie beruht auf einer deutlichen mässig leidenschaftlichen Rede und ist Kunst in jedem Sinne."

It was this element of design, of craftsmanship, of Kunst, so often specifically suspected by Goethe himself in the lyrical poet, that had now become for him a permissible and even indispensable feature of the novelist's purposes. By developing an awareness for it in his own work he had, step by step, from *Werther* to nearly the end of his life perfected not merely his innate skill at telling a story, but his mastery of the perspectives of fiction and the plausible poetic symbols that would enable him to render his ever more complex view of reality. Goethe had never shared the belief in the rational empiricism of the seventeenth and eighteenth centuries, in the unambiguous evidence of the surface; yet he never abandoned his faith in the symbolic translucence of the observable world. His fiction, not unlike his scientific pursuits to which it is closely and essentially related, indicated his efforts at finding the most advantageous point of view from which the observable evidence might be examined, evaluated or, at any rate, represented. By bringing a poetic, a multiple, intelligence to bear upon the tangible world, and by illuminating the familiar figure or incident, he reveals something of their barely suspected complexity. With Goethe there begins the interest in the symbols of variety, of depth and incongruity, that concerns the modern novelists; but unlike them Goethe could still provide that perspective of symbolic depth without obliterating the realistic surface. It is an enviable advantage that distinguished him from us. Yet, as he points in his maturest fiction to several credible orders of reality held together by his comprehensive vision of the whole, he anticipates something of that sense of a differentiated universe that has since become the very condition of our lives.

Wilhelm Meisters Lehrjahre

by Georg Lukács

Goethe's *Wilhelm Meister* is the most significant product of the transition in the history of fiction between the eighteenth and nineteenth century. It contains the characteristics of both of these periods in the development of the modern novel, ideologically as well as artistically. We shall see that it is no coincidence that the final version was completed during the years 1793–95, at the time when the revolutionary crisis of transition between the two epochs reached its climax in France.

It is true that the beginnings of this novel go back much farther. The conception and perhaps the first attempts at composition can be ascertained as early as 1777. By 1785 six books of a novel entitled *Wilhelm Meisters Theatralische Sendung* had been written down. This initial draft, lost for a long time and by a happy coincidence found only in 1910, offers us the best opportunity to show precisely in which respects, artistic and ideological, the *Lehrjahre* represents a characteristically transitional work.

The first version was conceived and shaped throughout in the spirit of the young Goethe. At the heart of this version stands—just as in *Tasso*—the problem of the relationship of the writer to the bourgeois world, a problem already brought into sharp focus in the rebellious atmosphere of *Werther* at the beginning of the Weimar period.

If problems of the theater and of dramaturgy completely dominate the first draft of the *Lehrjahre,* the theater signifies the freeing of a perceptive soul from the drab, prosaic confinement of the bourgeois world. Goethe says of his hero: "The stage became for him a place of healing, since there he could see the world in a nutshell, since he could gaze in astonishment, as if in a mirror, at

"Wilhelm Meisters Lehrjahre." From *Goethe und seine Zeit,* by Georg Lukács (Neuwied am Rhein: Hermann Luchterhand Verlag, 1964), trans. L. Evans and Victor Lange. Translation © 1968 by Prentice-Hall, Inc. Reprinted by permission of the publisher.

his own feelings and what he hoped to achieve, at his friends and brothers as though they were heroes, and see, in any weather and comfortably sheltered, the immeasurable glories of nature."

In the later version the issue of life and the theater is enlarged to include the humanistic education of the whole person within the world of bourgeois society. When in the *Lehrjahre* the hero irrevocably decides to join the theater, he reflects: "What good does it do me to produce good iron, if I myself am full of dross, and what good does it do me to bring order to a country, if I am always at odds with myself?" And his insight at the time, that the complete development of his human capabilities can under the given social conditions be realized only through the theater, becomes the central motive of his decision. Thus theatrical and dramatic production are here only the means to a free and comprehensive development of the human personality.

It is in keeping with this conception of theater that the plot of *Lehrjahre* goes beyond the theater itself, that the theater is for Wilhelm Meister no longer a "mission" ("Sendung"), but merely a transitional phase. The theatrical life, to which the entire first draft had been devoted, is now expressly considered by the mature Wilhelm to be a mistake, a detour on the way toward his goal. The new version is broadened to include an account of the whole of society. It is true that even in the earlier *Werther* a picture of bourgeois society had been presented, but more as a reflection of the rebellious subjectivity of the hero. *Theatralische Sendung* is far more objective in its method of presentation; yet, its conception allows only the presentation of those social forces and types which are directly or indirectly connected with theater or dramatic writing. Goethe's breakthrough, in content as well as form, to an objective portrayal of the whole of bourgeois society, therefore is not fully accomplished until the *Lehrjahre*. This novel was immediately preceded by the short satiric epic poem "Reineke Fuchs" (1793), a little masterpiece in which Goethe presents a comprehensive satirical picture of the emerging middle-class society.

Thus the theater now becomes merely one aspect of the whole. Goethe retains much of the first version: most of the characters, the plot outline, a number of individual scenes, etc. But with genuine artistic instinct he removes everything from the first draft which had been necessary to justify the central significance of the theater (including the performance of the play Wilhelm himself had written, the detailed account of his poetic development, the confrontation with French classicism, etc.). On the other hand, much of what was only of episodic significance in the first version is now elaborated and resolutely placed in the foreground—particularly the performance of *Hamlet* and the related discussion of Shakespeare.

All this appears only to underscore the significance of the theater, but this is in fact not Goethe's intention; for the matter of Shakespeare now far transcends the sphere of the theater itself. Shakespeare now becomes the great teacher, whose aim is the full realization of a humane personality; his plays are models of how the development of personality was achieved during the great period of humanism and how such a development should be accomplished in the present. Any stage performance of Shakespeare was in the late eighteenth century, of necessity, a compromise: Wilhelm Meister fully realizes how greatly Shakespeare towers above the technical limitations of the theater, and strives in every way possible to save the essential Shakespeare. The high-point of Wilhelm's efforts in the theater—the performance of *Hamlet*—therefore becomes an illustration of the fact that the theater and dramatic writing, indeed, all literature is only one aspect, one part of the all-important, enveloping complex of education, of the development of personality, of humanity.

Thus the theater is now, in every respect, only a phase of Wilhelm's experience. The actual portrayal of society, the criticism of the middle class and the aristocracy, the presentation of an exemplary humanistic life can be developed only after transcending the theater as a way to humanity. In *Theatralische Sendung* the portrayal of society was altogether related to the theater. Wilhelm's criticism of the pettiness of middle-class life was made in the light of his poetic aspirations, and the aristocracy was seen only in its role as patron. In contrast, in the *Lehrjahre*, Jarno replies to Wilhelm's description of his bitter disappointments with the theater: "Do you know, my friend . . . that you haven't described the theater, but rather the world, and that I could find enough characters and plots for your harsh views in all classes of society?" This method of portrayal is used not only in the new second part of the novel, but also in the re-working of those earlier parts that concern the theater. Thus Friedrich Schlegel, immediately after the publication of the *Lehrjahre*, commented upon the famous scene in the castle: "with a fatuous camaraderie and generously overlooking the tremendous gulf that separates them socially, the count greets (one of the actors) as though he were his colleague; the baron, in his intellectual silliness, and the baroness, in her moral meanness, cannot be outdone by anyone; the countess herself presents at best a pretext for the most pleasant display of finery; and the aristocrats, apart from their rank, are superior to the actors only in that they are more thoroughly vulgar."

The realization in this novel of Goethe's humanistic ideals proves again and again the necessity of "assigning to birth and class the nullity which belongs to them as soon as we are concerned with basically human issues" (Schiller). The portrayal as well as the criticism of the various classes and their representatives always proceed in *Lehrjahre* from this central standpoint. Criticism of the middle class is therefore not merely criticism of specifically German forms of pettiness and narrowness, but also a critique of the capitalistic distribution of labor, of excessive specialization, and of the destruction of the human being by this distribution of labor. The middle-class citizen, says Wilhelm Meister, can not be a public figure: "He may gain respect and, if need be, cultivate his mind; but his personality is lost in the process, no matter what he affects to be. . . . He may not ask himself: what are you? but only: what do you have? what intelligence, what knowledge, what ability, how much wealth? . . . let him cultivate particular capacities in order to become useful, because it is assumed that harmony cannot or should not be in his character, because, in order to make himself useful in one way he must neglect everything else."

It is this humanistic view that determines Goethe's "glorification of the aristocracy," which has so often been emphasized by bourgeois literary historians. It is true that Wilhelm Meister, in the same context from which we have just quoted a few sentences, speaks at length about the fact that the aristocratic life may remove those very hindrances to a free and complete development of the personality, hindrances which he condemns in bourgeois life. But in Goethe's eyes, the aristocracy has value only as a stepping stone, as a favorable condition for the development of personality. Even Wilhelm Meister—let alone Goethe himself—clearly sees that a step is not in fact necessarily made from this stepping stone and that these opportunities by no means always transform themselves into reality.

On the contrary, Goethe's humanistic criticism of society is directed not merely at the capitalistic distribution of labor, but also at the constriction and distortion of the human character in any form of class consciousness. We have referred to Friedrich Schlegel's judgment of the "glorified" aristocrats of this novel. Wilhelm Meister himself, directly after the scene in the castle, passes judgment on the aristocrats: "He for whom inherited riches have created an easy life . . . becomes accustomed to considering these possessions to be his first and foremost concern; the values of a truly humane life do not become clear to him. The behavior of the aristocracy toward the less fortunate, indeed toward their peers, is determined by purely external advantages; they permit anyone to display his title, his rank, his clothes and his carriage, but never his merits."

Naturally, the second part of the novel presents an essentially different picture of aristocratic society. Goethe there portrays, especially in Lothario and Natalie, the realization of humanistic ideals. It is true that these figures are somewhat paler than the more problematic ones. But through Lothario's life Goethe shows with extraordinary clarity how he envisages the opportunities which noble birth and inherited wealth offer for the well-rounded development of a personality. Lothario has traveled throughout the world, but he has also fought at the side of Washington in the War of Independence; when he gains possession of his properties, he voluntarily sets as his goal the liquidation of feudal privileges. This continues to be the direction of the plot throughout the second half of the novel. It ends with a series of marriages which, from the standpoint of a class society, are misalliances, i.e. marriages between aristocrats and members of the middle class. Schiller is entirely correct in recognizing in this move the proof of the "nullity" of class in the light of humanistic ideals.

But the revision of the first version presents not only a new view of an aristocracy which has become humanistic and been joined with the middle-class; it no less affects those sections that remain *specifically* concerned with the theater. In the first version, Philine is only a moderately important minor figure. In the second version, she may not play a much more extensive role, but her character is given a new dimension of depth. She is the only figure in the novel who possesses a spontaneous, natural humanity and harmony. Goethe supplies her character, by virtue of a remarkable realism, with all the characteristics of plebeian shrewdness, dexterity, and adaptability. But her light-hearted craftiness is always bound up with a fundamentally sure human instinct: she is never untrue to herself, she never cripples or distorts herself in all her frivolity: it is most interesting to see that it is Philine who expresses Goethe's own deepest feeling for life, his attitude toward nature and men, that "amor dei intellectualis" which he took from Spinoza. When the wounded Wilhelm, who has been saved by Philine, wants to send her away because of moral scruples, she laughs at him: "You're a fool," she says, "you'll never grow wiser. I know better than you what is good for you: I'm staying, I won't move from this spot. I've never counted on the gratitude of men, so I won't count on yours, and if I love you, what business is that of yours?"

In a similar way, although with a completely different human and artistic emphasis, Goethe enhances in the *Lehrjahre* the figure of old Barbara, the match-making servant of Wilhelm's first love, Marianne. In the early scenes her unsympathetic characteristics are presented sharply and drastically. But in the scene in which she informs Wilhelm of Marianne's death, her accusation of the society which drives an impecunious woman to sin and hypocrisy and then to destruction assumes truly tragic grandeur.

The realization of humanistic ideals offers in the *Lehrjahre* not merely a standard by which to judge the various classes and their representatives, but becomes the very measure and driving force of the plot itself. For Wilhelm Meister and several other figures of this book, the effort to realize humanistic ideals is the more or less conscious mainspring of action. Naturally, this cannot be said of all the figures in the novel, perhaps not even of the majority. Understandably enough, most of them act from egotistical motives, and seek their more or less honorable advantages. But the way in which the success or failure in the pursuit of such goals is handled in the novel is always intimately connected to the realization of humanistic ideals.

Goethe offers us a maze of entangled lives: he portrays those who, through their guilt or innocence founder tragically; he creates figures who waste their lives; he renders figures in whom the specialization brought about by the capitalistic division of labor ossifies one or the other feature of their personality to the point of caricature and stunts the rest of their humane character completely; he shows that the lives of others pass in irrelevancy, in pointless fragmentation, without a compelling central activity that gives unity to their personality and that always moves the whole man at once. By interweaving all these lives according to this humanistic criterion, by recognizing it and it alone as the measure for the conduct of one's life, and by treating as insignificant everything else— any success, any actual attainment of set goals—he conveys his *Weltanschauung* in the concrete and lively terms of narrative action.

Thus he places the individual and the fulfillment and development of his personality in the very center of the novel, and this with a clarity and precision attained by few other writers. Naturally, this *Weltanschauung* is not the personal property of Goethe: it pervades all of European literature since the Renaissance and forms the very center of the literature of the Enlightenment. But the unique feature of Goethe's novel consists in the fact that, on the one hand, he elaborates this *Weltanschauung* with an emphasis and awareness that is underscored philosophically, emotionally, and dramatically, so that it becomes the driving force of the whole fictional world. And the singularity of the work lies no less in the fact that Goethe places before us the attainment of the completely developed personality as a concrete experience of concrete people in concrete circumstances, a fulfillment merely dreamed of by the Renaissance and Enlightenment, and in a bourgeois society bound always to remain utopian. . . .

To have shown through the medium of a work of art the actual possibility of accomplishing the humane goals of the bourgeois revolution is the new and characteristic contribution of Goethe's novel. The realization of this ideal in action as well as the demonstration of its essentially social character becomes Goethe's chief concern. He insists that the human personality can develop only in activity and activity is always the impact of men upon each other within society. As a clear-sighted realist Goethe cannot, of course, expect that bourgeois society as he knows it, particularly the miserable and undeveloped Germany of his day, could conceivably move toward the fulfillment of these social ideals. It is in fact impossible for the social character of humanistic activity to emerge organically from any realistic interpretation of bourgeois society; therefore this social consequence cannot, in a realistic portrayal of this society, appear as a spontaneous, organic product of its own inherent movement. On the other hand, Goethe feels with a clarity and depth as have few other men before or after him that these humane ideals are the necessary products of the social evolution. However antagonistic the bourgeois society itself may be towards these ideals in everyday life, they are in fact the products of that social evolution; they are indeed its most valuable cultural result.

In keeping with this contradictory basis of his social philosophy, Goethe constructs in the novel a kind of "island" within bourgeois society. It would be superficial to consider this invention to be merely an escape. The portrayal of a humanistic ideal (which in a bourgeois society must remain utopian) is bound to have something of an escape character about it. For no realistic writer can combine the attainment of the humanistic ideals with an effective portrayal of the *normal course* of events in bourgeois society. The Goethean "island," however, is a group of human beings who are active in the community. The life of each of these is developed realistically from concrete social conditions and premises. Not even the fact that they find their way to each other and eventually join can be described as unrealistic. If Goethe resorts to stylization it consists of his giving to this group—not without some irony—certain ritualistic features, and of trying to regard it as a sort of society within society, as a germ cell of the gradual transformation of bourgeois society as a whole—much as the great socialist Fourier imagined that if his fabulous millionaire were to permit him the founding of a phalanstery, this would lead to the spread of his brand of socialism all over the world.

The convincing effectiveness of Goethe's "island" can be achieved only in the course of the development of human beings. Goethe's supreme artistry lies in his dealing with all the problems of humanism—the positive as well as the negative—in the concrete conditions of life and the concrete experiences of certain figures. The humane ideals never appear in a static utopian, existential form, but as psychological functions and aspects of the plot, as phases in the development of specific individuals at specific, crucial turning-points of their life.

Yet, this sort of realistic rendering of the humanistic ideals does not mean the elimination of intellectual purpose. On the contrary, Goethe logically develops certain ideas of the Enlightenment: he attaches extraordinary importance to the processes of education, to the conscious direction of human development. The somewhat contrived device of the Tower, the ceremonious letters of instruction, etc., merely serve to underscore this purposeful, pedagogical principle. Goethe implies by discreet characterization and with a few short scenes, that Wilhelm Meister's development is from the very beginning supervised and specifically directed.

It is true that this education is unusual: it seeks to train men who will develop their qualities in freedom and spontaneity but with due regard for the effects of chance as well as planning. It is for this reason that warnings are ceaselessly uttered against any faith in "destiny" or fatalistic resignation, and that the educators in the novel again and again emphasize their scorn for all moral "commandments." Human beings must not slavishly obey any enforced morality, but become socially mature by virtue of free and organic action; they should bring the development of their individuality into harmony with the happiness and the interests of their fellow-men. The moral scheme of *Wilhelm Meister* is an emphatic—though tacit—attack upon the moral theory of Kant.

Accordingly, the ideal of the "beautiful soul" is central to these parts of the novel. It appears specifically for the first time in the title of the sixth book as "Confessions of a Beautiful Soul." But we would mistake Goethe's intentions and miss his subtly ironic accents, if we were to take the canoness as the true embodiment of this ideal. The "beautiful soul" represents for Goethe the harmonious union of consciousness and spontaneity, of worldly activity and a fully developed inner life. The canoness, however, is as much a subjective, purely "inward" character as most of the other searching figures of the first part, as Wilhelm Meister himself, or Aurelia. This subjective seeking which often withdraws into pure inwardness, forms the—relatively, but only relatively, justified—opposite pole of the empty and scattered busyness of Werner, Laertes, and even of Serlo. The turning point of Wilhelm's education is, precisely, his rejection of this life of subjectivity and inwardness which Goethe (and later Hegel in his *Phenomenology*) condemns explicitly as vacuous and abstract. The criticism of the canoness is offered with great discretion. But the tendency of Goethe's criticism becomes obvious when we recognize the place of this interlude within the structure of the novel, and note the fact that these confessions are offered to Wilhelm by Aurelia, at a moment when he himself is threatened with tragic destruction, as a mirror of his own crisis of sensibility. At the end of the confessions Goethe is somewhat more specific: we learn that the abbé, the chief representative of Goethe's educational principles, has in their childhood kept Lothario, Natalie, and others away from the canoness so as to remove them from her influence. It is in figures such as Lothario and Natalie and in Wilhelm's own aspirations that the true character of a "beautiful soul," the harmony between inwardness and activity, is fully represented.

However, the polemic purpose of *Wilhelm Meister* is directed not only at the two false extremes described above; it is also a declaration of war against romantic tendencies. The new "poesy of life" embodied in the individual who actively masters life, the poesy for which Goethe himself longed so profoundly was, as we have seen, everywhere being threatened by the "prose of capitalism." We have been able to observe Goethe's ideal of humanity in its struggle against this age of prose. Yet, Goethe condemns not only the prosaic life as such, but also the blind revolt against it. The blind revolt, the false poesy of Romanticism, consists for Goethe in its very "homelessness" in bourgeois life. This homelessness may of course, have a seductive poetic appeal: it is an instinctive, spontaneous form of rebellion against the prose of capitalistic life. However, it is exactly by its spontaneity that this poesy is merely seductive but not truly productive; it does not lead to a victory over prose, but only to its evasion, a thoughtless indifference to its problems—while the power of the prosaic life continues undisturbed.

Goethe's efforts at defeating such fruitless romanticism determines the whole novel. Wilhelm's infatuation with the theater is the first phase of this struggle; the account of a romantic sort of religion in the "Confessions" is the second. Mignon and the harpist, homeless, poetic figures move through the novel as the very embodiments of the romantic spirit. . . . It is due to the seductive beauty of these figures that most German romantic poets overlooked Goethe's discretely accentuated but nevertheless palpable polemic intention, and that *Wilhelm Meister* became the much copied model of romantic ficton. Only Novalis, intellectually the most consistent of the early German romantics, clearly recognized the polemic tendency of Goethe's novel and therefore bitterly criticized it. *"Wilhelm Meister,"* he said, "is in fact an embarrassing and silly book . . . intensely unpoetical in its substance, however poetical its form . . . The political intention is overriding. . . . Poetry is the harlequin of the whole farce. . . . The hero only retards the establishment of the gospel of political economy. . . . *Wilhelm Meister* is, in fact, a *Candide* directed against the poetic experience." These sharply critical sentences reveal a more genuine understanding of Goethe's anti-romantic intentions than the many enthusiastic imitations of Mignon and the harpist. . . .

The struggle of Goethe the humanist is directed against any kind of dissolution of reality in dreams, in merely subjective imaginings or ideals. His chief concern, like that of every great novelist is the struggle between ideals and activity and the eventual realization of these ideals. We have seen that the decisive turning point in Wilhelm's education is precisely his rejection of a purely inward, purely subjective attitude towards reality, of his groping toward an understanding of objective reality, toward activity in a concrete community. *Wilhelm Meisters Lehrjahre* is in fact a novel of education (*Erziehungsroman*); its theme is the practical education of man toward a practical understanding of reality. . . .

Goethe was convinced not only that the ideals of a humane life are deeply rooted in human nature but that they could, if slowly and with difficulty, be achieved in the bourgeois society which was emerging after the French revolution. He recognized the palpable contradictions between the ideology of his humanism and the realities of a capitalistic society, but he never considered them as basically antagonistic or *a priori* irreconcilable. . . . That Goethe was profoundly aware of this contradiction is obvious from the extraordinarily subtle and profound irony with which he developed the latter part of *Wilhelm Meister*. The humane ideals are now realized through the cooperation of a group of consciously pedagogical-minded individuals in a closed, "insular" society. The substance of these efforts as well as the hope of their eventual fulfillment reflect Goethe's deepest convictions. The theories developed by the abbé and, in turn, ironically criticized by Natalie and Jarno, are Goethe's own; and it is not by chance that Goethe, on the one hand, makes the conscious direction of Wilhelm's (and others') education through the members of the Tower the most important feature of the plot, but that he treats this conscious enterprise, on the other hand, almost as a game, as something which the group may have taken seriously at one time, but which it has by now outgrown. . . .

Philosophically, then, *Wilhelm Meister* stands on the dividing line between two epochs: it portrays the tragic crisis of bourgeois ideals of humanity and the beginnings of their (as yet, utopian) realization, beyond the framework of bourgeois society. . . . The style of *Wilhelm Meister* clearly reflects this transitional character. It contains obvious elements of the novel of the Enlightenment and the epic poems of the post-Renaissance period, such as the "artificial machinery" of the Tower or convenient devices for the continuity of plot such as mistaken identity or accidental encounters. But if we carefully examine the artistic process by which Goethe transformed the *Theatralische Sendung* into the *Lehrjahre*, we recognize that he evolved elements which later became decisive in the novel of the nineteenth century: he concentrates the action upon a few dramatic scenes and achieves a close connection between figures and events. This was later, in theory and practice, offered by Balzac as a characteristic difference between modern fiction and that of the seventeenth and eighteenth century. If we compare the manner in which Goethe introduces figures such as Philine and Mignon in *Theatralische Sendung* and in *Lehrjahre* we can easily recognize this "dramatic" purpose; it is no mere technical shift: some of the figures are now richer and more complex and have a greater psychological range and tension. . . . On the other hand Goethe aims at a more resolute and more differentiated rendering of what now seems essential to him. He trims the episodic parts, and those that he retains he relates more specifically and more elaborately to the main action. . . .

With all this he approximates the structural principles of the novel in the first half of the nineteenth century, but only approximates. If Goethe wishes now to portray more complicated individuals and more complicated relationships between individuals than the seventeenth and eighteenth century novel permitted (and as he had himself intended in the first version), this sort of complexity has, of course, little or nothing to do with the analytic character of the later realistic novel—or, indeed, with Goethe's later *Elective Affinities*. He models his figures with extraordinary delicacy and yet endows them with a classical sort of concreteness. Figures like Philine and Mignon who achieve emotional presence and vitality with the most economical artistic skill, are unique in world literature. . . . The art of portraying the most significant and the most complicated with a light hand, sensual, pithy, and unforgettably vivid, reaches in *Wilhelm Meister* a high-point of narrative art. The totality of society was portrayed earlier and especially later by a more comprehensive and extensive realism; in this respect we can compare Goethe in *Wilhelm Meister* neither with Le Sage or Defoe, nor with Balzac or Stendhal. For Le Sage is dry, Balzac is confused and overladen when placed beside the classical perfection of Goethe's writing and the litheness of his composition and characterization.

In his correspondence, Schiller has repeatedly and with great perception pointed to the singular stylistic accomplishment of this extraordinary novel. He calls it in one place "calm and profound, lucid, yet unfathomable like nature herself." It never relies merely upon the technical excellence of Goethe's writing, but springs from a vision of culture that sustains the lives and relationships of human beings. If the style is both delicate and discrete, graphic and clear, it is because Goethe's view of man and his relationships rests upon a carefully considered and genuine understanding of human nature. . . . With superb mastery Goethe grasps the essential qualities of a human life, delineates its typical and common features as well as the differentiating energies, provides something like a carefully organized pattern of all these relationships, differences, and nuances, and is able to translate these elements into lively and revealing action.

The figures of this novel are preoccupied with the struggle for the ideals of humanism, and particularly the issue of the two false extremes of behavior—radical subjectivism and pointless activity.

It is impressive to see how Goethe, beginning with Lothario and Natalie, who represent the rejection of the erroneous extremes, displays his gallery of "doers," from Jarno and Therese to Werner and Medina; no two of these characters are alike, yet they are not differentiated by merely pedantic, intellectual or analytical devices; without explicit comment, a hierarchy of human values and an approximation of the humanistic ideal is firmly established.

This art of portraiture, whose excellence no other modern novelist has achieved, although some have in other respects surpassed Goethe, represents an imperishable legacy. It is a legacy of considerable and pressing importance, for the steady, balanced, and yet concrete portrayal of the intellectual and psychological processes is one of the most urgent tasks that Socialist realism will have to fulfill.

Goethe and Antiquity:
The Helen Episode of Goethe's
Faust

by Karl Reinhardt

All that Goethe felt about the Greeks, all the meaning he saw in them, all he hoped they would mean to the future, he laid down in the second part of his *Faust,* in a dramatized form we may call, with his own words, an "open secret." We have but to consider the relevant scenes, the so-called Helen episode, at the end of the first act and in the third act—the second being concerned in its entirety with the "classical Walpurgis night"—in order to grasp the intimate, and almost magical relationship he had with that world of the past.

The action is strange, even if compared with the Faust tradition. There Faust was involved with the apparition of Helen in two adventures: in the first, Faust presents her to the emperor and his court in a magical performance; in the second, he engages in a lascivious love affair with the pagan spirit that was Helen.

The scene corresponding to the first of these adventures in Goethe's *Faust* is of a most acute tenseness. It was given its definitive form at a late date, but its conception goes back to a much earlier period. Goethe's Faust, assisted in his sorcery by Mephistopheles, acts before the emperor on a magical stage, and there he evokes a pantomime of the rape of Helen by Paris. At once, however, the phantom Helen seems to him to be the only reality, and all that is reality around him seems but phantom. His jealous passion causes a tremendous explosion. In the tumult, Mephistopheles

"Goethe and Antiquity: The Helen Episode of Goethe's *Faust*" by Karl Reinhardt. From *Goethe and the Modern Age,* ed. Arnold Bergstraesser (Chicago: Henry Regnery Co., Inc., 1950), pp. 38–49. Copyright 1950 by Henry Regnery Co., Inc. Reprinted by permission of the publisher.

shoulders his swooning companion, the victim of his own sorcery, and carries him away with a *bon mot*. The audience had meanwhile been glossing the performance with rather pretty banalities.

This first appearance of Helen is a mute one, and thus the second appears all the more brilliant by its eloquence. Here the poet indulges in the pleasure of making her speak. She speaks a supreme, a magic Greek: a German Greek never heard before. She proves to be beauty personified even in her speech. She speaks like the heroine of an Aeschylean tragedy. This, too, is a performance, but there is no more reference to the audience. As to the action, the precision of the first one is relaxed. It seems rather vague, rambling, turgid. The more it advances, the more absurd and impossible it becomes. Thrice the stage changes by magic. Each time the conflict is at its height, magic intervenes and weakens the illusion. Magic plays the role of what in Attic tragedy is the *deus ex machina*.

What an absurd action altogether! Helen, accompanied by a chorus of captured women, has just returned to Sparta from Troy. Sent ahead by Menelaus to prepare an offering to the gods, she enters the palace, but, startled by some horrible vision, immediately rushes out again. Within she had met the ugliest of all masks, an old woman, her housemaid—a new mask of the devil, as we are told at the end. Both her entrance and return recall the opening of a tragedy of Aeschylus, the *Eumenides,* wherein the priestess of Apollo enters the temple and rebounds in the same way, having seen within the dreadful goddesses of revenge.

Goethe's style is quite in keeping with the content. The terrible old woman confirms Helen's fears: Menelaus, there is no doubt, will kill her; the preparations for an offering to the gods are the preparations for her death; she herself will be the sacrifice. The chorus laments in utter desperation. Greek tragedy in its excessive choral pathetic form comes to life again, but in what an absurd situation!

The Gordian knot is cut by magic. The only escape, the old woman suggests, is to withdraw to a mountain castle. The queen agrees. The classical surroundings are transmuted into medieval ones, and Faust, dressed as a medieval duke, accompanied by his knights, receives the queen with all the ceremonial of the age of chivalry. The language, too, changes accordingly; rhyme replaces the Greek meters.

But once more the scene changes; it becomes an idyllic landscape peopled with shepherds and their flocks, a scene partly recalling the bucolics of Virgil, partly suggesting the classic landscapes of the seventeenth century. Above all, however, this scene shows a vision of a golden age in which nature and man are united in serenity and harmony. A new Arcadia is called into existence, to become no less a part of Goethe himself than had ancient Greece earlier in the Helen drama:

> Primeval woods! the strong oak there is regnant. . . .
>
> *Altwälder sind's! Die Eiche starret mächtig. . . .*

This Arcadia is the scene of the accomplished love between a chivalrous Faust and the Greek heroine.

Time passes. Behind lovely ivy-covered bowers Helen and Faust enjoy their bliss. Soon a young voice is heard. Euphorion, the beloved son of the happy couple, grows up with magic speed, like young Mercury in the myth—a wonder of beauty and grace, dancing, singing, leaping, playing the lyre, catching young girls, longing to become a hero. But there is some magic restraint on him: he is forbidden to fly, and, while trying to do so, tilts, falls and dies like a new Icarus. At the same moment, Helen vanishes from Faust's arms. He holds nothing but her garments. Changing into clouds they lift him into the air and carry him away. The epilogue, spoken by the old woman, interprets the metamorphosis:

> The garment let not go! . . .
> It is no more the Goddess thou hast lost,
> But godlike is it.
> 'Twill bear thee swift from all things mean and low
> To ether high, so long thou canst endure.
> We'll meet again, far, very far from here.

> *Das Kleid, lass es nicht los. Da zupfen schon*
> *Dämonen an den Zipfeln, möchten gern*
> *Zur Unterwelt es reissen. Halte fest!*
> *Die Göttin ist's nicht mehr, die du verlorst,*
> *Doch göttlich ist's. Bediene dich der hohen,*
> *Unschätzbarn Gunst und hebe dich empor:*
> *Es trägt dich über alles Gemeine rasch*
> *Am Aether hin, solange du dauern kannst.*
> *Wir sehn uns wieder, weit, gar weit von hier.*

As to the remains of Euphorion, tunic and lyre, Mephistopheles, taking his true shape again, recommends them as apparel for new schools of poetry.

Here, too, the play ends in a catastrophe, but one different from that of Helen's first appearance at the emperor's court: something lives on that is eternal. The end of the first Helen episode was sarcastic, the end of the second is sublime. We may consider the whole act an allegory. It is more than an allegory, but we may start from this preliminary statement: it allegorizes the acceptance of the highest values of antiquity by modern times. In so far as the time of Goethe was potentially ready to accept these values, the allegory is of general significance.

To begin with, the general trend was a most favorable one. Goethe's life coincided with the period of European classicism. The time between his birth and his death saw the beginning, the climax, and the decline of a most comprehensive predilection for things Greek. In poetry, art, architecture, furniture, clothing, this tendency was so strong that more than once, it seems to us, in spite of its self-consciousness, or because of it, it became a mask. Goethe's own house on the *Frauenplan* in Weimar, with its Empire- and Biedermeier-decorated rooms crowded with plaster figures, looks like a trim little museum, displaying the time's tendency of style with its ideals borrowed from the Greeks to adapt them to the narrowness of homely urban dwelling. If you recall but the names of Winckelmann, Canova, David, Ingres, you will grant that in his predilection for the Greeks Goethe only shares the prevailing taste.

Apart from this general view, however, Goethe's relationship to the Greeks has another aspect. He conceived of it as a gift peculiar to him. It would be easy to find many utterances of his in which the difference is stressed. For instance, referring to the *Iliad,* he says: "There is no one living now and no one will be born, who will be able to judge this poetry."

You may, by the way, recognize the same distinction even at the end of the Helen act: on the one hand, the celestial aspect, Faust's mystical elevation caused by Helen's garments; on the other hand, the terrestrial pendant, the satirical distribution of Euphorion's *"exuviae"* (clothes) among the industrious schools of contemporary poetry.

Goethe must have felt something personal about his relationship to the Greeks, something like a revelation, varying through his life, but never abandoning him. At first it was more like an anticipation and a longing or a striving: "With my soul longing for the land of the Greeks . . ." he says at the beginning of *Iphigenie*. In his middle years it was more like a feeling of discovery and possession, of clear intuition of the essential, of a revelation of beauty. Toward the end of his life it was an ever-increasing feeling of mystery. His concept of the Greeks developed parallel with his concept of nature.

Now the belief of Goethe's time on which its general tendency toward the Greeks depended was based on approximately the following views: Nature itself seemed to lead toward the Greeks, just as the Greeks seemed to lead to nature; the very core of nature was considered to be "noble simplicity and quiet grandeur"; the evidence that these three—nature, simplicity, and grandeur—were the same, seemed to be given by the Greeks. Goethe, the greatest admirer of the Greeks that ever was, would in so far not be at variance with his time.

And yet no one but Goethe has ever been seized by so personal, as it were so magical an experience of the interrelation between the Greek past and the European present. It is not by chance that magic plays so enormous a part in the Helen episode. It has a meaning here even deeper than its meaning in the first part of *Faust*. Recall but a few of the magic symbols Goethe here employs: tripod, key, sinking and raising, Faust's shamanlike travel to the timeless realm of the Mother Goddesses. Goethe must have felt, you will admit, that his own thinking followed a path quite different from ordinary historical or aesthetic categories. He was sure that he himself possessed the magic key, and he believed that it was the only right one. This key is a symbol for that personal experience from which the scene of Helen's resurrection was created.

But before going on, we must return to another source of Goethe's work. Goethe was perhaps the first to become conscious in a creative sense of the traditional historical world. He saw it as something still remaining but already beginning to vanish. He became aware of it, growing up in the atmosphere of the old town in which he was born, with its vanishing flavors, with its reminders of the Middle Ages, partly revolting, partly delightful. Goethe was the first in whom the sentimental consciousness of his time embraced the still extant historical tradition. Certainly in this regard, too, he had had some predecessors. But it would be hard, I think, to find others who expressed such a feeling of traditional surroundings in terms as intense as, for instance, those in some scenes of the first part of *Faust*. One line often involves a whole world:

> How from the window of the sacristy
> Upward th' eternal lamp sends forth a glimmer . . .

> *Wie von dem Fenster dort der Sakristei*
> *Aufwärts der Schein des ewigen Lämpchens flimmert . . .*

Needless to say, Shakespeare was not yet so remote that there could be no sense of close relationship between old Frankfurt and the world disclosed to Goethe by the English poet.

Goethe was endowed with two contrasting gifts to a greater degree than anyone else. He alone had the power of calling into existence at the same time two entirely different spheres, one so near, the other so remote in space and time; one still sensible and living in Goethe's own memory, the other to be acquired by witchcraft, as Helen is to be rescued from death and oblivion. The first of these gifts is the romantic, the second the classical. The first is connected with everything surrounding the young German girl, Gretchen, the second with all the splendor accompanying the apparition of the Greek goddess. In this drama of Helen two opposite worlds struggle against each other. Then a reconciliation comes about, a new horoscopic conjunction—whatever the sense, be it historical, personal, or utopian. By conquering Helen, Faust rescues her from the restraint of age and time; he defeats the power of Menelaus, teaches Helen to speak in rhymes, then marries her and has a son. . . .

But there is still a third root of the Helen drama to expound. In spite of his superhistorical greatness, Goethe ever remained faithful to his youth. His youth was the time of the rococo. The rococo tradition, still embodying the baroque, stayed with him throughout his life. In his latest poetry the rococo charm and fancifulness still survived in contrast with the tendencies of his contemporaries. He even achieved a new spiritualized rococo, a development which his great humanist friend Wilhelm von Humboldt would hardly have understood. Whatever the reason, Goethe relieved him of the task of criticism by concealing the manuscript of the second part of *Faust*. He did not want even his friends to read it.

But of the rococo element of his personality he could not make a subject of poetic creation, as he did of the romantic and the classic. The rococo worked within him as a principle of form. Since he could not give to it the form of a story or an action, it worked the more strongly as an element of style. Last but not least it supplied him with music. From the point of view of style, the second part of the Helen episode is a libretto for an opera. The various sections follow each other in a circle. The tragic note of the scenes of Helen's return is relieved by an idyllic movement. This, however, turns abruptly into another tragic passage, though of an opposite type. The poetical composition here is so musical that only a full orchestra could add anything to it. The play starts in the style of Aeschylus; it ends in the last great style of modern theatrical tradition, in a pathetic "baroque."

At first encounter much of the diction here may seem turgid, depending on one's philosophy of style. But we must listen not merely to the words, but to the music of the verse.

The rococo influence goes even further. The combination of dance, solo dance and counterdance with music, the vocal trio of Euphorion, Helen and Faust, the modern balletlike function of the chorus, show the same influence. What at first sight may perhaps seem maudlin sentimentality—the apparition of the flowery youth Euphorion with his lyre, the homage to the fallen Byron, the whole finale with its symbolic transmutations, the garments becoming clouds—all these point in the same direction. Nevertheless, from the viewpoint of style, this rococo conclusion by no means resulted from the intention of deliberately contrasting the beginning with the end.

Until now we have been considering the synthesis of those three elements: the Greek, the medieval, and the rococo or baroque. We have also stressed that magic power brings about their conjunction. Magic, we saw, plays the *deus ex machina*. It renders possible the impossible. And the impossible is the chief function of poetry: "I love him who strives after the impossible." This means: magic remains no longer only the function of the devil. Maybe the devil, too, has something to do with magic. But on the whole, in the Helen drama, magic, instead of being a part of the negative spirit, becomes productive. In the first act Faust was crushed by the power he had invoked; in the third act he is the superior, the magnanimous man, the gentle lover. No more are words like these spoken: "The spectral drama thou thyself hast made." The apparitions are no longer subjective. Both style and content are intensified. All the riches of fancy are displayed, but in what an objective manner! The first act cannot be understood without the third, the "explosion" without the "marriage."

There remains one more aspect of no less importance, the connection between magic and irony. For instance, there are remarkable differences between the real, the historical rococo style and Goethe's form of it. The Goethean rococo shows an admixture of personal irony. With regard to the antique ingredient it is the same. Its very abstruseness and absurdity makes the action, which is magical, at the same time ironic. The transition into the grand-opera style required some preparatory modulations and ironic overtones. They are already found in the part written in the tragic Greek meter, and even among the most tragical passages:

> Thereafter further came my lord's imperious speech . . .

> *Sodann erfolgte des Herren ferneres Herrscherwort* . . .

In spite of all this high-spirited magnificence, Goethe is always inclined to make fun of it—most secretly. The whole play, we must not forget, remains a "phantasmagoria." Helen herself is not quite sure of her existence; she swoons sometimes:

> It was a dream, as even the words themselves declare,
> I vanish hence . . .
> (She sinks into the arms of the chorus.)

> *Es war ein Traum, so sagen ja die Worte selbst,*
> *Ich schwinde hin und werde selbst mir ein Idol.*
> (*Sie sinkt dem Halbchor in die Arme.*)

The Aeschylean style is not simple, rather it is exaggerated. But in all the exaggeration, as far as it is legitimate, some playfulness is concealed. And yet there is some basic difference between the irony of Goethe and the irony of the Romantics, for instance: Goethe's irony is a matter of form, not a matter of background or content. Responsibility, allegiance to the calling he felt to be his, remains in the foreground of Goethe's mind. There is, however, in Goethe's irony a yielding to conventions—to conventions of society as well as of the theatre and of the various genres of poetry, conventions even of his own. The more he resorted to esoteric means, the more he abided in the exoteric with good grace. Conventions may even become a spell. The magic player is attached to them. Greek tragedy too is a convention, is something "as if," *als ob*. And what a convention is grand opera!

Now the whole Helen drama, from the beginning almost to end, remains a masque of ghosts. The masque, however, is still a hidden, not an open one. The masque continues to the end. There is a sudden general unmasking. *Demaskierung;* the chorus turns into elemental spirits, Helen into the shadow she was, and the ugly old housemaid, the manager of the whole, into the devil himself. The devil enters the proscenium, expanding into an enormous shape. During the masque, the ceremony and declamation never fail to show some more or less ironical hints (philologists and classicists must not read too much of their own seriousness into Goethe's Helen play). Each line contains some ambiguity, some ironic ambivalence. For example, Phorkyas' speech:

> Ye Phantoms! Like to frozen images ye stand,
> In terror thus from Day to part, which is not yours.
> Men, and the race of specters like you, one and all,
> Renounce not willingly the bright beams of the sun.

> *Gespenster!——Gleich erstarrten Bildern steht ihr da,*
> *Geschreckt, vom Tag zu scheiden, der euch nicht gehört.*
> *Die Menschen, die Gespenster sämtlich gleich wie ihr,*
> *Entsagen auch nicht willig hehrem Sonnenschein.*

But if you were to ask me: Arcadia? Isn't Arcadia a "convention," too? I should reply: No! By no means! Arcadia is a realization, the purest image of godlike patriarchal mankind, the highest thinkable achievement of the unity of man and nature.

> Primeval woods! The strong oak there is regnant,
> And bough crooks out from bough in stubborn state;
> The maple mild, with sweetest juices pregnant,
> Shoots cleanly up, and dallies with its weight.

> *Altwälder sind's! Die Eiche starret mächtig,*
> *Und eigensinnig zackt sich Ast an Ast;*
> *Der Ahorn, mild, von süssem Safte trächtig,*
> *Steigt rein empor und spielt mit seiner Last.*

And a little farther on:

> So was Apollo shepherdlike in feature,
> That other shepherds were as fair and fleet;
> For wherein such clear orbit moveth Nature,
> All worlds in interaction meet.[1]

> *So war Apoll den Hirten zugestaltet,*
> *Dass ihm der schönsten einer glich;*
> *Denn wo Natur im reinen Kreise waltet,*
> *Ergreifen alle Welten sich.*

---

[1] The translation, it seems to me, does not render the meaning correctly. Where nature rules in such a clean circuit, not soiled by human violence, untouched and undisturbed by the developments of history, there "all worlds," the divine and the human, are in harmony and embrace one another.

Perhaps Arcadia too had been a convention, in the rococo or in the time of *As You Like It;* here, with Goethe, it becomes a vision. Poetry triumphs over irony.

Nevertheless, there is a progress in the movement of the conventions, in the development of the styles and ages, not only in the historical sense. In the beginning of the play, in the Greek tragedy, Helen is but a prey of conquerors, lovers, revengers. She is a victim of destiny. But this tragedy with its classical form is not the real one. Greek tragedy is, in the light of our days, a phantom. Real tragedy begins just when the phantom tragedy would seem to be over. So Helen herself, as an allegory, becomes tragic. Love, real love, teaches her to become a mortal. Hence the relevance of the teaching scene. Rhyme, as Goethe suggests, may be an invention of love:

> Canst thou to me that lovely speech impart?
>
> 'Tis easy; it must issue from the heart.
>
> And if the breast with yearning overflow,
>
> One looks around, and asks—
>
> > Who shares the glow.

> *So sage denn, wie sprech ich auch so schön?*
>
> *Das ist gar leicht, es muss von Herzen gehn.*
>
> *Und wenn die Brust von Sehnsucht überfliesst,*
>
> *Man sieht sich um und fragt—*
>
> > *wer mitgeniesst.*

And then—she is improving; she is already rhyming in the middle of each line:

> I feel so far away, and yet so near;
> And am so fain to say: Here am I! here!

> *Ich fühle mich so fern und doch so nah,*
> *Und sage nur zu gern: da bin ich! da!*

But a ghost on the way to becoming a mortal—doesn't that look like a type of story we know quite well? "Once there was a mortal who found or gained or conquered a fairy, and they fell in love and were happy and had children, until by some misfortune or mistake the magical spell by which she lived was broken, and she disappeared. The mortal never forgot her." Instead of an allegory, you may consider the whole Helen episode from another viewpoint, with no less reason, to be a fairy tale or a folk-lore story. The allegory becomes a saga or, if you will, the saga is involved in artificial and symbolical meanings. But it is from the saga that the action derives, as well as the emotion, the sweetness, the tenderness, and the tragedy of the end. One of the earlier schemes for the play made the allusion even more perspicuous; there it was a magic ring that lent her a mortal existence.

It is in the shape of such a fairy tale or saga that Goethe has dramatized the mystery of his relationship to the ancients. "A fairy once was called by love, by magic of a mortal, the most beautiful fairy of all; but the son of the mortal transcended the limits of mortals, and she faded away. Yet there remained from her a power of transfiguration . . ."

Goethe's legacy to posterity with regard to the Greeks is laid down in the epilogue:

> The garment let not go! Already twitch
> The Demons at its skirts . . .
>
> *Das Kleid, lass es nicht los. Da zupfen schon*
> *Dämonen an den Zipfeln . . .*

Goethe's Conception of Form

by Elizabeth M. Wilkinson

'In the sciences', Goethe observes, 'it is greatly rewarding to seek out the inadequate truths already possessed by the Ancients and develop them further'.[1] With this seeming paradox we are at the heart of his attitude to intellectual inquiry. In what sense may a truth be said to be inadequate? It is here said to be so in the more immediate sense that some insight of a man of science may not quicken, or may not survive long enough in the intellectual climate of his age, for its implications to be fully explored. Before its generative force is spent, it is elbowed out by others which more nearly meet the needs of the moment. It remains inadequate because it still awaits clarification in detail and the test of precise application. But implicit in this paradox, too, is Goethe's conviction that the perception of truth is not the monopoly of any one mode of thinking. Ritual, myth, religion, philosophy, as well as earlier, more naïve, epochs of scientific inquiry, have all bequeathed truths to mankind. It is one of the secrets of Goethe's successful living that he did not withdraw his allegiance from these just because they could not command the assent of his purely discursive intelligence. They had been discovered as answers to older needs of the human mind, and some unerring wisdom taught him that these do not atrophy as new needs develop. They live on side by side, not essentially incompatible, but at war, even to the point where sanity

"Goethe's Conception of Form" by Elizabeth M. Wilkinson. From *Goethe, Poet and Thinker*, by Elizabeth M. Wilkinson and Leonard A. Willoughby (London: Edward Arnold [Publishers] Ltd., 1962). Copyright © 1962 by Edward Arnold (Publishers) Ltd. Reprinted by permission of the author and the publisher. The essay originally appeared in *Proceedings of the British Academy*, XXXVII (July, 1951), p. 175ff., "Annual Lecture on a Master Mind."

[1] *Maximen v. Reflexionen* (ed. Günther Müller, Stuttgart, 1943), 895. The reader is here referred to this particular edition because its arrangement of Goethe's 1,200 odd aphorisms so clearly exhibits that "polar" movement of his thought which I am at pains to bring out in the opening pages of this essay.

is threatened, unless appropriate satisfaction can be found for both. Goethe found it by transforming his mode of assent. Much that could no longer, without intellectual dishonesty, be accepted literally, as fact, he accepted transliterally, as symbol. In this, as in much else, the Either/Or attitude was repugnant to him in its crudity. He reserved the right, and developed the mastery, of free movement among the mansions of his mind, weaving his way, with immense flexibility of response, between the symbolic and the factual: between memories of childhood piety, or intimations of the divine, and sober investigation of natural process, between metaphysical insights and robust common sense, between literal truths and those transformations of myth and ritual which live on in art and in the sense of occasion.

Thus reason was safeguarded. But not by the denial of rationality. To mistake this flexibility for indeterminate vagueness, a kind of intellectual chiaroscuro, is to court disaster from the unexpected sharpness of some of his distinctions. The swiftness of his transitions from one mode of response to another, at the sovereign instance of appropriateness, may dazzle the eye of the beholder; the responses themselves are differentiated to a fine degree. Thus he insisted[2] that myth and legend have no place in science; or if used for purposes of illustration, then it must be, like all analogy, with clearly metaphorical, not factual, reference—a distinction not always strictly observed by more orthodox scientists. To confuse these symbols with the objects or processes they symbolize is to foster superstition, which, he allowed, has indeed its place in life, but in the realm of poetry and imagination,[3] not among the abstractive techniques of rationalized knowledge. In other words, one mode of thought may illuminate and support another; it can never do duty for it. A famous aphorism of his begins: 'Everything worth thinking has already been thought'; but it continues: '*our* endeavour must be to think it through again'.[4] And this rethinking proceeds by what Goethe called successive transpositions. From time to time the human mind evolves new leading concepts, develops new methods, which by their very nature are provisional, to be superseded by others when their work is done.[5] But only in this way are new insights ever achieved, old 'inadequate' truths given precision and application, and the challenge of the present moment answered.

[2] *Maximen,* ed. cit., 1056, 1058.
[3] Ibid., 606.
[4] Ibid., 1174.
[5] Ibid., 926.

To those who, appalled by some of its accompanying effects, would call a halt to the physicist's method of exploring the universe, Goethe offers no genuine support. They may invoke, and it is salutary to do so, his misgivings about the rise of technology, his suspicion of the atomistic reduction of nature to quantitative symbols, his concern at the decline in man's power to apprehend, through disciplined and concrete intuition, the forms of natural phenomena as they present themselves, in all the fullness of their qualitative variety, to sense-experience. But the picture is misleadingly incomplete if it includes no indication of his undismayed acceptance that good and evil are fatefully interlinked, and that truth may well arise as a by-product of error.[6] Thus we might construe as an illiberal setting of his face against further inquiry the dictum that 'even discerning minds do not see that what they are trying to *explain* are in reality primary facts of experience, incapable of further reduction', were it not followed *at once* by the saving corollary: 'Yet this pursuit of explanations may be all to the good, for without it the search for knowledge would be abandoned far too soon'.[7] The style of his thinking is, in fact, essentially dramatistic, and in presenting it we must see to it that both antagonist and protagonist have their say. To his *in*sistence that science is held back by its preoccupation with what is neither knowable, nor worth knowing,[8] we must oppose his categorical *re*sistance to the dangerous prejudice of putting any mode of scientific inquiry under a ban.[9] His contention that the highest happiness of a rational being is to have explored the accessible, and quietly to revere the inaccessible,[10] has to be parried with its evident counterpart that man must persist in his belief that the incomprehensible is comprehensible, for otherwise he would cease to explore.[11] And we must make it clear that when the author of this unending dialogue speaks to us *directly*, he does so in statements which either synthesize, or hold in balance, the contraries involved. As in the aphorism: 'Whatever emancipates the mind without giving us control over ourselves is dangerous',[12] where explicit statement of the reserves in his loyalty to intellectual enlightenment conceals implicit exhortation to render it foolproof by enlightenment of another sort. Or in these concerning man's

[6] Ibid., 888.
[7] Ibid., 1040, 1041.
[8] Ibid., 934.
[9] Ibid., 985.
[10] Ibid., 873.
[11] Ibid., 875.
[12] Ibid., 82.

proper relation to the past: 'Authority—without it man cannot exist, yet it brings error as well as truth in its train',[13] or 'Ancient fundaments one respects, but one must never forfeit the right to start laying fresh foundations elsewhere'.[14]

'The mighty taker', Klopstock once called Goethe in a moment of acrimony. And so he was. But his strength, and his originality, derive from the productive tension between taking and rejecting. Indeed we might get a fresh angle on this Teutonic sage by applying the concept of 'perspective by incongruity' and assigning him to what Mr. Kenneth Burke[15] calls the 'comic' order of thinkers— by which synonym for sceptical, dialectic, humanistic, he would suggest that to be an accepter-rejecter in a world which goes in for whole-hearted accepters or out-and-out rejecters is a pretty funny thing to be.[16] I don't know that Mr. Burke has ever thought of including Goethe in his 'comic' frame. But it's where he belongs. For he is neither wholly orthodox nor wholly heretical. He moves dialectically between ironic scepticism about progress and unshakable devotion to the further adventuring of the human spirit, between steady conviction of the hypothetical nature of all knowledge and firm belief in truth, between the sanction of authority and wholesome reaction against it, between allegiance to the past and assent to the future.

It is in something of this same spirit, I suggest, that it would be profitable to re-examine his own conception of form at this particular point of time. For form is in the air—indeed on the air. Whether we tune in to a talk on the molecular structure of synthetic fibres, the processes of the human brain, the making of history, or recent work in sociology and linguistics, this powerful medium for the popularization of ideas speaks to us of *patterns*. The scientist, it seems, no longer thinks only atomistically, in terms of ever more precise analysis into smaller and smaller particles of matter, but also formally, in terms of complex systems of relationships, systems from which the observer himself can no longer be rigorously excluded. By 'explanations' he no longer means tracing the very springs of nature, but, more modestly, arranging nature in a coherent *order*. The symbols for communicating these notions have

[13] Ibid., 1183.

[14] Ibid., 1177.

[15] In *Attitudes toward History*, New York, 1937.

[16] This is how S. E. Hyman (*The Armed Vision*, New York, 1948, p. 357f.) explains Kenneth Burke's choice of the word 'comic' to describe this attitude of ambivalence.

changed accordingly. The layman is invited to think of nature less as an engine than as an algebra,[17] and of himself less as an animated machine than as a pattern. He hears this word so often that, as J. Z. Young suggested in his Reith Lectures, he could easily fall to thinking of himself as a carpet—Sherrington's likening of brain-activity to an 'enchanted loom' might support the fancy—and this error has to be forestalled by frequent reminders that it is a pattern of constantly *changing* relations. Stability of structure, individual identity is, it seems, a property not of material particles, but of *form*. It is perhaps not surprising that in this climate of thought the arts and the sciences, after a longish estrangement, should show signs of drawing together again. The artistic and the scientific imagination are compared now as much as they are contrasted. A poet and an astrophysicist[18] can find common ground for an exchange of their views of nature. And there is at this moment[19] an exhibition of the natural shapes and structures revealed by modern science, entitled 'Growth and Form' in tribute to that great scientist D'Arcy Thompson, but arranged by the Institute of Contemporary Arts.

I often catch myself thinking: 'Goethe said as much'. I may remember that the loom was his favourite symbol for the processes of nature, within man and without; recall his aphorism: 'The phenomenon is not severed from the observer but inextricably implicated and involved in him';[20] or 'Pushing problems aside which can only be explained dynamically is bound to result in mechanistic modes of explanation';[21] or his unwavering conviction that the laws of art and nature are fundamentally the same. But, of course, he did not say *as much*. He said either more or less—according to how you look at it. His knowledge was more varied, and far more coherent, than that of any specialist today; but it was less exact—in the scientific sense of the word 'exact'. For what we now call exact knowledge can only be obtained by an approach to nature which is the very antithesis of his; by isolating and immobilizing things under the artificial conditions of experiment, and analyzing them

[17] I borrow this phrase from J. Bronowski's review of Viscount Samuel's *Essay in Physics, The Observer*, 15.IV.1951.

[18] Walter de la Mare and Dr. Martin Johnson. Their exchange of ideas, lasting over a period of years, was discussed by the latter in a broadcast on 13.II.1951 (Third Programme).

[19] I.e., at the time of writing. Cf. *Aspects of Form*. A Symposium, ed. L. L. Whyte, issued on the occasion of this Exhibition. London, 1951.

[20] *Maximen*, ed. cit., 1020.

[21] Ibid., 1109.

with the precision of mathematical calculation. But thereby phenomena which he deemed incapable of further reduction *have* been
further reduced. The pursuit of 'explanations', in the older sense
of a search for ultimate causes, has, in fact, as he foresaw, given
man immense control over nature, for good, and not only for evil.
And if thought seems to be swinging round to what preoccupied
him, dynamic explanations of forms in movement, it is a swing
round, not back—the appropriate image is Goethe's spiral, not
Nietzsche's cyclic recurrence—round at a level of far greater exactitude and detail. Nevertheless, this turn of events does mean
that his insights have new actuality, that he speaks to us in accents
more urgent than perhaps to any generation, during his lifetime or
since.

Inside Germany there has been growing awareness of this for
thirty years or more. No less than four editions of his scientific
works were prepared independently during the twenties.[22] His concepts and methods have been developed in the field of botany by
Wilhelm Troll and his pupils and in the field of literary criticism
by Günther Müller and the morphological school. The impulse
they gave to the theory of perception evolved by the *Gestalt* psy-
chologists and to Viktor von Weizsäcker's work on the relation between sense-perception and motor-activity, if less explicitly acknowledged, is none the less apparent. Of the value of much of this work
there can be no doubt, though one feels that some of Goethe's own
warnings can never be too often invoked: warnings about the danger, always imminent in our longing for order, of leaping from
observable fact to inadequate theory, of mistaking the scaffolding
for the building, the hypothesis for knowledge, of succumbing to
the domination of phrases and substituting analogies for phenomena, of generalizing prematurely from one field to another.[23]

Outside of Germany the tendency is all the other way, and as
thinker he is usually relegated to a position of at most historical
interest. The language barrier is of moment. Few are equipped to

[22] *Goethes Morphologische Schriften,* ed. Wilhelm Troll, Jena, 1926; *Goethes
naturwissenschaftliche Schriften,* ed. Rudolph Steiner, Dornach, 1926; *Goethes
Schriften Über die Natur,* ed. Günther Ipsen, Leipzig, 1928; *Goethes naturwissenschaftliche Schriften,* ed. Waldemar V. Wasielewski in vol. 36 of Goethe's
Werke, Berlin (Bong), 1929.

[23] See, f. i., *Maximen.* ed. cit., 1042–84, the remarks with which he prefaced his
Theory of Colour, or his short essays on scientific method, e.g., *Der Versuch als
Vermittler von Objekt und Subjekt, Erfahrung und Wissenschaft, Erfinden und
Entdecken.*

offer us, as the late Agnes Arber did,[24] both an impeccable translation of his *Metamorphosis of Plants* and an expert assessment of its
standing as botany; fewer still to transcend the technical details of
their subject and, in a survey ranging from Aristotle to the present
day, to show us, as she has shown, Goethe's contribution to the
natural philosophy of plant form.[25] The non-German scientist
tends on the whole to be more chary of relating his findings to a
general theory of knowledge. But a too ardent scepticism is no less
inept than over-enthusiasm. Where separate fields of study are
moving independently to conclusions similar enough to provide a
point of contact, it seems almost perverse not to explore possibilities of integration. For, as Goethe says,[26] we should not call our
knowledge a mere patchwork of disjointed fragments if we did not
possess the concept of wholeness. And at such moments of conver-
gence thinkers of the past, with their more unified and less distracted vision, may well provide us with principles for organizing
the scattered results of experimental knowledge. What is needed is
a blend of boldness and caution. In borrowing Goethe's eye for
connections, we must proceed with nothing less than his care for
distinctions; knowing how to separate not only the false from the
true, but adequate truths from those still awaiting demonstration;
remembering that to elevate him into dogma is not only alien to
the profoundly undogmatic temper of his own mind (despite his
blind spot about Newton) but comes uncomfortably near to fulfilling his ironic prophecy that it would not be long before people
started believing in him and quoting him as if he were gospel.[27]

But why should we turn to Goethe in particular? Has he anything more to offer us than, say, Aristotle for whom form was a
master concept in all branches of knowledge? I think he has. For
Goethe was not only a discerner of form; he was a maker of it, and
a maker of an immense variety of forms. It has been said, by no less
an authority than Sir Charles Sherrington, that if it were not for
Goethe's poetry we should not trouble about his science.[28] And this
is true. But not in the sense intended. His poetic mind does indeed
constitute the interest of his scientific work, not because he thinks
as a poet when he is supposed to be thinking as a scientist—he

---

[24] *Goethe's Botany. Chronica Botanica*, Waltham, Mass., X, 2 (1946).
[25] *The Natural Philosophy of Plant Form*, Cambridge, 1950.
[26] *Maximen*, ed. cit., 885.
[27] In conversation with J. Falk, 28.II.1809.
[28] *Goethe on Nature and Science*, Cambridge, 1942, p. 23.

moves freely between both these modes of thought—but because his extensive first-hand experience in the two spheres makes him uniquely qualified to evolve a conception of form embracing both art and nature. ✳

And he has yet a further qualification which is often overlooked in treating of his view of form: his profound comprehension of *how* he made it. This is not to say that he plucked the mystery out of creation. The 'mighty visitation unimplored' remained to the end a token of grace before which he bowed his head in awe. But if the cause of inspiration was not to be explained, the form of its operations could still be explored. His lucidity about the creative act is reminiscent of a Flaubert, a Gide, or a Valéry—and all three were, in fact, fascinated by the records of it he has left. But the marvel is that in him this knowledge was not destructive of spontaneity. The muse who in his youth 'dictated to him slumb'ring', so that he must leap from his bed and scrawl his 'unpremeditated verse' diagonally across the page,[29] still deigned to bless him at sixty with lyrics of such mysterious power that we are not surprised when he tells us that one of them 'came' to him at midnight, unheralded and unsought.[30] But she was more gracious still. Perhaps as a reward for long years of unremitting poetic labour, she granted him, just before his death, a measure of power to 'command' his inspiration, to descend, fully waking, into that unconscious stream where poetry has its source—'a mysterious psychological development which might be worth looking into' was his comment upon this new mode of productivity in a letter to Wilhelm von Humboldt.[31] But he had been preparing for it since his late twenties when he first began to turn a watchful eye on the involuntary movements of his mind, fostering in himself a kind of awareness which could *observe* his spontaneous activity without inhibiting it. 'I must observe more closely the cycle in me of good and bad days', he wrote in his diary when he was thirty;[32] 'inspiration, technical working out, ordering—it all alternates and follows a regular course'. His interest clearly embraced more than the activity of composition; he was intent on discerning the whole pattern of his mental processes. For the same diary entry continues: 'Good humour, depression, strength, elasticity, weakness, composure, and desire, likewise.

[29] *Dichtung und Wahrheit*, IV, 16; JA, XXV, 10.
[30] The poem *Um Mitternacht*.
[31] 1.XII.1831.
[32] 26.III.1780.

With patience I ought to be able to discover the time and order of my own cycle'. And the last words he ever wrote[33] are still concerned with what he calls these 'ultimate mysteries', with the secret, intricate connections between conscious and unconscious, awareness and spontaneity, with the strange duality of man, whereby, to be wise, he must never cease to hearken to the involuntary promptings of his nature and yet, by taking thought, can learn, in some measure, to guide their direction and so bring to full realization the inherent *form* of his being.

What Goethe, then, brought to the investigation of forms outside himself, whether of art or of nature—rock, cloud, or crystal formations, plant metamorphosis or comparative anatomy—was inside knowledge of the formative process at work in his own mind, an objective awareness of his own subjectivity. Looking at nature within himself he found that the psychological laws operating there were not a denial of the laws of external nature, but their fulfillment, and what he offers us is a unified conception of a formative principle transcending the dichotomy of subjective and objective experience.

But Goethe has also something different to say to us from Aristotle because, by virtue of his historical position, many of the problems which preoccupied him were already conceived in terms in which we still conceive them today. He lived, as a young man, through the surging excitement of the revolution which was taking place in man's whole way of thinking: the change to a dynamic view of the universe. The world into which he was born was a world of static forms. The established sciences were the separating ones—*Scheidekunst* the eighteenth century called chemistry—which immobilized in order to weigh and measure, and, with the precision instruments of Newtonian physics, translated the moving forms of sense-experience into the immutable formulae of mathematics. But the coming sciences were those dealing with the continuity of living organisms—not with being, but with becoming. The venerable idea of an unbroken hierarchy of forms, from the lowest to the highest, the Great Chain of Being, had been transferred from philosophy to the fields of biology and history, and there was shaping in men's minds, not so much a *theory* of evolution—the theory came later and is far less of a change than this imaginative revolution which prepared it—but a mental image, a view of the world

---

[33] In a letter to v. Humboldt of 17.III.1832, which is a commentary on the conscious commanding of inspiration referred to in his earlier letter of 1.XII. 1831.

in which process, growth, and development are basic. Before this time to speak of evolution meant simply increase of size, the swelling of the primary cell which, according to the doctrine of pre-formation, or *emboîtement,* already contained in miniature the entire animal or entire homunculus. But from now on it began to mean the changes in the life-cycle of an individual organism, and the idea, familiar to us now, but not in itself easy to grasp, of one form gradually changing into another and yet somehow retaining identity.

And the society Goethe moved in as a boy was a society still dominated by the forms and conventions of French classicism: finite forms, of static grace and symmetrical proportions, produced by artists who thought of themselves as craftsmen, modestly imitating the finished products of nature, or improving upon them in accordance with traditional rules to evolve what they charmingly termed a copy of *la belle nature*; an art to be measured against fixed norms and judged by the prevailing standards of good taste and good sense. But by the time he was twenty he was caught in the flood-tide of the new dynamic mode of thinking and the morphological approach to the study of cultures originated by Vico in his *Scienza Nuova,* but which Goethe had straight from the mouth of that other great progenitor of the historical method, Johann Gottfried Herder. From him he learnt to appreciate works of art in appearance so irregular, fragmentary, individual, even idiosyncratic, that by rationalistic standards they had been reckoned formless and barbaric: Gothic architecture and the Gothic Shakespeare, the primitive songs of backward peoples, the Dionysiac origins of the Greek dithyramb. Once referred back to their origins, however, seen in historical perspective as products of a certain soil, climate, and cultural environment, these could be understood as highly characteristic organisms, forms not finished perhaps, but becoming. The artist, he now heard, was no mere imitator, but an original genius, manifesting in his activity the very processes of natural creation; and the standards for judging his work were no longer absolute norms, external to the individual work in question, but laws inherent within it, relative, and accessible only to the genetic method.

Goethe was thus the immediate heir of various, and conflicting, conceptions of form. From each he took what he needed and rejected what was alien to him. What attracted him in the doctrine of 'inward form', deriving from Plotinus, and just then made available through its revival by Shaftesbury (though he also came across it in his reading of Giordano Bruno), was the idea that form is it-

self the principle at work in a living organism. It enabled him to
dispense with the thought, repugnant to any artist, of form as a
mere vessel for the containing of essence or spirit; or the related
theory, proceeding from the mechanistic sciences, of the form of
anything being the purely passive configuration of the elements
composing it, produced by an agency which is something other than
form, by energy or forces. It taught him, too, that form is something
different from symmetry, and so provided him with a new criterion
for judging works of art. But his encounter with this exciting new
notion did not oust his appreciation of traditional outward forms;
it revitalized it. It never led him into excusing sheer formlessness
on the grounds that a work had plenty of content! After his first
brief and intense surrender the unifying activity of his mind prevailed, and by the time he was twenty-five he was pointing out to
his more formless contemporaries of the Storm-and-Stress movement
that 'inner form is the form embracing all forms', transcending, but
including, outer form.[34] He might agree that, in Sir Thomas
Browne's phrase, 'the outward figures of a thing, plant or person
hang as signs or bushes of their inward form'; but never with that
more extravagant Neoplatonism which thought such outward figures *mere* reflections of inward essence. Nor did he ever fall victim
to those implications of the doctrine, which still dominated the
Romantics and have been the bane of much German criticism and
aesthetics since: the notion that form, as the principle of mind, suf-
fers an inevitable loss of perfection when, as Plotinus has it, it *de-
scends* into matter, or, as Shelley puts it: 'the most glorious poetry
ever communicated to the world is but a feeble shadow of the original conception of the poet'. Goethe's answer to this is already implicit in the brief comments he wrote in 1775 for the German translation of that impudent challenge to classicism, Louis Sébastien
Mercier's *Nouvel essai sur l'art dramatique*; it is explicit in his late
criticism of Plotinus himself: 'The created product is not less than
the creating mind. It is the advantage of living creation that what
is created can be of greater excellence than its creator'.[35] His awareness of his own creative process taught him early that an artist's
material medium is already a factor in his original conception, that
a form is not there, complete and insubstantial in his mind; if it
comes to him, whole, by sudden inspiration, then it is already in
terms of his medium; otherwise he wrestles with his medium until
he discovers and realizes a form.

[34] *Aus Goethes Brieftasche*; JA, XXXVI, 115.
[35] *Maximen*, ed. cit., 769.

What Goethe, then, did was to take over from the Neoplatonists the idea of form as a process at work even in the inmost parts of an organism, and fuse it completely with the idea of form as outward shape. The one is not the *cause* of the other; they are completely reciprocal. Inner structure determines outward shape and outward shape inner structure.[36] As he puts it in his *Lectures on Comparative Anatomy*,[37] the development or non-development of any one member affects the whole body, as this and its needs affect each single member. All the parts work in and through each other.

And if inner form is not separable from outer form neither is organism from environment. A living thing, he says in the preface to his *Morphology*,[38] is not a single unit but a plurality. Some of its elements are already joined together when it comes into being. But growth consists of a constant interchange of its own elements with elements of the environment, a taking-in and a giving-out, an incessant re-arrangement of patterns in all directions. What is formed is immediately broken down and re-formed. Stable identity derives not from the unchanging elements, but from the pattern which survives all their changes. Thus there is no hard and fast boundary between an organism and its surroundings, but a continuity. Again, Goethe took all he could from the new genetic method with its emphasis on environmental conditions; but he never fell into what Coleridge calls the 'sophism' of mistaking conditions for causes. He points out[39] that neither the statement that the fish is fashioned for living in water, nor the statement that it adapts itself to living in water, really reflects the actual state of affairs. It is better to say that the fish exists in and through water. There is no before or after in his formative process, in the sense of cause and effect. Nature fashions from outside inwards and from inside outwards, and the study of any living thing involves a study of all the reciprocal relations between organism and environment, considered not only genetically but *sub specie formae*.

The only actual definition Goethe ever gives of 'form' is tackled on semantic lines: 'For the whole complexity of existence of an actual being, German has the word *Gestalt*'.[40] Alive to the static quality of this word of past-participle origin, he continues: 'In

---

[36] *Versuch einer allgemeinen Vergleichungslehre* (1792); JA, XXXIX, 130.

[37] *Vorträge über die drei ersten Capitel des Entwurfs einer allgemeinen Einleitung in die vergleichende Anatomie* (1796); ibid., 163.

[38] In the section headed 'Die Absicht eingeleitet'; ibid., 252.

[39] *Versuch einer allgemeinen Vergleichungslehre;* ibid., 130.

[40] 'Die Absicht eingeleitet'; ibid., 251.

using this expression, however, we abstract from what is in constant flux and assume that the collection of parts we call an identity is finished and fixed in its character. But if we consider natural forms, we find that nowhere does anything stable or completed occur. Rather is everything suspended in precarious balance. Wherefore the German language is wont to use, appropriately enough, the word *Bildung* both of the form produced and of the process of formation'. But here is no niggling obsession with the problem of the meaning of meaning! Having made his distinction with care, he at once sanctions the use of the word *Gestalt,* provided that we always remember that it is an abstraction of something which in actual experience is never stable for more than a moment.

The subject Goethe developed, and christened, for the study of living forms in process of constant change and transformation was *Morphology.* By it he understood not only a branch of botany or biology, which is the meaning it still has today, but an independent science. It would, as he conceived it, make use of the findings of all the other sciences, including the quantitative results of physics and chemistry. For he was not, as is often asserted, opposed to analytical methods. On the contrary, he states explicitly, and on many occasions, that every means of investigating nature is legitimate and useful. But what he himself was interested in was not the identical elements, the atoms or nuclei, which are nature's material, but the multifarious patterns in which they manifest themselves, so that what is identical in substance can appear in forms utterly dissimilar;[41] just as in his study of plants and animals he never ceased to marvel at nature's power to modify identical organs, so that in form and function they appear not only different, but even opposed.[42] The business of morphology was what he called 'synthesis'; by which he did not mean putting together again all the parts that analysis had laid out side by side, but starting with living wholes and studying them in the light of the information about them that other sciences can provide; or, put the other way round, co-ordinating the scattered findings of the other sciences under the unifying aspect of form.[43]

The problems of morphology are so difficult precisely because of the great demands they make on the personality of the scientist. By what means is one to grasp the full complexity of an organism—

[41] Ibid., 252.
[42] E.g., *Vorträge über vergleichende Anatomie; * ibid., 170.
[43] His conception of the scope and function of morphology **is set out in his** *Betrachtung über Morphologie überhaupt* (1795); ibid., 133ff.

not just its external appearance but its internal organization, the interworking of all the parts in and through the whole? And not just the organism as we see it at any given moment of time but the cycle of its development from the beginning of its life-history till its end, including transformation into something totally unlike in appearance, as, for instance, the metamorphosis of a chrysalis into a butterfly? Goethe thought it could only be done by what he called *Anschauung,* intuitive contemplation, if you like, though both these words have something misleading about them. It involved first a subtle technique of the eye, indispensable for the apprehension of developmental processes; but the role of the mind's eye is no less important. The analytical thought involved is considerable too; for all the findings of the physico-chemical study of organisms have to be borne in mind. It is, as Agnes Arber puts it in an illuminating discussion of this tricky problem,[44] a combination of mediate knowledge *about* with the immediacy of knowledge *of,* a fusion of conceptual reason with thought which is visual and tactual. Intuition, on the other hand, might suggest the sudden flash out of the blue. But, vital and indispensable as that is, it is but one moment in the sustained process of *Anschauung,* a moment for which Goethe reserved the term *aperçu,* defining this as one link in a chain of observation and thought.[45] Goethe developed the technique of *Anschauung* into a methodical discipline and a fine art; it was by means of it that he made the discoveries he did about the forms of animals and plants.

The bringing of order into all the variety of individual forms thus grasped was achieved by Goethe in two complementary ways: by comparison and by the use of type concepts, the former a source of genuine inspiration to later workers in the field, the latter still a subject of much dispute. The archetypal concept, as *he* used it, involved a free movement between deduction and induction, even as *Anschauung* involved a constant alternation between analysis and synthesis. The procedure was to compare individual forms until the mind was sufficiently saturated with them for an archetype to emerge which then, in its turn, served as a regulative organ of perception in the comparison and ordering of further forms. Though abstractions, therefore, these archetypes or, as he called them, *Urphänomene,* were never purely mental abstractions; they still partook of sensuous experience. Nor were they static conceptions like Platonic ideas; they were capable of modification as new

[44] *The Natural Philosophy of Plant Form,* ed. cit., p. 209.
[45] *Maximen,* ed. cit., 1168.

forms were investigated. Goethe could never linger long in a schematic world. His immediate impulse was to find sensuous embodiment for his abstractions. Hence his instinctive movement to *sketch* his *Urpflanze*, that essence of 'plantness', a gesture incomprehensible to Schiller who was more at home in the realm of abstractions and could not imagine such an apparent contradiction in terms as a sensuous idea.[46] But so sensuous were Goethe's ideas that he— naïvely in the view of idealist philosophers—half hoped, though never in all seriousness, that he might come across his type-plant in the gardens of Palermo. Hence, too, his passionate attachment to that garden-love of his—which had come all the way from Kew!— *Bryophyllum calycinum*, because, in its strange mode of reproduction, it seemed to him the very image and symbol of the activity of metamorphosis.

Obviously the natural sciences can achieve results without considering the problem of *Gestalt*. They have done. Whether they will ever be able to effect any unification of their knowledge without coming to grips with questions of form in a systematic way is another matter. But in criticism and aesthetics form is the central issue, which it is impossible to avoid. And in the present chaotic state of literary studies in particular, Goethe's morphological principles could have both clarifying and unifying effect—provided they are applied with discrimination. It is all very well to say that he realized that there is no essential difference between form, not only in the crystal and the bone, in the leaf and in the cloud, but also in the painting and in the poem. But this is misleading. True, he is always coupling art and nature, once even with a single article, which in German almost has the effect of hyphening them: 'Die höchste und einzige Operation der Natur und Kunst ist die Gestaltung'.[47] But just as often he insists that art has its own laws. It is the handling of likeness and difference that he manages so superbly. There is no question of an identity of art and nature. It is a matter of analogy, or homology, as the scientist would say today; and analogies, as Goethe is always insisting, though indispensable for the communication, and even for the acquiring, of knowledge, defeat their own ends if pressed too far.

We should do well to clear our minds first of what he did not mean when he said that a work of art is like a work of nature. He did not mean such biologization of art as can be found, for instance, in the *Avant-propos* to the *Comédie Humaine*—the contrast is

[46] Cf. *Erste Bekanntschaft mit Schiller, 1794;* JA, XXX, 391.
[47] Letter to Zelter, 30.X.1808.

appropriate since Balzac is there drawing explicitly on the theories of Geoffroy Saint-Hilaire, the French biologist whose methods of tackling nature were, as Goethe publicly acknowledged, so like his own. Nor did he mean the rendering in art of the visual forms of nature, neither of external shapes nor of internal structures. Such forms may indeed inspire the artist. They inspired Goethe himself in his middle period. But that is not what he had in mind when he said that the laws of art and nature are fundamentally the same.

What he did mean was, firstly, that a work of art must be treated as an unalterable fact. 'What the poet has created must be taken *as* he has created it', he said in one famous conversation;[48] 'as he made his world, so it is'. The Abbé in *Wilhelm Meisters Lehrjahre*[49] gives us an all too familiar picture of the opposite procedure: 'Most people treat finished works of art as though they were made of putty. According to their own preferences, prejudices and whims, they would have the chiselled marble remodelled, massive walls pulled out or in; a painting must teach, a drama edify, and everything must be anything but what it is . . . They reduce it all to what they call effect, and everything is relative to their own feeling and taste'.

Secondly, in a work of art as in a natural organism the organization of the parts is always according to the principle of what Goethe calls subordination. The relationships are never those of mere succession or co-existence, the single part affected only by its immediate neighbours. Each several one not only determines, but is determined by, all the others, and all are subordinated to a dominant tendency which is more than their simple agglomeration. The pattern they make has a mysterious life of its own; for the whole is more than, and different from, the sum of all its parts. Hence no examination of a part in isolation can ever be valid in its conclusions; nor an account of external proportions ever do justice to the form. For no more than in a work of nature is outward shape separable from inner patterning.

But for such principles to be fruitful in their application the critic must have the differences between art and nature constantly in mind. First and most important is the difference of material. Morphological criticism which, in discussing a work of art, does not take account of the *substance* in which the formative principle is there at work lands itself in that species of organism aesthetics which is content to speak in terms of cells and fibres and never gets

[48] With H. Luden, 19.VIII.1806.
[49] VIII, 7; JA, XVIII, 352.

down to talking in terms of words and tones, paint and canvas, clay or stone. Not that there is anything wrong with biological analogies for purposes of illumination. But they can never yield any measure of precision.

Secondly, the relations of natural forms are in constant flux and change. Those of art-forms are stable. As Goethe puts it in his essay on Winckelmann,[50] man, the victim of transience in himself and in the forms among which he dwells, is yet endowed with the power to create forms which endure. It is perhaps ironical that we can only continue to live in the world we inhabit by abstracting stability from the forms of change; whereas we endow art with life by attributing movement, growth, and function to relations which are in fact stable. It is this illusion of movement which makes it possible to apply to art the same morphological principles as to nature; and the sense of its being an illusion—a frank, an honest illusion, as Schiller would say—must never be absent from criticism.

And thirdly, art has what Goethe called *Gehalt*. This is perhaps best rendered by *import,* for it is not to be confused with content, as this is often understood. The objects, figures, and scenes represented, the paraphrasable prose sense which can be abstracted from literature, these, for Goethe, are all as much a part of the artist's material, his *Stoff,* as the stone or the clay, the brush, paint, and canvas, the words and the tones. They are the potential which takes on the specific actuality of form. Once all this heterogeneous material is fashioned by the artist it constitutes *Gestalt*—all of it. *All* the patterns, or systems of relations, work on each other. Sound patterns, rhyme, rhythm, colour, and shape do not simply work together as form and *contain* images, ideas, characters, objects, and themes which are to be thought of as meaning or content patterns. What, then, is *Gehalt?* A *Gestalt* of nature has no import. Its whole complex of existence is its *Gestalt,* which is expressive of nothing but itself. It is, if you like, its own import. But a *Gestalt* which is a work of art is expressive of feeling, of the elusive but familiar patterns of our inner life, those transient experiences which are expressible in no other way. This is its *Gehalt*. And this import is immanent within the *Gestalt,* implicit in it, and never to be made explicit by being translated into any other set of terms.[51]

---

[50] JA, XXXIV, 17. Cf. too his poem *Permanence in Change.*

[51] For a fuller discussion of this problem see E. M. Wilkinson—' "Form" and "Content" in the Aesthetics of German Classicism,' *Stil–und Formprobleme in der Literatur.* Vorträge des VII. Kongresses der Internationalen Vereinigung für moderne Sprachen und Literaturen in Heidelberg 1957. Heidelberg, 1959.

Must we, then, despair of saying anything about a work of art at all? Goethe encourages us to think that we need not. 'The true mediator', he says,[52] 'is art itself. To speak about art, therefore, would seem like trying to mediate the mediator; and yet by doing so, much that is valuable has accumulated'. For what we *can* speak of is not the *Gehalt* but the *Gestalt*—and that is the whole value of the analogy with works of nature. We can try to discover the relations of the parts to each other and to the whole; partly by *Anschauung*, and partly by analysis. Again with his approval: 'Don't be discouraged by having to take the poem to pieces as it were', he wrote to a friend,[53] I know of no other way of proceeding from a general to a specific appreciation'. The procedure advocated was essentially the same as for works of nature: a constant to and fro between analysis and synthesis—synthesis not in the sense of putting together the results attained by attending to the parts, but in the sense of looking at the whole again in the light of all the detail discovered.

When I tell the young people I teach that form is essence, they raise a sceptical eyebrow or become vocally querulous. And it is understandable; for we are at the tail end of a reaction against that attenuation of the meaning of the word *form* which was the result, though not the intention, of the movement of art for art's sake. But if one comes from Goethe's conception of form it is impossible to think otherwise. For it embraces all the forms of the natural world, animate and inanimate. And because for him the habitual distinction between form and function has no reality—function, he says, is existence thought of as activity[54]—it also comprises all modes of animal and human behaviour; not only that non-spatial structure, the form of the individual personality, but social forms, the art of living one with another, that delicate, indefinable, and easily disturbed pattern of relationships which we call 'good form', and which Goethe so much admired in those young Englishmen who frequented his house[55]—more for the sake of his daughter-in-law's charms than for the privilege of consorting with the greatest mind of Europe! It is wide enough to include the harmonious proportions and exquisite symmetry of his *Tasso* and the jumble of styles and verse which is *Faust*. His definition of *Gestalt* has been described

[52] *Maximen*, ed. cit., 536–7.
[53] K. L. v. Knebel, 21.II.1821.
[54] *Maximen*, ed. cit., 36.
[55] Cf. L. A. Willoughby, 'Goethe Looks at the English,' MLR, L (1955); esp. p. 482.

as peculiarly anti-Classical. It would be truer to say that it includes and transcends the Classical. There is room in it for the Romantic and even for the Surrealist. And it does not force us into tiresome arguments about the relative value of form and content. For if Goethe insists that form is everything, he does not do so because he thinks it more important than content, but because it is the *condition* of content, because he knows that without form there can be no artistic content. Nor does it impose on us a false opposition between the formal and the genetic approach to works of art. On the contrary, his morphological approach takes up into itself the genetic method by examining questions of origin in the light of all-predominating considerations of form. At the moment at which he lived it would have been easy for him to fall into that exclusive preoccupation with sources and influences, with the biographical and social conditions of literature, which prevailed during the nineteenth century, and to become a prey to the critical relativism which ensued therefrom. He did not. Just because of his preoccupation with form as a dynamic, developing system of relationships, he achieved what Hugo von Hofmannsthal has called 'the majestic equipoise of his mind between the relative and the absolute', and so anticipated the balance which a present generation of critics is still struggling to effect.

But to set forth Goethe's conception of form in summary fashion gives no hint of its resonance in his actual work. For it pervades all his writings, verse as well as prose, not only in the sense that conceptual statements of it are incorporated into his philosophical poems; it is implicit in the structural relations of the language itself. Consider those verses in which an infinity of personal experience of metamorphosis had coupled with ancient memories of Heraclitus, and with more recent reading of the work of a Basel brain-specialist on the unstable flux of bodily and mental states,[56] to precipitate a poetic statement of the transience of all things, in which romantic melancholy modulates into classical acceptance. In the fourth verse he comes, then, to the changefulness of our own body. This hand which even now in generous impulse stretched forth to bring solace, even that has changed:

> Jene Hand, die gern und milde
> Sich bewegte, wohlzutun

[56] For details see the notes to the poem *Dauer im Wechsel* in Emil Staiger's edition of Goethe's *Gedichte* (Zurich, 1949), II, 463f.

Das gegliederte Gebilde
Alles ist ein andres nun.

This articulated structure—'das gegliederte Gebilde'. The feeling of completion in the past participle combines with the collective *Gebilde* to give the sense of a complex finished structure; and yet all the movement of *bilden*, the activity of formation, is retained in *Gebilde*. Does poetic language here not in fact render that simultaneity of changefulness and continuing identity for which he despaired of ever finding an adequate symbolism?

Or think how he elevates the rhetorical device of oxymoron into an instrument of philosophical thought, as when he speaks of 'innate merits'—'angeborene Verdienste' [57]—as masterly a rendering of the paradox of personal development as is Keats's 'negative capability' of the paradox of artistic power. What questions it raises of whether we can achieve anything at all unless we are right by nature! What recognition of the arduous responsibility of realizing native endowments! There lies the merit. In this phrase, grace and endeavour both receive their meed, even as they do in *Faust*.

Nor can such abstractive exposition convey the ironic reservations, or the mild acceptance of our human condition, which kept him from ever becoming the slave of his theories. It is characteristic that his finest distinctions are usually followed by a saving 'And yet' or its equivalent—as in this concession to popular appreciation: 'Form is a mystery to most people . . . hence they pick out the odd line to quote or discuss; and yet this has its value, for something of the whole is in every part'.[58] Or this, on the necessity for patience in the academic teacher: 'We young students listened all agog for the story'—it was Herder reading *The Vicar of Wakefield*. 'To me it was all real and alive. But he was impatient that we had no eye for the form, and had missed the significance of a change from the third to the first person. He would have had us regard it strictly as a work of art; but we were still at that youthful stage when it is appropriate to respond to a work of art as if it were a work of nature.' [59]

But above all such an account misses the dramatic tension of Goethe's quest for forms. It leaves us with the impression of a mild old gentleman sitting there in the backwater of a small German

[57] *Dichtung u. Wahrheit*, III, 11; JA, XXIV, 34.
[58] *Maximen*, ed. cit., 561–3.
[59] *Dichtung u. Wahrheit*, II, 10; JA, XXIII, 257f. I hope that this paraphrase catches the gist and tone of a passage too long to quote in full.

capital with his collection of plants and bones, emitting from time to time exhortations about the importance of form to a Romantic generation which rarely heeded them. But what gives depth and tension to his love of order is his experience of chaos. Still at seventy-three he knew what it was, in anguish of heart, to feel the world of forms he loved so well and had done so much to discover—dissolve, more than that, cease to matter. Let someone else get on with the job of exploring the forms of nature is what he really says at the end of his great Marienbad Elegy, and leave me to my affliction of soul. But this experience of a world bereft of forms, when time and place shivered to atoms and the normal congruence between self and surroundings snapped, found its precipitate not, as with our present-day Existentialists, in his thought, but in his poetry. His Werther, when misery overcomes him, feels as though a curtain has been rent before his soul, and that same landscape, which was even now filled with significant forms, turns into a meaningless flux, a self-devouring monster. His Tasso in extremity feels the edifice of his existence crumble into a terrifying heap of rubble and doubts his very identity. And Faust in his descent to the Mothers must traverse a void of nothingness. Mephisto tries to give him an idea of what it means: Can you imagine the final desolation of utter solitude? Were you to swim to the boundless ends of the ocean, you would still see *something*—sun, moon, and stars, and the waves, those most transient of forms, each moment taking shape and surrendering it again. But down there on the way to the Mothers—nothing.

> Und hättest du den Ozean durchschwommen,
> Das Grenzenlose dort geschaut,
> So sähst du dort doch Well' auf Welle kommen,
> Selbst wenn es dir vorm Untergange graut.
> Du sähst doch *etwas.* Sähst wohl in der Grüne
> Gestillter Meere streichende Delphine;
> Sähst Wolken ziehen, Sonne, Mond und Sterne;
> *Nichts* wirst du sehn in ewig leerer Ferne . . .   *6239–46*

Yet this passage through waste and desolation is to the very archetypes of formation and transformation. For that is what the Mothers are. A strange word! And it moves Faust strangely too. The implication is that the source of forms lies partly in man himself. In searching for them he must search too within himself, and at his most original depths. And that, indeed, is how Goethe saw it. We are committed to the world in which we find ourselves—*angewiesen* is the word he uses—'engaged' in existence. And existence throws out a challenge to us to create forms in collaboration with nature. It is an unending dialogue between us. Nature speaks to us;[60] but what we discover depends also on how we respond. To understand her language, just as to appreciate the language of art, we have to see to it that our minds are flexible and formative too.[61] For if there is no form within us, we shall not find it outside us.[62] What this view implies is an increase of responsibility in our encounter with the world. And a responsibility chiefly towards ourselves. The discovery of forms, Goethe is always insisting, is a matter of choice no less than a matter of understanding. And if we do not discover them, the loss is ours. For where there is no form, there is no meaning. And it is significant that at those moments of crisis when his heroes experience a loss of meaning through the disintegration of forms, they simultaneously experience a loss of power. For where there is no form there is no power either. Which perhaps explains Goethe's affection for a phrase from the *Liber Basiorum* of the sixteenth-century poet, Johannes Secundus:

Vis superba formae.

[60] *Vorwort zur Farbenlehre;* JA, XL, 61ff.
[61] Ibid., p. 63. Cf. *Vorwort zur Morphologie.* 'Die Absicht eingeleitet'; ibid., 252.
[62] *Wilhelm Meisters Lehrjahre,* VIII, 7; JA, XVIII, 352.

On Goethe's *Faust*

by Erich Heller

What follows is the second half of the essay "Faust's Damnation: The Morality of Knowledge," from Erich Heller, The Artist's Journey into the Interior. *Although this section of the essay deals mainly with Goethe's Faust, it concludes with a brief discussion of Paul Valéry's and Thomas Mann's variations on the ancient theme. Their works not only complete the "vicious circle" of the story's unhappy endings—a consummation of the "morality of knowledge" seemingly avoided "for good" by the Enlightenment—, but also illuminate important aspects of the meaning of Goethe's dramatic poem. In its entirety, Heller's essay is concerned with the historically changing attitudes toward the ethics of knowledge, changes of mind that are shown by "the transformations of meaning which the story of Dr. Faustus has undergone since this 'insatiable speculator' and experimenter made his first appearance in literature," namely as the damned hero of the German Faust-book published in 1578. After a few years the "despicable blackguard" of Lutheran Germany emerged in Elizabethan England as the "tragic hero" of Marlowe's play; and this promotion signalled the beginning of an epoch in which "the notion of a possible sin of the mind gradually disappeared." This is why Lessing, the great man of the German Enlightenment, was bound to fail in his attempt to recast the story in the spirit of intellectual optimism, the mode of thought that dominated the philosophy of the eighteenth century. It was, writes Heller, an enterprise "about as promising as it would have been for the French Revolution to adapt Macbeth to the belief that the murder of monarchs was supremely desirable." Lessing himself seems to have recognized this later when he said that "anyone who today should try to represent such a subject . . . would be courting failure."*

. . . This was in 1777; but more than half a century later, in 1831, Goethe, at the age of eighty-two, brought such precarious courting to one of the most celebrated consummations in the history of literature: he sealed a parcel that contained the manuscript of the at last concluded Part II of his *Faust*. The *"Hauptgeschäft,"* the main business of his life, as he was in the habit of referring to it during his last years, was done; or rather, Goethe willed that it should be done: the seal was to protect it above all from his own persistent scruples and dissatisfactions. As death approached, he was determined not to meddle any more with this *Sorgenkind,* this problem-child of his. Also, the parcel was not to be opened for the time being because, as Goethe wrote five days before his death, the hour was "really so absurd and confused" that he was convinced his "long and honest effort in building this strange edifice" would be ill-rewarded. "It would drift, fragments of a shipwreck, towards barren shores and lie buried in the sandy dunes of time." Yet once, during the last two months of his life, he broke the seal again to read from the manuscript to his beloved daughter-in-law, and afterward promptly confided to his diary that this reading had made him worry once more: should he not have dealt at greater length with "the principal themes"? He had "treated them, in order to finish it all, far too laconically." Touching words! Goethe felt he had been in too much of a hurry when he disposed of his "main business"—over which he had spent more than sixty years. It would almost seem that Lessing was right in suggesting that the age itself did not allow anyone to succeed in writing *Faust;* and Goethe's fears were, of course, justified. Indeed, the "absurd and confused" epoch did not know what to make of his *Faust II,* but this was not altogether the fault of the readers: Goethe's rendering of the "principal themes" was certainly not innocent of confusion.

In many a letter, written during his last months, he warned his friends not to expect too much of the withheld manuscript, above all not to look forward to "any solutions." He referred to his *Faust II* as "these very serious jests," and said that as soon as one problem appeared "to have been solved in it, it revealed, after the manner of the history of world and man, a new one demanding to be puzzled out." True enough; for we are left with no end of puzzles when the curtain comes down upon Faust's entelechy, his immortal self, saved, not without the intervention of the inscrutable grace of God, through having kept his promise to strive eternally and never to content himself with any achievement on earth. But has he really fulfilled the famous condition of his salvation? Not quite, if we consult the plot; for there it would seem that Faust has been smuggled into Heaven, like precious contraband, by angelic choir boys who have snatched his soul from the Devil, the legal winner, while distracting his attention with their seductive beauty. But if we allow the surpassing poetry of the final scene to make us forget the letter of the wager, then again it would appear as if Faust had merely struggled in vain throughout his life to be rid of what was, regardless of his activities, his inalienable birthright in Paradise. Even by uttering the fatal words of ultimate contentment which, according to the Mephistophelian bet, were to commit his soul to eternal damnation; even by declaring himself satisfied with the last gift of the Devil—the magic transformation of pestiferous swamps into fertile land upon which he would found a republic of free men—he could not prevail upon the Upper Spheres to let him go to Hell. The damning utterance, with which in the end he renounces his eternal striving, is gleefully registered by Mephistopheles, tasting the fruit of victory; but it must have fallen upon deaf ears in Heaven: up there it is held that he has striven eternally all the same, and is therefore, with a little helping of divine grace, worth saving.

This, of course, is callous and blasphemous talk. It is unseemly to speak like this about Goethe's *Faust,* which justly has survived the blatant inconsistencies of its plot as one of the greatest poetic creations of the world. But it is a legitimate way of speaking about the *dramatic* and *theological* pretentions of the work. Part II is no drama whatever; and for Goethe to persist—and against what inhibitions!—in bringing it to a kind of dramatic and theological conclusion was a decision of quixotic heroism. In one sense Lessing stood a better dramatic chance with his abortive *Faust* than Goethe. Lessing's hero was singlemindedly dedicated, against all phantom appearances, to the pursuit of Knowledge and thus was an obedient servant to the God of the philosophers.

But Goethe's Faust? The complexities of his moral character are unresolvable. He is an ungovernable theological problem-child, and presents no simple alternative of good or evil to the Goethean God, who, far from being the God of the philosophers, seems not even to know his own mind. At one point the Devil, who ought to be familiar with God's ways, speaks of the divinity as if indeed the divinty were Lessing:

> *Verachte nur Vernunft und Wissenschaft,*
> *Des Menschen allerhöchste Kraft,*
>
> . . . .
> *So hab ich dich schon unbedingt—,*

meaning that Faust will be his, the Devil's, easy prey through the very contempt in which he holds man's supreme faculties: reason and scholarship. Yet is it true to say that Faust despises knowledge? Have we not learned from his first monologue that, despairing of all merely human knowledge, he has called upon black magic to help his ignorance and initiate his mind into the innermost secret of the world:

> *Dass ich erkenne, was die Welt*
> *Im innersten zusammenhält.*

However, at many another point it would seem that not only has he done with the pursuit of knowledge, but, contrary to the Devil's enlightened judgment, pleases God by nothing more than his unwillingness ever to be weaned from his *"Urquell,"* the very source of his unreasoning and restless spirit—that spirit which prompts him, in translating the Bible, to reject *logos* as the principle of all things, nurtures in his soul the desire to be cured of all *"Wissensdrang,"* the urge to know, and drives him from his quiet study into the turbulent world to suffer in his own self, unimpaired by knowledge, all the sorrows allotted to mankind, and to rejoice in all its joys. True, as he enters Heaven, the chant of the cherubic boys welcomes him as their teacher; for he has learned much:

> *Doch dieser hat gelernt,*
> *Er wird uns lehren.*

But it is with some concern for the celestial peace of the blessed children that one contemplates the possible substance and manner of his instruction.

Despite all these perplexities and confusions, Goethe's *Faust* is incomparably closer to the original Faust-book than would have been Lessing's. Despite the perplexities? Because of them! For Lessing's *Faust* would have been the generous and nobly simple-minded reversal of the Lutheran writer's morality of knowledge: the sixteenth century's damnation was salvation to the eighteenth. The Devil? Black magic? Bizarre souvenirs, picked up in some unclean exotic place by Reason on its grand tour through History. Goethe was incapable of such enlightenment. His morality of knowledge was infinitely complex, tangled up as it was, inextricably, with his moral intuition that man was free to commit sins of the mind: he could be lured toward the kind of "truth" that was deeply and destructively at odds both with his true nature and the true nature of the world—a moral offense against the order of creation. And this, surely, is a belief which Goethe shared with the author of the ancient legend of Dr. Faustus. Goethe had the historical impertinence to oppose Newton; and he said, and tried to prove, that Newton was wrong. What he truly meant was that Newtonian physics was false to human nature; and this is what he did say when he was not proudly determined to beat the physicists at their own game. Truth, for him, was what befits man to know, what man is *meant* to know; and he was convinced that the dominant methods of scientific inquiry were "unbecoming" to man, a danger to his spiritual health and integrity because they reduced the phenomena of nature to a system of abstractions within which their true being vanished, yielding nothing to man except empty intellectual power over a spiritually vacuous world: a power that was bound to corrupt his soul. And therefore Goethe said, outrageously: "As in the moral sphere, so we need a categorical imperative in the natural sciences." Provocatively and significantly, he even had the courage to play the crank by expressing uneasiness about microscopes and telescopes: "They merely disturb man's natural vision." And when his Wilhelm Meister for the first time gazes at the stars through a telescope, he warns the astronomers around him of "the morally bad effect" these instruments must have upon man: "For what he perceives with their help . . . is out of keeping with his inner faculty of discernment." It would need a superhuman culture "to harmonize the inner truth of man with this inappropriate vision from without."

The perplexities of Goethe's *Faust* are due, firstly, to Goethe's inability—which he had in common with the sixteenth-century writer of the first Faust-book—to divorce the problem of knowledge from the totality of man's nature, to separate the aspiration of his mind from the destiny of his soul; and they are due, secondly, to Goethe's inability—which he had in common with his own age—unambiguously to demonstrate this totality and this destiny, that is to say, to *define Human Being.* This is why his Faust, so confusingly, is now a man who has embarked upon a desperate quest for knowledge, now a man who curses knowledge as a futile distraction from the passions' crying out for the fullness of life, and now again a man who reaches his *"höchster Augenblick,"* his highest moment, in the renunciation of his search for both knowledge and passionate self-fulfillment, in the resigned acceptance of his social duty to further the commonwealth of man. Because Goethe was the profoundest mind of an epoch dispossessed of any faithful vocabulary for the definition of Human Being, he was possessed by two overpowering and paradoxical intuitions: that man's *being* was definable only through his incessant striving to *become* what he was not yet and was yet *meant* to be; and that in thus striving he was in extreme danger of losing himself through his impatient and impetuous ignorance of what he was. Therefore, Faust's soul was an unfit object for any clearly stated transaction between Heaven and Hell, and the definitive bargain of the first Faust-book had to be replaced by a wager whose outcome was left in abeyance. If Faust ceased to strive, he would be damned; but he would also be damned if, in his ceaseless quest for himself and his world, he overstepped the elusive measure of his humanity. Yet in the drama itself, Faust could only be damned *or* saved. Thus Goethe had to reconcile himself to the dramatic absurdity of a salvation merited both by the endlessly uncertain voyage and the contented arrival at an uncertain destination. An uncertain destination: for the Faust who believes he has arrived, is a blind and deluded man, taking for the builders of a great human future the diggers of his grave. It is as if the honesty of Goethe's precise imagination had forced him in the end to disavow, with terrible poetic irony, the imprecision of the dramatic plot. And indeed, had it not been for the grace of God, or for the Promethean youth who designed the plot of *Faust,* Goethe, in his old age, might well have damned his black magician. For it was the man of eighty-two who wrote the scenes (as if at the last moment to obstruct the workings of salvation) where Faust's involvement in the satanic art is truly black and satanic: the scenes in which his mad lust for power and aggrandizement kills the very goodness and innocence of life, this time without a trace of that saving love which, long ago, had left him with a chance of ultimate forgiveness even in his betrayal of Gretchen.

When after all the paraphernalia and phantasmagoria of imperial politics and high finance, of science laboratories, classical incantations and mystical initiations, of which most of *Faust II* is composed, the last act begins, we seem to be back, unexpectedly, in the world of Gretchen: in the shadow of linden trees, at the little house and chapel of a faithful old couple, Philemon and Baucis, contentedly living near the sea on what is now Faust's estate. Just then they are visited by a mysterious wanderer whom many years ago they had hospitably put up and helped after the shipwreck he suffered in the nearby shoals—a distant relation, no doubt, of those gods or divine messengers who, in the *Metamorphoses* of Ovid, are the guests of Philemon and Baucis, or, in the *Acts of the Apostles,* chapter XIV, preach to the inhabitants of Iconium and Lystra. Now he has come to thank them once again and to bless them. Through this scene we enter the realm of inexhaustible ambiguity in which

Faust's end and transfiguration are to be enacted. The neighbor-
hood of the two old people's cottage has been much improved by
Faust's land-winning enterprise. Where once the stranger had been
cast ashore, there stretch now green fields far into what used to be
shallow sea. This certainly seems to be to the good, and Philemon,
the husband, praises the change lyrically and admiringly; but his
wife views it with misgivings. Surely, it was a miracle, but one that
was performed in godlessness. Floods of fire were poured into the
ocean and human lives recklessly sacrificed in order to construct a
canal. Moreover, Faust, the owner of the new land, seems to be, for
no good reason, intent upon driving them from their house and
garden; and so they all enter the chapel, ring its bell, and kneel
down to pray. And as Faust, in the park of his palace, hears the
bell—the very same "silvery sound" which had once announced to
the lost traveler on the beach the closeness of his rescuers (and it
was, we should remember, "the celestial tone" of church bells that
on a certain Easter morning had called Faust back from desperation
and made him withdraw from his lips the suicidal cup of poison)—
as Faust now hears the sound of simple piety ring out from the hill,
he curses it as a reminder of the petty limits imposed upon his
power, and in a senseless rage commands Mephistopheles to remove
the couple to another place. They and their guest perish as Faust's
order is carried out, and house and chapel go up in flames.

Yet while Faust's most damnable crime is being committed, the
scene changes to the tower of his palace where the watchman
Lynceus intones the song that is one of Goethe's most beautiful
lyrical creations:

> *Zum Sehen geboren,*
> *Zum Schauen bestellt . . .*

ecstatically affirming the beauty of everything his eyes have ever
seen—"whatever it be":

> *Ihr glücklichen Augen,*
> *Was je ihr gesehn,*
> *Es sei, wie es wolle,*
> *Es war doch so schön!*

It is hard to imagine profounder depths for poetic irony to reach
than it does at this moment of change from that show of absolute
evil to this absolute affirmation. And what vast expanses of irony
are compressed into the brackets which Goethe inserted after the
exultant celebration of the world's beauty—a beauty which no evil

can diminish. "Pause" is written between those brackets. Pause, indeed! For the watchman's recital continues with the observation that his duties on the tower are not only "aesthetic" in nature; and instantly he registers "the abominable horror" threatening him from out of "the darkness of the world":

> *Nicht allein mich zu ergetzen,*
> *Bin ich hier so hoch gestellt;*
> *Welch ein greuliches Entsetzen*
> *Droht mir aus der finstern Welt!—*

from out of that dark world where Faust's servant, Mephistopheles, in the course of executing his master's megalomaniac orders, unthinks, as it were, the very thoughts of charity, compassion, and peace, shattering the luminous sphere whence, by Goethe's symbolic design, had once emerged the shipwrecked stranger. It is as if the "whatever it be" of that absolute affirmation had not been meant to include the evil of a world ravished by the black magic of godless power. And as in the whirls of smoke that drift from the burning house, the demons of human failure form—like avenging Erinyes appointed by the slain wanderer—and as one of them, the spirit of Anxiety, approaches Faust to strike with blindness him who had "run through life blindly," his eyes are at last opened; and he utters a wish that is not a magic conjuration but almost a prayer:

> *Könnt' ich Magie von meinem Pfad entfernen,*
> *Die Zaubersprüche ganz und gar verlernen .*

If only he could rid himself of magic and utterly forget how to invoke it! There is more consistent drama in the brief sequence of these scenes than emerges from the bewildering totality of the poem, more dramatic occasion for either damning Faust because of his evil-doing as a magician, or for saving him because of his desire to abandon the evil practice.

It is the theme of black magic through which Goethe's *Faust* is linked, in almost a sixteenth-century fashion, with Goethe's morality of knowledge. What, we may well ask, can black magic mean to Goethe's sophisticated mind? The black magic of *Faust* is the poetically fantastic rendering of Goethe's belief that evil arises from any knowing and doing of man that is in excess of his "being." Man aspiring to a freedom of the mind fatally beyond the grasp of his "concrete imagination," seeking power over life through actions that overreach the reaches of his soul, acquiring a virtuosity inappropriately superior to his "virtue"—this was Goethe's idea of *hubris,* his divination of the meaning of black magic. Absolute activity, activity unrestrained by the condition of humanity, he once said, leads to bankruptcy; and "everything that sets our minds free without giving us mastery over ourselves is pernicious." He saw something spiritually mischievous, something akin to black magic, in every form of knowledge or technique that "unnaturally" raises man's power above the substance of his being. In his *Faust* black magic almost always works the perverse miracle of such "desubstantiation." Whether Faust conjures up the very spirit of Nature and Life, the *Erdgeist,* only to realize in distracted impotence that he cannot endure him; whether the body politic is being corrupted by insubstantial paper assuming the credit that would only be due to substantial gold; whether Homunculus, a synthetic midget of great intellectual alacrity, is produced in the laboratory's test tube, a brain more splendidly equipped for thinking than the brains that have thought it out: the creature capable of enslaving his creators; or whether Faust begets with Helena, magically called back from her mythological past, the ethereal child Euphorion, who, not made for life on earth, is undone by his yearning for sublimity—throughout the adventures of his Faust, Goethe's imagination is fascinated, enthralled, and terrified by the spectacle of man's mind rising above the reality of his being and destroying it in such dark transcendence. This, then, is black magic for Goethe: the awful art that cultivates the disparity between knowledge and being, power and substance, virtuosity and character; the abysmal craft bringing forth the machinery of fabrication and destruction that passes understanding.

In the last two *Fausts* of literary history, Paul Valéry's and Thomas Mann's, the gulf, most dreaded by Goethe, between knowledge and the integrity of being, between virtuosity and the sanity of substance, has become so wide that even the Devil seems to be lost in it: for the human soul, in the hunt for which the Devil has always sought his livelihood, is in an extreme state of malnutrition. But the mind lives in formidable prosperity and has no need to raise loans from Hell for indulging even its most extravagant ambitions.

Valéry has called his sequence of variations on the ancient theme *Mon Faust;* and indeed his Faust is more *his,* more the possession of the author who has created the frigid paragon of aesthetic intellectuality, Monsieur Teste, than he is the Devil's. Yet this is by no means to the advantage of his spiritual prospects: these are as

gloomy as can be. For if he does not lose his soul, this is only because he has none to lose. In the affluence of his intellectual riches,
he *is* the lost soul, just as Mephistopheles is a lost devil in the face
of a human world overflowing with self-supplied goods of the kind
that was once the monopoly of Hell. The Hell-supplied wings of
the eagle are in demand no more. As Ivan Karamazov before him,
so Valéry's Faust shows the Devil that he is an anachronism: his
existence was based solely on the unenlightened belief that "people
weren't clever enough to damn themselves by their own devices."
But those days have gone. "The whole system," Faust says to Mephistopheles, "of which you were the linchpin, is falling to pieces. Confess that even you feel lost among this new crowd of human beings
who do evil without knowing or caring, who have no notion of
Eternity, who risk their lives ten times a day in playing with their
new machines, who have created countless marvels your magic
never dreamt of, and have put them in the reach of any fool. . . ."
And even if Mephistopheles were not on the point of being starved
out of the universe for want of human souls, this Faust would still
have nothing to gain from a bargain with him. His intellection is
as strong as he could wish, and he knows what he does when he dismisses his hellish visitor as, after all, "nothing but a mind" and
therefore, he adds: "We could exchange functions." It is as if he
had said: *"Cogito ergo sum in profundis"*—"I think and thus I am
in Hell already"; or "I know and therefore I will not live"—the
uncanniest cancellation of the first Faust-book as well as of the
Cartesian ontology. Moreover, the passion with which Goethe's
Faust assails the innermost secret of the world is dissolved by
Valéry in *ennui,* the unkeen expectation of an emptily precise answer to be given by some Homunculus or electronic bore.

If Valéry's Mephisto, the "pure mind," has become unemployable
as a seducer in a society of satiated intellects and emasculate souls,
Thomas Mann has found a role for him which brings the literary
history of Dr. Faustus to a conclusion that is definitive in its per-
versity: the Devil is now the giver of a soul. It is he who supplies
feeling and passionate intensity to a Faustian genius whose soul
and being had been frozen into rigidity by the *cogitare,* the chill of
intellectual abstraction, and whose art was, therefore, the art of
purely speculative virtuosity. The musician Leverkühn, Thomas
Mann's Dr. Faustus, has, like the epoch whose music he composes,
despaired of any pre-established harmonies between the human
mind and the truth of the world; and having lost any such faith,
he exists in a state of total despair. Not for him the music of "sub-

jective harmony," the music of souls supported by the metaphysical assurance that in their depths they mirror the eternal and sublime verities of Creation. For Leverkühn, life, to its very core, that is, to its innermost void, is absurd and chaotic; and if the human mind goes on, absurdly and yet stubbornly, to insist upon some semblance of order, this order has to be constructed from nothing by the sheer obstinacy of the abstractly logical imagination. Therefore, this imagination reflects only itself and not some dreamt-of consonance between the self and cosmic harmonies. Beethoven was mistaken; and so Leverkühn announces his desperate plan to compose a piece of music that would take back, "unwrite," the greatest of all musical celebrations of the "subjective harmony," the Ninth Symphony: the Ninth Symphony is not true, or true no more. But if it is not true, then neither is Goethe's *Faust*, the poetic equivalent in subjective harmony to that choral dithyramb; and just as Thomas Mann makes his composer revoke the Ninth Symphony, so he himself revokes Goethe's *Faust* by writing the book of Faust's damnation. For Goethe's *Faust*, despite its unresolvable doubts and ambiguities, and despite its holding back, confusing, and obstructing redemption until it can only be had in a riot of poetic contradictions—Goethe's *Faust* yet embodies the faith that Faust is saved: for he aspires to that self-realization through which, by metaphysical necessity, he loyally realizes the will, order, and ultimate purpose of the cosmos itself. It is by virtue of the "subjective harmony" that Faust's infinite enthusiasm, time and again confounded, must yet triumph in the end over Mephisto's ironical, cold, and logical mind—the supremely detached mind that on one great theological occasion had won its detachment, once and for all, by denying the design of Creation.

Precisely such a mind is owned by Leverkühn; and therefore the music he writes is detached, ironical, cold, and logical, composed within a mathematically austere system which has been ingeniously calculated to conceal, or transcend, or hold at bay, the chaos within and without, the subjective dissonance that has taken the place of the subjective harmony. Indeed, it is a soul-less music; and the most scandalous idea in Thomas Mann's scandalously profound book is this: a soul is finally bestowed upon this music by the Devil. When Mephistopheles calls on the composer to ratify the pact long since concluded in Leverkühn's embrace of the prostitute who gave him the "disease of genius," the visitor from Hell remarks: "They tell me that the Devil passes for a man of destructive criticism." It is, of course, Goethe who has made him believe this by portraying

Mephistopheles as cynicism incarnate, out to distract Faust's enthusiastic inspiration. But now the Devil emphatically disclaims this reputation: "Slander and again slander . . . What he wants and gives is triumph over it, is shining, sparkling, vainglorious unreflectiveness!" And he does fulfill his promise: Leverkühn's last and greatest work, "The Lamentation of Dr. Faustus," the choral work he composes on the verge of madness and in protest against the Ninth Symphony, using as his text the first German Faust-book, is even stricter in form and more ingenious in calculation than his preceding compositions; and yet it is, for the first time, abandoned self-expression, an ecstasy of desperation, a panegyric of the inner abyss. "Subjective harmony," the lost soul of music, is recovered— a soul without hope. For the re-established harmony is now fixed between the subject and that dispensation by which he is unredeemable. "Being" has been returned to "doing," and substance to virtuosity: but "being" means being damned, and the substance is the stuff of Hell. This music is the mystical consummation of distraught godlessness, the emergence of a soul from the alchemy of its negation. "After all," says Thomas Mann's Devil, "I am by now [religion's] sole custodian! In whom will you recognize theological existence if not in me?"

Thus ends the eventful story that has led from the damnation of Dr. Faustus through his liberation to his damnation. It was Goethe's desire to arrest it in the middle of its journey by teaching the "insatiable Speculators" his morality of knowledge. His failure deserves the most thoughtful attention.

Goethe would have found much to love in the story, written 2,500 years ago, of a Chinese sage who once met a simple man, his better in wisdom. The sage, seeing how the man watered his field in a very primitive manner, asked him: "Don't you know that there is a contraption called a draw-well, a kind of machine that would enable you to water a hundred such little fields in one day?" And he received this reply: "I have heard my teacher say: He who uses machines, conducts his business like a machine. He who conducts his business like a machine, will soon have the heart of a machine. He who has the heart of a machine, has lost all certainties of the spirit. He who has lost the certainties of the spirit, must needs sin against the meaning of life. Yes, I do know such machines as you speak of, but I also know why I shall not use them."

Undoubtedly, Goethe would have applauded the wisdom of this story. Yet the "modern man" in him would also have known that he could not live by its lesson. After all, he greeted with enthusiasm the plans for the Panama Canal and found no more fitting symbol for Faust's renunciation of magic than his assuming the position of a welfare engineer. The ambiguities of his *Faust* provide the measure of his lasting dilemma, a dilemma that is bound to stay with us. But the refusal to contemplate it on a level beyond the expediencies of science, technology, and statesmanship would deny the essential freedom in which we may still—no, not resolve the tension but sustain it without despairing. If, as even Goethe's *Faust* might teach us, grace cannot be merited by man, he may yet try to earn his hope. Goethe's intuition of the "categorical imperative" that is needful in the pursuit of knowledge can be articulated but vaguely. Yet this is no reason for preferring the exact prospect opened by that scientific earnestness and moral frivolity which would hear nothing of the inexact morality of knowledge. For that exact prospect is monstrous in its exactitude: a race of magician's apprentices who, as the one in Goethe's poem *"Der Zauberlehrling,"* are about to perish in the floods they themselves have released by the magic formula; a horde of cave-dwellers, their souls impoverished by machines and panic helplessness, sheltering themselves from the products of their titanically superior brains.

It is a vision from the first German Faust-book. Dr. Faustus was taken to the place he had bargained for and, so we read, "thereafter it became so sinister in his house that no one could live in it."

Goethe and the Natural Sciences

by Willy Hartner

The highest would be: to understand that everything real is theory in itself. The azure color of the sky reveals to us the basic law of chromatics. Do not try to go behind the phenomena; they themselves are the doctrine.

In these words, written a few years before his death, the aged Goethe once more laid down his creed, the essence of his philosophy of science, as a watchword and a warning to the generations to come. During the hundred and twenty years which have elapsed since, the annals of natural science have recorded the greatest victories, the most revolutionary material progress which mankind thus far has lived to see.

The scientists did not heed Goethe's word. More eagerly than ever, they competed in inventing hypotheses about what is *behind* the phenomena. By means of practical experiments and theoretical ratiocination, a state of domination of the forces of nature has eventually been reached which no doubt is fascinating and captivating, but at the same time also bewildering and frightening.

If we consider exclusively material facts and actual achievements, as is the habit common to all our heralds of progress, a few words could suffice to characterize the importance of Goethe as a scientist.

By a systematic investigation of the skulls of animals as well as of embryonic and adult human skulls, Goethe discovered the intermaxillary bone of man. It must, however, be stated that Vesalius had seen at least the palatal suture of this bone in skulls of children and hence obviously must have been aware of its existence.

In 1791, at the Lido near Venice, Goethe found the fragments of a sheep's skull. A careful examination of them led to the discovery that the skulls of mammals can, or must, be interpreted as consisting of enlarged and transformed vertebrae. For reasons unknown Goethe did not publish his discovery until the years 1823 and 1824, in his *Contributions to Morphology*. Meanwhile, the biologist Lorenz Oken, to whom Goethe said he had spoken about his theory, had published it in his own name in 1807, asserting that the idea had spontaneously struck him while he was demonstrating the skull of a deer to some of his students. There arose from this one of those unpleasant priority contests in which the history of science is particularly abundant. The case was never completely cleared up. To us it is only of secondary historical interest, since the vertebral theory of the cranium is no longer maintained by modern biologists.

Although no discoveries in the strict sense of the word can be ascribed to Goethe in mineralogy (the goethite, it may be well to state, was not discovered by but only named after the poet), petrography, geology, palaeontology, or meteorology, Goethe's observations in these fields exercised a considerable influence and produced a stimulating effect on his contemporaries. In some respects he even anticipated certain later theories which proved extremely fertile, such as Darwin's theory of the origin of species. As an example I refer to his observations on the skeleton of a primigenial ox (*Bos primigenius*) uncovered from the turf near Hassleben. In his *Contributions to Morphology*, he compared the fossil remnants with the skeletons of the various living species. He ventured to assert that the latter are, speaking in terms of evolution, the offspring of the former. Moreover, he claimed that the particular shape of the horns was produced by selective breeding, and thus set forth the principle of selection no less than forty-odd years before the great English naturalist published his magnum opus in which this central principle was elevated to a dogma.

In the unfortunate scientific contest between the Neptunists and the Vulcanists, by which the development of geology was severely hampered for a long time, Goethe subordinated his natural instinct and his prior convictions to the authority of the highly reputed mineralogist A. G. Werner, and went wrong. He was no less wrong when, having finally wearied of the endless struggle concerning the origin of basalt, he composed the following verses:

Amerika, Du hast es besser

> *Als unser Kontinent der alte;*
> *Hast keine verfallenen Schlösser*
> *Und keine Basalte—*

"America, thou farest better than our old continent; thou hast no ruined castles and no basalt." He would surely not have written these lines had he known that the Palisades on the Hudson River near New York are cut out of enormous masses of basalt and that, in the far west of the New World, thousands of square miles are covered with this same species of rock that bear witness to gigantic volcanic eruptions in earlier geological periods.

Observations and statements of very considerable importance are found in Goethe's *Metamorphosis of Plants*. By this work he laid the foundation of a new biological discipline: comparative morphology.

As for the most famous of Goethe's scientific works, the *Farbenlehre* or *Theory of Chromatics*, it must be said that later developments proved him wrong and confirmed the correctness of Isaac Newton's *Optics*, which Goethe had tried to refute and to replace by his own work. In more than one respect, science was sufficiently advanced even in Goethe's time to prove the erroneousness of his assumptions and assertions, and his contemporaries did not fail to point out the weaknesses of his theory.

Thus, taking account only of material facts and assuming the authority of historical judges, we might say that Goethe's scientific achievements are considerable in some of the many fields of his interest, whereas in others they are practically negligible, or even negative.

Statements to this effect can be found in great number. I need not say that they are just as insufficient when made about Goethe as they are about Copernicus, Kepler, Galileo, or any other of the pioneers of science. They were all children of their time. They all made mistakes, even mistakes they could have avoided. They all had predecessors, and none of their theories and discoveries was born like Pallas Athene, from the head of Zeus.

It would be futile to indicate a definite date for the awakening of Goethe's "interest" in the phenomena of nature. From his early youth he conceived the various manifestations of life, nature, and art as forming one great and comprehensive unity. All his works— his poetry no less than his writings on natural science—bear witness to his conviction that man and nature are one and the same, that they are identical. To him the question of how far man's spiritual existence is dependent on man's own personality or on the "external world" is meaningless. "I have never distinguished between the two," he says. It is therefore also essentially wrong to distinguish between Goethe as a poet and philosopher and Goethe as a naturalist or natural scientist. To Goethe, the whole of nature reveals itself as an eternal interrelation and interaction of antagonistic elements by which life as well as death and destruction is produced. Who would not immediately think of the overwhelming words in which the Earth Spirit expresses the idea of all-comprising unity:

> *In Lebensfluten, im Tatensturm*
> *Wall' ich auf und ab,*
> *Wehe hin und her!*
> *Geburt und Grab,*
> *Ein ewiges Meer,*
> *Ein wechselnd Weben,*
> *Ein glühend Leben:*
> *So schaff' ich am sausenden Webstuhl der Zeit,*
> *Und wirke der Gottheit lebendiges Kleid.*

> In the tide of life, in Action's storm,
> A fluctuant wave,
> A shuttle free.
> Birth and the Grave,
> An eternal sea,
> A weaving, flowing
> Life, all-glowing:
> Thus at Time's humming loom 'tis my hand prepares
> The garment of Life which the Deity wears.

At first sight it might seem strange that the philosopher to whom Goethe feels most deeply indebted is the one whose static, mathematically (*"more geometrico"*) constructed system one would expect to be utterly repugnant to the poet's dynamic view: Baruch de Spinoza. Perhaps we should interpret this fact as one of the greatest, and simultaneously most fertile, misunderstandings. Perhaps, I may add, Goethe was aware of it himself, but was anxious to keep it a secret and to try to forget about it. It was the feeling of man's identity with nature and of both fusing together into one great unity which appealed to Goethe's mind. To quote his own words: "Here I found that my passions came to rest. A great and free view of the perceptual and the ethical world seemed to open. . . . I devoted myself to this reading and felt by self-contemplation that I had never seen the world so clearly."

In his letter to Sömmering of August, 1796, dealing with Sömmering's essay on the "organism of the soul," Goethe classified himself as an "empiricist and realist." But a few months later, in a letter to F. H. Jacobi, he writes: "You would no longer find me such a rigid realist. It is of great advantage to me that I have become more familiar with the other modes of thinking which, though they will never really become mine, I still need very badly for practical purposes, as a supplement to my one-sidedness."

No doubt Theodor Ziehen is right in attributing this change to the increasing influence of Schiller. It is well known how, in the summer of 1794, Goethe explained to Schiller his ideas concerning the metamorphosis of plants and, while sketching on a sheet of paper the characteristic features of a symbolic plant, did not hesitate to call this an "experience." Schiller, however, being a trained Kantian, shook his head and answered: "No, this is no experience, this is an idea." Goethe, who had not yet forgotten his old grudge against Schiller, retorted: "I must say I appreciate having ideas without being aware of it, and even seeing them with my own eyes."

What Goethe has in mind when calling himself a "realist" is that his natural philosophy takes its start not from the observing subject, but in a much higher degree from the object to be observed. This approach, which is completely characteristic of Goethe's scientific studies throughout his life, is the one which Schiller as well as Fichte calls "realistic." Schiller, in his essay *On Naïve and Sentimental Poetical Composition* written in 1795 and 1796, says that the realist "with regard to theory is characterized by a dispassionate spirit of observation and a strong attachment to the uniform testimony of the senses," and Fichte defines the realist as one who holds that the ego arrives at its notions in a passive way, or receives them as effects produced by the objects. As Ziehen also pointed out, as early as 1793 Goethe had laid stress on the subjective conditions of perception, as is evident from his essay, "Experiment as a Mediator between Object and Subject." There he says: "Nobody will deny the fact that, in natural science as well as in all other undertakings of man, experience has, and must have, the very greatest influence; no less, however, will anybody impugn the high and, so to say, creative and independent power inherent in the psychic forces by which those experiences are perceived, summed up, set in order, and given form."

It has sometimes been said, even with regret, that Goethe was not a philosopher at all or that, at the most, we are entitled to call him an eclectic. This statement, if not entirely untrue, is at least misleading and susceptible of being misunderstood.

In the first place, it is true that Goethe did not work out a philosophical system of his own which he laid down in bulky volumes. There arises the question whether the title of philosopher must be reserved only to the "professional" who offers such a fully developed theoretical system to his contemporaries and to coming generations, or whether he also deserves it whose life and work are nothing but the exterior symptoms or precipitations of a very definite and consistent philosophical attitude.

Second, it is a mere question of definition as to what we mean by the term "eclecticism." It is generally understood as the practice of selecting from various sources what seems best for one's aims, and of fusing the elements together so as to form a new, though not original, system. As each new philosophical system inevitably stands in some relation to the systems of earlier thinkers, rejecting some of their propositions as faulty and accepting others as correct, it will sometimes be hard to trace a well-defined mathematical boundary between the eclectic and the original philosopher. One single synthetic conclusion can suffice to prove the originality of a thinker whom we otherwise would classify as a mere eclectic. Still, in most cases a very definite feeling will guide us as soon as we dive into the ideas of a philosopher; thus neither the eclecticism of Cicero, nor the originality of Spinoza or Kant will ever be seriously doubted. No better definition of eclecticism, by the way, could be adduced in this connection than Goethe's own:

> Where eclecticism originates from the inner nature of man, it is good. There are many who, according to their natural inclinations, are half Stoics, half Epicureans. It will therefore not seem strange that they absorb the principles of both systems and try to combine them with each other as well as can be done. An entirely different phenomenon is the lack of spirit which, in default of any proper inner guidance, like a jackdaw carries to its nest everything that haphazardly offers itself. Thus, being dead from the beginning, it becomes totally irrelevant to a vital, animated whole.

Why then should we apply a different measure to Goethe? Within our wider perspective, he, and perhaps only he, is a man whose life and work reflect a thoroughly consistent philosophy of great, or even unique, originality. His indebtedness to earlier thinkers as well as to his contemporaries is beyond doubt. No less obvious, however, is the extraordinary independence with which he handles the concepts and ideas of his predecessors and pours them into a "system," or rather a "vision," which is entirely his own. This, though he hardly ever makes it explicit in coherent words, lies open to everybody who retains enough of his own original directness of thinking to understand—or should I rather say, to feel what Goethe aims at. Sometimes one will get as much by reading between the lines as by trying to catch the sense of the written words only. It will help one's understanding to remember particularly two of Goethe's words: "I should like to stop talking altogether. I should like to speak as Nature does: merely in signs"; and, "Earlier centuries had their ideas in the form of imaginative vision, ours has its ideas in the form of concepts . . . the great ideas of life were then seen as forms, patterns (*Gestalten*), as gods . . . then *productive* or creative power was greater, today destructive power or the art of dissection."

In June, 1794, Goethe wrote a letter to Fichte asking him to "reconcile" him with the philosophers, the need for whom he "had always felt without having been able to come to terms with them." This has to be understood as an attempt to get a clear picture of the contemporary trends of philosophy, especially of epistemology. With certain restrictions, Kant's *Critique of Judgment* had appealed to Goethe's mind. He expressly referred to Kant's statement about the close relationship between poetry and the comparative study of natural science, both of which, the philosopher holds, are controlled by the same power of discrimination. On the other hand, Kant's *Critique of Pure Reason* always remained alien to Goethe.

Spinoza, whom I mentioned before, does not enter into the picture in this connection. By reading him, Goethe attains the state of meditation and introspective vision which is the starting point of his mental activity. But Spinoza of course does not yield the basis for epistemological reasoning. It is love that unites Goethe with the great Jewish philosopher, and love often softens critical analysis.

Of Plato, Goethe possessed a relatively thorough knowledge, yet he was never a Platonist. All the attempts which have been made to derive Goethe's ideas of the *type*, which is the carrying idea of his natural philosophy, altogether from Plato's *ideas*, have failed, and had to fail. The *type* plays an increasingly important part in Goethe's reasoning from his trip to Italy (1786–88) onward. After having undergone some change—due largely to Schiller's influence —this concept assumed its definite shape only in the last two decades of his life. Although Goethe himself tells us on one occasion that he is occupied with "hyperphysical considerations," this does not imply that his idea of *type* lies on the same transcendental plane as the Platonic *idea*. Goethe's types are immanent in nature, they are derived from and exist only within experience. But it seems justifiable to assume that Plato's doctrine of ideas stimulated Goethe and led him to adapt the Platonic concept to his own way of thinking.

A considerable, though merely accidental, similarity is noticeable between the Goethean type and the Aristotelian *morphe* or *eidos* in so far as both are principles of formation immanent in nature and both become manifest in homologous (in Goethe's terminology, "analogous") organisms. But the differences are more than the similarities: Aristotle arrives at his concept of *morphe* and *eidos* by way of ratiocination, not, like Goethe, by "vision," and his seeking for primary reasons is repugnant to Goethe. Goethe's attitude was, as we stated in the very beginning, not to look *behind* the phenomena; therefore, whenever he uses the Aristotelian term "entelechy," he conceives it as *"ein Stück Ewigkeit,"* "a piece of eternity," permeating and animating bodies like the Indian Atman or the Chinese Tao.

While Goethe in the beginning adhered to a moderate dualistic concept of nature, though not in the Platonic sense, it was early superseded by a monistic view which went so far as to exclude even a clear distinction between subject and object. Thus he writes in 1801 in a letter to Jacobi:

> If philosophy's first aim is to separate, I cannot get along with it . . . ; but if it unites, or rather elevates our original feeling of being united with nature, and if it transforms it safely into a deep, calm contemplation in whose eternal *syncrisis* and *diacrisis* we perceive a divine life—although we are not granted the pleasure of living it— then I welcome philosophy.

And this monistic view—to throw another sidelight on my statements—confirms Goethe in his old love of Spinoza, who had given him the clear formulation of his leading idea: *"Deus sive natura."* This love finds its highest expression in an earlier letter to the same Jacobi (1786), where Goethe says:

> He who wills the highest must will the whole. He who treats of spirit must presuppose nature; he who speaks of nature must presuppose, or implicitly deal with, spirit. Reasoning cannot be separated from what is being thought, and will is inseparable from what is being moved. Thus I become more and more closely attached to the God-worship of the atheist Spinoza, and leave to you everything that is called religion.

As a consequence of Goethe's monism, we understand that the principle of unification, of reducing the infinity of observable facts to a minimum of simple phenomena, is the essence of his philosophy. This principle is obvious no less in his writings on the problems of nature than in his poetical works. His *Urphänomene* (original phenomena) and his types are only one—certainly the most important—manifestation of his monism.

Goethe's epoch possessed no knowledge whatever of geological periods. The evolution of life on earth was believed to have been compressed into the inconceivably short period of the few thousand years that had elapsed since the creation of the world according to the Bible. Hence, obviously, no "historical" approach to those questions can be traceable until the last years of Goethe's life.

By keeping this in mind we can avoid the grave error of interpreting the Goethean types as having a primarily historical, evolutionary meaning, as being intended to represent the earliest, and, at the same time, the most primitive specimen from which all later varieties have originated. Neither Goethe's idea of the *Urpflanze* (original plant) nor the *Urstier* (primigenial ox) permits of such an interpretation. What he envisions, and actually is looking for, is not the historically older form, speaking in terms of evolution, but the primitive form, which is characterized as consisting of only the simplest irreducible elements.

As late as 1786 he believed it possible to find the *Urpflanze* as a living species. Then the concept undergoes some change. He conceives of an abstract, intellectual *Urpflanze*, perceptible by the senses. Finally, in his old age, the idea becomes a "law" of formation, though, as he wrote to Johannes Müller in 1829, a law "to which the perceptible world offers nothing but exceptions"—in other words, a very strange law.

Concerning the idea of the primigenial ox, which occurred to Goethe on the occasion of the unearthing of the skeleton near Hassleben, it cannot be denied that it has a closer relation to the theory of evolution and even anticipates the concept of selective breeding. This seems logical when we recall that Goethe's occupation with this problem too falls within the last period of his life and practically coincides with the time of his "law of biological formation."

Coming back now to our initial survey of Goethe's merits and errors, which I composed in the style of a positivistic historian of science, most of the statements made there are of such a superficial nature that they can hardly be of serious interest. Both Lamarck and Darwin are, directly or indirectly, indebted to Goethe. This is beyond doubt. But it does not follow that Goethe can be called a forerunner of either. In particular, Darwin's phylogenetic conception, which is an essential feature of his theory, is entirely his own; it cannot be found in Goethe, hardly even in rudimentary form.

Still, Goethe stands as the first who intuited the great unity of nature and declared his unshakable belief in that unity by a thousand poetic and prose testimonies. This finds its clearest expression in his discovery of the intermaxillary bone. Vesalius had noted the palatal suture and marked it down—one of the many anatomical details by which he enriched the knowledge of his time. But it was far from his mind to draw conclusions from this discovery—even the conclusion that man *has* the *os intermaxillare*. So far as he was concerned, this was only one of four hundred bones. Goethe, on the contrary, *knew* before starting out on anatomical investigations that man could not possibly form an exception to the rule, and hence must have the intermaxillary bone. His preconceived conviction led him to the discovery, and this in turn confirmed his belief in the general unity of nature which allows of no exceptions. Nothing seems more apt to illustrate the futility of statements concerning the priority of a discovery which do not take account of what it meant to the discoverer and to his time.

It would be beyond the scope of this essay to discuss *in extenso* Goethe's attitude towards mathematics. He had only a very limited mathematical training, and therefore was unable to appreciate the importance of the magnificent achievements made in mathematics from the seventeenth century to his days. One of the greatest among his contemporaries, Gauss, lived only a few hours' travel from Goethe's residence. It is possible that he did not even know the name.

It would, however, be erroneous to assume that Goethe condemned mathematics altogether. He was aware of the intrinsic beauty of mathematical method, though whenever he makes a concrete statement concerning it, it is evident that he understands practically nothing of it; he approved of mathematics only as far as it remained within its own abstract realm. In his essay "On Mathematics and its Abuse," Goethe says: "I have heard that people accuse me of being an adversary, an enemy of mathematics as a whole. Yet nobody can possibly have a higher appreciation of it than I, because it achieves just what I have not had the privilege of doing." I am tempted to say that he tolerated it in theory and admired it as "art for art's sake." Needless to say, this approach was contrary to the one which he applied in his own work. But he became suspicious as soon as mathematics emerged from its transcendental world as a tool in the hands of the physicists and naturalists.

Goethe no doubt also appreciated the scope of the development of physics, particularly of mechanics, which, starting with Kepler and Galileo, was crowned by the immortal discovery of Isaac Newton. He became his great scientist's irreconcilable adversary, not in the field of astronomy, in which Goethe never aspired to go beyond meditative vision, but in his theory of light, which Goethe considered almost a personal attack upon himself. It is not probable that Goethe was aware that Newton's law of gravitation, which Newton himself regarded as an unexplainable, original phenomenon, has a pretty close relationship to Goethe's own idea of the *Urphänomen* when not only the forms (*Gestalten*) but also the forces of nature are taken into consideration. Goethe, however, regards forces as immanent in, and inseparable from, forms, and hence he necessarily classifies Newton among the "dissectors." Furthermore, Newton's original phenomenon was presented not in plain words but as a mathematical formula, or ratio. To Goethe, this inevitably appears as an abstract concept, detached from the reality of nature, whereas he himself operates only with concrete entities, even when he searches for original phenomena. Among the *Urphänomene* he counts entities accessible to direct observation, such as matter, light, darkness, or the interaction of some of them, as of light and darkness, by which he believed (erroneously) color is produced.

If we leave out the numerical, algebraic side of mathematics, which the layman is far too much inclined to consider its main characteristic, then Goethe's scientific studies can be said to contain a considerable mathematical element. In his theory of chromatics he freely makes use of symmetry as an essential factor in his considerations. And his vertebral theory of the skull is the result of reasoning in typical terms of mathematical proportions. Starting from the histological similarity between the substances of the spinal marrow and of the brain, he realizes that the former must be to the latter as the vertebral column is to the skull. The anatomical evidence being susceptible of such an interpretation, the intuition becomes conviction. Oken, on the other hand, not being satisfied with this result, propounded the generalizing and absurd theory that the skeleton is nothing but a grown-out, ramified, and repeated vertebra, and that the latter is thus the preformed element of the skeleton: "the whole of man is a vertebral bone." This hypothesis, which floats in the air and has nothing in common with the natural, mathematical consideration mentioned, Goethe called "tumultuous, disorderly, and imperfect."

It follows from all we have stated so far that Goethe's approach is something peculiar to him, for it is neither deductive (observation is the starting point) nor inductive (not laws but phenomena are primarily sought for). In spite of his appreciation of the achievements of the seventeenth-century scientists, he was at the same time stricken with horror when he viewed the consequences of their procedure, which he foresaw more clearly than any other of his contemporaries. Since it was the inductive method that had led to the enormous progress of mathematical physics, Goethe could not but consider it the primary reason why the conception of unity between inorganic matter and organic as well as spiritual life was destroyed.

It appears as the apotropaic gesture of a man who foresees the rise of a denaturalized, dehumanized, demonic age when three years before his death he jots down the following sarcastic assault on induction:

> I never ventured to apply it, not even to myself. I let the facts stand each by itself. But I sought for the analogous. And in this way, for instance, I arrived at the concept of the metamorphosis of plants. Induction serves only the purpose of the man who wishes to persuade. One admits two or three propositions and some inferences, and at once gets lost. . . .
>
> It is difficult to protect oneself against it and to free others from such fetters and to lead them back. Skepticism must first become dogmatic; then new adversaries to it will arise again. For even skepticism must either allow problems to remain unsolved, or solve them in such a way that human intelligence becomes alarmed.

Sinister words of a dying prophet!

One work to which we have hitherto referred only casually calls for discussion: Goethe's *Chromatics*, the most bulky of all his scientific writings, comprising nearly fifteen hundred pages. It was a child of many sorrows, composed over two decades.

A panegyrist of the Olympian poet would do better not to deal with the *Chromatics* at all, or at least not to mention the polemical part, which fills one whole volume. Whoever succeeds in reading it is bound to be shocked and offended on every page, and is alternately filled with pain and disgust. It bears witness to the struggle of a man who sees the treasures of his life menaced by an enemy far superior to him in calm cunning, and who is therefore driven to defensive measures which normally he would find beneath his dignity.

The most elementary rules of honest scientific discussion are gravely violated. The dead adversary is not allowed to make coherent statements but is brutally interrupted right in the middle of his phrases, propositions, inferences. Goethe answers and refutes before Newton has finished. Repeatedly Goethe blames him for inaccuracy, or even dishonesty, where the fault lies in Goethe's own erroneous translation or interpretation. In one instance the question is about the invariability of the refractive power of the prism, or rather about Newton's correct statement that the distance of the point through which the light passes from the refracting edge of the prism is irrelevant to its refractive power. Goethe misunderstands the statement in the first place, then becomes aware of his error, but continues accusing Newton of having erred.

The painful impression on the reader is not effaced by the apologies Goethe makes to Newton in the *History of Chromatics,* which he composed after having finished the polemical and didactic parts of his great work. Throughout Goethe feels and acts like Tasso:

> *Nein, ich muss*
> *Von nun an diesen Mann als Gegenstand*
> *Von meinem tiefsten Hass behalten; nichts*
> *Kann mir die Lust entreissen, schlimm und schlimmer*
> *Von ihm zu denken—*

"No, from now on I must keep this man as the object of my profoundest hatred; nothing can repress my desire to think more and more evil of him."

Time and again, during the last hundred years, leading physicists have taken up the question of the validity and lasting importance of the work. Of these I mention only Hermann von Helmholtz, Wilhelm Wien, and Werner Heisenberg. They all agree that from the standpoint of modern physics Goethe's *theory* must be called wrong. At the same time, however, they also agree that his observations are of an admirable exactness, and each of them, in line with the change in viewpoint that occurs in his time, finds one or other of Goethe's conclusions worthy of praise. Heisenberg, in particular, makes the interesting remark that the only thing Goethe can be blamed for is lack of consistency, in so far as he attacked only Newton's *Optics* instead of claiming that all of his physics, including his mechanics and his law of gravitation, originated from the Devil. And Helmholtz says about Goethe's *Chromatics* that it "has to be regarded as an attempt to protect the immediate truth of the sensory perception against the attacks made upon it by the scientists."

Newton and Goethe approached the problem in diametrically opposite ways. To Newton, the simplest, primary or original phenomenon offers itself as a monochromatic beam of light produced by a series of complicated gadgets or instruments. To Goethe, light as a whole, the animating element *par excellence* which is the source of all life on earth, is the primary phenomenon.

It is too well known to be discussed here that Newton's theory is the only one that allows of a mathematical treatment by which predictions of any kind of phenomena not yet observed can be made with the desirable degree of exactness. As Goethe's theory does not fulfill the same requirements, science cannot but proclaim Newton's victory. Still, it is no less indubitable that Goethe's work has not only stimulated the artist's imagination, which was one of the author's chief aims, but has also actually borne fruits in the field of physiology.

In reality, the two hostile theories treat of different subjects and serve different purposes. Hence no comparison can result in a final statement as to right and wrong. After having watched for a hundred or more years the development of the struggle which eventually died out, we can safely state that it was all in vain; we now see more clearly than before that a contest was fought on two different planes whose intersecting line was far from the places regarded as the theaters of war.

There arises a final question: Are there any aspects of Goethe's theory that can be said to have a direct bearing on the most recent phase of modern physics, and if so, which? The answer has to be positive. Goethe's main argument against the theory of Newton was that the latter by his illicit "unnatural" methods of observation distorted the natural course of events and therefore was bound to lead to conclusions which could no longer be regarded as yielding a true picture of the natural phenomena. In other words, Goethe feared that the methods of observation applied might produce a disturbing effect on the object observed and thus falsify the results.

Goethe's fear proved unjustified as long as only macrophysical objects were under observation; for in that case an estimate of the disturbing effect can always be made with whatever degree of accuracy is desired and thus be taken into account. The picture, however, is radically changed when—as in nuclear physics—the microcosmos of the subatomic world is taken under observation. There the disturbing effect produced by our macrophysical methods is such that what we observe is not a picture of the "true" natural phenomenon, including a slight and calculable falsification, but the inseparable combination of the phenomenon itself with this disturbing effect which can be approximately of the same magnitude as the phenomenon proper. And as our instruments are necessarily always on the macrophysical level, there can be no hope that we shall ever succeed in observing the undisturbed natural phenomenon.

While in macrophysics it is always possible to make a definite statement as to a position *and* velocity of a moving object at any moment of time, a law of nature characteristic of microphysics prevents us from doing the same in the atomic world. Under "normal" conditions the subatomic objects, we may say, have only a "potential" reality. Only under observation do they assume a well-defined state and distinct properties. Thus, by measuring with high accuracy the place taken by a particle in a certain moment, we deprive ourselves of the possibility of simultaneously making any definite statement as to its velocity; we might just as well say that it has none. Correspondingly, a highly accurate measurement of the velocity of a particle prohibits the determination of its position; it would be even better to say that it has no well-defined position at all. Position and velocity thus are alternative aspects or manifestations of the particle's "potential reality" which are mutually exclusive. Through the experiment the particle can be forced to assume only one of them. This means no less than the invalidity of the law of causality in the subatomic world.

At the same time, this puts an end to the struggle of two centuries about the nature of light: Newton's corpuscular against Huygens' undulatory theory. The question is no longer about either-or; the problem has now found its solution in an as-well-as. To put it more clearly, the question today no longer reads, What *is* light and radiation in general? but rather, What can *become* of it? And the answer is, that in one case the particle's potential reality becomes manifest as a "wave" or as an undulatory process which allows of a measurement of velocity; in the other, as a corpuscle of which we can measure the position.

There is another subatomic phenomenon which is closely connected with the preceding: the impossibility of making any prediction on the future behavior of one individual particle under observation. We know, for instance, that the average time required for the spontaneous disintegration of 1 mg. of radium to half its weight is 1630 years. But nothing can be predicted as to the reaction of one individual atom among the many which make up the one milligram of radium. It may disintegrate in the next second or in a thousand years. But as soon as we take into consideration a large number of such particles, we are able to make the very exactest statements concerning the probability of their reacting in this way or that, of their remaining stable or disintegrating. This implies that causality in the microphysical realm is replaced by a statistical law. And it is due to the validity of this statistical law in microphysics that the law of causality is warranted in macrophysics.

The consequences which these discoveries may still have are beyond the imaginative power of ordinary man. Science is just entering upon the problems of biology seen from the point of view of nuclear physics. In a relatively short time we may obtain the most revolutionary answers to Goethe's and our own question concerning the unity of organic life and inorganic matter; by scientific research new light may be thrown on the problem of causality versus freedom of will, and thus even the highest, most sublime problem, that concerning the essence of spirit, may be brought nearer a solution.

Unity and Continuity in Goethe

by Leonard A. Willoughby

Any truly scientific observer, Goethe declares time and time again, must prefer to order his material rather than arrange it in arbitrary combinations. The difficulty is that both methods arise from one and the same property of the human mind: its power to see relations between things. So that man's strength is at the same time his weakness. Confronted with the universe in its immensity man seeks to discover order within it. If some unity is not immediately apparent to his reason, he has no compunction in calling upon belief, prejudice, whimsical fancy, and even folly, to bring him the relief of simplification.[1]

It is something of this sort that we are apt to do when faced with the rich and varied personality of Goethe. Overwhelmed by the prodigious length of his days, by the multiplicity of his activities, by the many facets of his being, by the sovereign ease with which he moves among the forms and styles of literary tradition, it is tempting to snatch at a label with which to docket him and so, to our mental satisfaction, dispose of this embarrassing fulness of natural vitality: Goethe, the Romantic; Goethe, the Nordic poet; Goethe, the victim of Classical tyranny; Goethe, the dynamic philosopher; Goethe, the moralist—or amoralist, in our English view even the libertine; Goethe, the *Fürstendiener;* Goethe, the reactionary Philistine; Goethe, the unrepentant individualist. There is no end. But if we should resist the temptation to force him into a pattern of our own devising, are we then to fall back on a bare chronicle of his life and works? Might there not be a way of satisfying our desire

"Unity and Continuity in Goethe" by Leonard A. Willoughby. From *Goethe, Poet and Thinker* by Elizabeth M. Wilkinson and Leonard A. Willoughby (London: Edward Arnold [Publishers] Ltd., 1962). Copyright © 1962 by Edward Arnold (Publishers) Ltd. Reprinted by permission of the author and the publisher. This essay was originally the Taylorian Lecture read at Oxford, 1946.

[1] Cf. esp. his essays, *Der Versuch als Vermittler von Objekt und Subjekt* and *Bedenken und Ergebung;* JA, XXXIX, 20, 35.

for significant order without reducing his richness and variety and without doing violence to the natural rhythms of his being?

Here Goethe's own approach to the complexity of the universe may well serve as a guide. For the layman the value, and the abiding interest, of his scientific works is in their method rather than in their conclusions. In them is revealed a mind fully conscious of its own processes. Goethe knows that he is as prone as anyone to make arbitrary combinations rather than to discover order; but he is on his guard against it and aware of the necessity of scrupulously testing and retesting the validity of the method he employs. Thus it would be useless, he says in the *Vorwort zur Farbenlehre*,[2] to try to express in words the being of any phenomenon. But what we can observe is the way it behaves, and a complete account of this would presumably comprise its being. Make a survey of all a man's activities, and a picture of his character will emerge. If we follow this hint, we shall cease trying to say *what* Goethe is and concentrate instead on discovering *how* he is. In doing this we shall be adopting the methods of that science which Goethe inaugurated and for which he coined the name morphology,[3] that is, the study of forms. It was an approach which he found indispensable for the study of organic nature; for the form of a living organism is not something static which we can hold in our hands. Its very essence is movement. The form of a plant is not just the shape we see before us. It is the whole cycle from its seeding to its fading, and it is only by grasping the pattern in this movement, the law which is at work in its growth, that we can grasp the plant as a whole at all.

Might it not, then, be fruitful to approach Goethe as he himself approached natural phenomena, sharing both his patient submission to things as they are and his conviction that, however great the complexity of nature, her variety is never chaotic nor her ways arbitrary? His constant concern was to keep his thought a flexible instrument, at once active enough, and receptive enough, to perceive the unity within her variety and the continuity within her changes, and thereby to apprehend her essential forms.[4]

In a *Self-portrait* of 1797[5] Goethe speaks of his manifold activities in a way which provides a key to their hidden connections. He tells us that the 'Mittelpunkt und Base' of his existence was the 'poetischer Bildungstrieb'. *Mittelpunkt,* that is in Goethe's language

[2] JA, XL, 61.
[3] *Vorwort zur Morphologie.* 'Die Absicht eingeleitet'; JA, XXXIX, 251.
[4] Ibid., 249, 252. Cf. *Maximen u. Reflexionen*: ibid., 103.
[5] JA, XXV, 227.

the organic centre, whether in a plant, a poem, or a human being, from which everything radiates, the unity from which all variety proceeds, the focal point which, once discovered, illuminates all the parts. *Bildungstrieb,* that is the impulse to form, the urge which bids him see form and make form. This, the 'poetischer Bildung-strieb', is then the centre to which all his activities, however diverse, are ultimately related. Once this is grasped, Goethe continues, all apparent contradictions resolve themselves. It is clear that he intended the stress to be a level one, bearing as much on *Bildung* as on *poetisch.* Any occupation in which he could discover shape of some kind was a challenge and a source of satisfaction: drawing, science, statesmanship, theatre-management, mining and agriculture, all these excursions of his mind were yet related to poetry by the element of form which they contained for him. If Goethe then goes on to describe these excursions as 'false tendencies', he does not mean that they could, or should, have been avoided. For Goethe, whose realm is the present, what might have been is always an abstraction and idle speculation. Nor does he mean that they were in any sense unfruitful. They were 'false starts' in the sense that he did not become a statesman or an artist. He remained a poet. But for the kind of poet he became this roundabout way was inevitable. Goethe reminds us again and again that every step in life appears now as progress, now as regress, according to the angle from which we view it. To think of his multifarious occupations as digressions, aberrations, or vagaries, will not help us to understand him as a whole. They are rather modifications and variations of one profound and central impulse, the impulse to form, and this *Self-portrait* is illuminating just because it embraces, without obliterating, the seeming antagonisms of his being. In the light of it we can understand very well that he could say on one occasion that his scientific activities 'sprang from his inmost being',[6] on another that his real happiness had been his 'poetisches Sinnen und Schaffen'.[7] For, as he told Eckermann,[8] he really saw all his achievements as symbols, and at bottom it mattered very little whether he had made pots or pans! The important thing was that any activity should give scope for his impulse to form.

At first the impulse expressed itself unconsciously. 'Unbewusst und aus innerem Trieb'[9] he sought unceasingly to grasp the ulti-

---

[6] *Kampagne in Frankreich;* JA, XXVIII, 155.
[7] In conversation with Eckermann, 27.I.1824.
[8] Ibid., 2.V.1824.
[9] *Anschauende Urteilskraft;* JA, XXVIII, 155.

mate forces at work in the universe, to discover

> was die Welt
> Im Innersten zusammenhält.

Faust would force his way into the secrets of nature by a supreme effort of the will:

> Du musst! du musst! und kostet' es mein Leben!

and he vainly attempts to apprehend these processes of nature in ecstatic vision:

> *Schau'* alle Wirkungskraft und Samen.

Already the poet's intuition goes unerringly to the unity which is within, and embraces all nature's complexity:

> Wie alles sich zum *Ganzen* webt,
> Eins in dem andern wirkt und lebt!

The same intuition which enabled him to grasp the inner workings of nature permitted him to discern the inner form of a work of art. Even so complex a structure as the Strassburg minster yielded its secrets to the urgency of this intuition. Where his contemporaries perceived only arbitrary confusion and meaningless ornamentation, Goethe discovered 'a thousand harmonious details' fused with organic necessity into a related whole. By recognizing the hidden forces inherent in its structure, he was even able to complete its unfinished form in his imagination—and, to his joy, have this act of creative intuition confirmed by the discovery of the original plans.[10] And so he could write in *Von deutscher Baukunst*:[11] 'As in the works of eternal nature, everything down to the tiniest fibre, all is form— *Gestalt*—and everything contributes functionally to the whole— *alles zweckend zum Ganzen*'. The very vocabulary is reminiscent of Faust's first monologues and reveals the identity of Goethe's approach to nature and art at this period. There is, of course, some difference. Faust, after all, has his vision of the forces of nature sitting in his dim-lit study, contemplating a sign. He by-passes the outward appearances of nature to seize her mystery with the inner eye; whereas Goethe returned again and again to the minster, looked at its every detail from every angle and in every light, until his eye was weary. Yet it was only when twilight descended, blurring the

---

[10] *Dichtung u. Wahrheit*, III, 11; JA, XXIV, 63.
[11] JA, XXXIII, 9.

details and throwing the masses into relief, that his inner eye took charge and discovered the secrets of its inner form. It was as though the spirit of Erwin von Steinbach had inclined to his pleading, as the Erdgeist had done to Faust's insistence.

How different was his relation to the outward forms and appearances of nature once he began his scientific studies in earnest. In his letters and diaries of the first ten years in Weimar we can watch the change happening. It is no longer just the elemental aspects of nature, seen through the veil of his own moods, which absorb him. Botany, geology, anatomy, zoology, they all taught him to look on even the most trivial and insignificant of natural phenomena with passionate interest. No longer is it just to pass the time, 'kalt zu seinem Zeitvertreib botanisierend',[12] as in Strassburg, that he collects stones and plants and fungi. Instead he even begs his friends to send him such specimens as were not available at home. The aim is still, as he told Frau von Stein in 1786,[13] the perception of the essential form by which nature contrives to bring forth her infinite variety. But no longer by Faust's visionary short cut. By patient and detailed study of each plant he will discover, first its individual form, then the basic form of plant life—'and, if there were time in the short space of a man's life I could extend this method to every sphere of nature'.[13] There is now no more Faustian straining of will and intuition. His mind is no less active, but it is a receptive activity. 'Everything forces itself upon me', he writes.[14] 'I no longer ponder upon it, it comes out to meet me'. This submission to the nature of the object is completed in the clear air of Italy which threw everything into sharp relief. He now felt that he was really beginning to 'see', where his whole life long he had been just 'groping about'.[15] More and more he learns to value what he possesses with his outer eye and to distrust the power of soaring and embellishing imagination to grasp essential form.

Yet there is clearly more involved than mere sense-perception when he discovers traces of the intermaxillary bone in man; or recognizes that the skull of vertebrates is a modification of the bones of the spinal column; or perceives that all the parts of the plant, except root and stem, are modifications of the leaf; thus showing that the vegetable and animal kingdoms are governed by the same principle of metamorphosis, of morphological change. Goethe

[12] *Von deutscher Baukunst;* JA, XXXIII, 4. Cf. letter to Frau v. Stein, 31.X.1778.
[13] 9.VII.1786.
[14] To Frau v. Stein, 20–23.XII.1786.
[15] Ibid., 25.I.1787; 19.I.1788.

called such flashes of intuition *aperçus*.[16] The term might make us
think of visions such as Faust's; but there is a vast difference. An
aperçu is not achieved by some effort of the imagination with the
eye turned away from the object. It is rather a middle link in an
organic succession, arising only after much observation and leading
inevitably to further observation and checking.[17] An *aperçu* is the
product of thought so closely permeated by sense-perceptions that,
as Goethe once said, 'his perception was itself thinking and his
thinking perception'.[18]

The characteristics of Goethe's scientific attempts to discover
form are summed up in his *Vorwort zur Morphologie:*[19] 'to apprehend the outward, visible, and tangible parts of any living phenomenon in their relation to each other, to interpret these as indications of its inner form, thus grasping the phenomenon as a *whole*
—*das Ganze in der Anschauung beherrschen'*, Thus intuition—the
act of 'seeing-into'—has been assigned a definite place in his scientific method. It is no longer charged with emotion, but permeated
by thought.

But Goethe's science does not stop short at the apprehension of
forms. He penetrates into the forces which govern the forms—'les
forces sous les formes', as Paul Valéry, with the perspicacity of the
poet-scientist, puts it in his centenary *Discours en l'honneur de
Goethe* (1932). He is as fascinated by these forces as ever he was.
But from being vague pantheistic vital activities they can now be
identified scientifically. He can isolate them and call them by name:
Polarität and *Steigerung,* the two 'grosse Triebräder aller Natur',
as he called them to Kanzler von Müller in 1828.[20] By a kind of
symbolic extension Goethe may see these forces at work in every
sphere of human life. But the important thing is that he had first
perceived them sensuously as demonstrable facts of the physical
world—*Polarität* in the phenomenon of the magnet, *Steigerung* as
intensification and concentration in his experiments with colours
and with plants. Again, we might think we had come full circle, to
Faust's 'Kräfte der Natur'; and again we should be wrong. They
are now '*Triebräder* der Natur'—their nature and function established by the years of observation and experiment which have inter-

---

[16] *Dichtung u. Wahrheit,* IV, 16; JA, XXV, 20.
[17] *Maximen u. Reflexionen;* JA, XXXIX, 60.
[18] *Bedeutende Fördernis duch ein einziges geistreiches Wort;* JA, XXXIX, 48.
[19] JA, XXXIX, 251.
[20] Letter of 24.V.1828. WA, II, 11, p. 10; JA, XXXIX, 349.

vened. It is rather full *spiral* that we have come—round to an original position at a higher level.

The changes of method in Goethe's search for form are profound and important. But the thread of continuity running through all the changes is evident in the persistence of the world *schauen,* modified into its compound *Anschauung* and into its foreign form *aperçu.* And the outward and visible signs of this continuity are the brightly-coloured threads of recurrent images which persist throughout his writings. One he was specially fond of using, he tells us in the last letter of his life,[21] was that of weft and warp—'ein Gleichnis, das ich so gern brauche'. *Weben* is the image which from the beginning comes spontaneously to his mind whenever he thinks of ceaseless activity, whether of man, nature, or art. In his vocabulary, so influenced by Luther's bible, *weben* and *leben* are synonymous, and it is natural that Gretchen's busy daily round, her 'häusliches Beginnen', should be symbolized by the picture of her at the spinning-wheel. The image of *weben* is even implicit in the 'Zäserchen' of the Strassburg minster, the tiny fibres which go to make up its fabric. Faust is lost in wonder as he contemplates the inweaving of vital processes; Werther is prostrate as he thinks of their mutually destructive aspects. Yet the image which springs to the lips of each is the same—'Himmel und Erde und ihre webenden Kräfte'. The Erdgeist embraces both the creative and the destructive aspect, 'Geburt und Grab', in a pictorial elaboration of the whirring loom of time, weaving 'the living garment of God'. 'Poetry', Goethe says in one of his maxims,[22] 'gives intimations of the mysteries of nature and seeks to resolve them through an image'. This intimation that nature herself was the prime weaver was then confirmed by his scientific discoveries. In his *Vorwort zur Morphologie* he is still using the image 'schaffendes Gewebe' to describe the constant self-renewal of tissues in plant and animal life. And the modern scientist who has penetrated beyond Goethe to the molecular structure of tissues can find no better image to describe it than 'this gigantic textile business'. Such pregnant images as *weben* Goethe was wont to carry with him for forty or fifty years. Constantly renewed in his imagination, they took on different shape without changing their essence. In an essay of 1820, *Bedenken und Ergebung,* he takes up again those lines of the *Urfaust* where Mephistopheles mocks at the 'Gedankenfabrik' of philosophy by comparing its elaborations to those

[21] 17.III.1832.
[22] JA, XXXIX, 114.

of a complicated weaving-machine. But where Mephistopheles could only mock, Goethe now reaches to the central and ultimate problem where science and philosophy meet: to the reconciliation of thought with experience, the one independent of time and space, the other confined within them. To look too closely at this problem seems to him the way that madness lies. Therefore, he says, 'let us take refuge in the sphere of poetry and sing an old song with slight variations':

> So schauet mit bescheidnem Blick
> Der ewigen Weberin Meisterstück,
> Wie ein Tritt tausend Fäden regt,
> Die Schifflein hinüber herüber schiessen,
> Die Fäden sich begegnend fliessen,
> Ein Schlag tausend Verbindungen schlägt.
> Das hat sich nicht zusammen gebettelt,
> Sie hat's von Ewigkeit angezettelt,
> Damit der ewige Meistermann
> Getrost den Einschlag werfen kann.

The older Goethe is constantly making this transition from one kingdom of the mind to another, from poetry to science, from philosophy to religion, and from each or all of these ever again back to poetry. Not, indeed, in any mystical blurring of these disciplines, not because he would confuse their separate methods, but with the single view of one who has, as he said of himself, 'separated enough to combine and combined enough to be ready to separate again'.[23] It is not that sublime sense of being one with the oneness of the universe which comes to us when we are young, not a primal unity, but the return to ultimate simplicity of one who has penetrated through to the vantage-point where all the realms of knowledge are seen as coloured reflections of the one truth which is life. He now couples in one sentence scientific and poetic *aperçus*. He declares that beauty is 'eine Manifestation geheimer Naturgesetze';[24] and when he now comes back to Gothic architecture he can say in a new, and fuller, sense that it is like 'the works of eternal nature'. For he is seeing it with an eye sharpened by his insight into plant morphology. His earlier intuition has been confirmed by knowledge. He now knows what he sees.[25]

[23] JA, XXXIX, 350.
[24] *Maximen u. Reflexionen;* JA, XXXV, 305.
[25] *Von deutscher Baukunst* (1823); JA, XXXV, 236f. Cf. *Dichtung u. Wahrheit*, II, 9; JA, XXIII, 202–6.

The interpenetration of science and poetry comes out in the poems he wrote on scientific subjects—*Metamorphose der Tiere* or *Entoptische Farben*—or when he prefaces his *Farbenlehre* with a quotation from the Book of Job; or, most striking of all, when in a review of a scientific work he quotes from one of his most personal poems, the *Marienbader Elegie*.[26] But this interpenetration can be more intimate still. In some of his late poems where the content is remote from science there are lines so charged with the accumulation of his scientific experience that they radiate a quality unique in lyric poetry. That much-quoted line from his poem, *Urworte Orphisch,*

> Geprägte Form, die lebend sich entwickelt,

is not just a fine phrase embodying a philosophical truth about man's destiny. The secret of its perpetual power is, surely, that it mediates between the worlds of nature and of spirit. It is a perfect rounding-off for this oracular poem with its mystical and astrological symbols. But it has its roots in the natural world, and the metaphor corresponds at every point to that law of metamorphosis which is at work in every living organism. Or in the line from *Selige Sehnsucht,*

> Die dich zeugte, wo du zeugtest,

the insistent repetition of *zeugen* not only serves to point the contrast between the physical begetting in 'the coolness of the love night' and the spiritual consummation of the 'Flammentod'. In its precise sequence of generation ('which begat thee, where thou didst beget') it also announces nature's indifference to the life of the individual once he has fulfilled his purpose of perpetuating his kind.

But it would be very wrong if, in our desire to see unity in Goethe, we seemed to imply that he lacked the tensions which are the source and condition of all life. The difficulty when we speak of unity is not to confuse it with simple harmony, not to imagine a uniform movement in one direction. The problem is not one that would have arisen for Goethe, since for him the idea of unity, whether in himself or in the universe, was inseparable from that of polarity. The universe is undoubtedly one; but it is equally certain that we experience it in terms of opposites: light and darkness, left and right, subject and object, body and soul, matter and spirit. For Goethe these are not mutually exclusive opposites. On the contrary,

[26] *Maximen u. Reflexionen;* JA, XXXVIII, 263.

each is unthinkable without the other. They imply not dualism but duality. They are the poles of an all-embracing unity, as interdependent as the rhythm of breathing in and breathing out. And this is another image which runs through the whole length of Goethe's writings, from the fragment of a *Roman in Briefen* of 1772,[27] where it expresses the flow and recoil within the emotion of love, to a poem of the *West-Östlicher Divan* of 1814, where it is the occasion for praise of life as it is, with all its ups and downs:

> Im Atemholen sind zweierlei Gnaden:
> Die Luft einziehn, sich ihrer entladen.
> Jenes bedrängt, dieses erfrischt;
> So wunderbar ist das Leben gemischt.
> Du danke Gott, wenn er dich presst,
> Und dank' ihm, wenn er dich wieder entlässt.[28]

It is a commonplace that a man nowhere so clearly reveals the fundamentals of his being as in his style. And the sense of polarity, of opposites within unity, so permeates Goethe's thought and feeling that it is reflected in the very structure of his language. There is his love of coupling together in syntactical unity words which, by their meaning, pull away from each other in different directions. An adjective will qualify a noun of opposite meaning; the lover in *Werther* is 'der glückliche Unglückliche'.[29] Forty years later in the exquisite poem, *Nicht mehr auf Seidenblatt,* lovers everywhere and eternally are 'jene Glücklich-Unglücklichen'. The two opposites are here brought into even closer union by the dropping of the adjectival ending, and it is as if, by the use of the hyphen which binds them, Goethe would demonstrate to us visually that these poles, happy/unhappy, are the very condition of loving. Or, again, he will describe his own state of mind as compounded of 'meditative carefreeness and warm coldness'.[30] In *Dichtung und Wahrheit,*[31] trying to catch the whole of what Friederike Brion had meant for him, he writes: 'thoughtfully gay, naïve and self-aware, lighthearted and far-seeing, qualities which seem incompatible, yet in her were united'. By paradox he seeks to express the whole, not, as he pointed out, because truth lies between two extremes, but because it embraces them both. At first he seems to do it unconsciously,

[27] GA, IV, 263.
[28] JA, V, 7.
[29] JA, XVI, 105.
[30] To Sophie v. La Roche, 1.IX.1780.
[31] III, 11; JA, XXIV, 9.

as when he lets his Werther say that in this world things are rarely settled by Either/Or—'In der Welt ist es sehr selten mit dem Entweder Oder getan' [32]—but in later life it became a deliberate method of attacking difficult problems. No words, he thinks, are delicate and subtle enough to communicate experience, and the need for paradoxical expressions corresponds to a profound need of the human mind to operate with antitheses if it would get at an important truth.

His linguistic use of subject and object reveals more clearly still the absence of dualism even on the deepest levels of his thought. We are apt to think that because we say '*I* know *it*' the separation of subject and object actually corresponds to our own experience in the act of knowledge. But Goethe, like Coleridge, knew that this separation is merely an instrument, though a highly useful instrument, of analytical thought, and that during the experience itself subject and object are so instantly united that we cannot say to which of the two priority belongs.[33] 'I' for Goethe never has the overweening importance that it has so largely assumed in our Western subjectivism. He can easily let the perceiving subject slip into the role of grammatical object, and give the active part to the object perceived by turning it into the grammatical subject of the sentence. Thus, to express his perception of the form of the plant, he will say: '*It* forces itself upon *me* . . . *it* comes out to meet *me*'.[34] Asked how he knew that the tower of the Strassburg cathedral had been wrongly restored, he does not say '*I* discovered it', but 'the tower told *me*'.[35] It was in this sense that he could say: 'It was not *I* made my poems, *they* made *me*.'[36] Or, of certain legendary themes that he later made into poetry: '*they* embedded themselves deep in my mind.'[37] Nothing could reflect more clearly that subject and object are but polar opposites of a single unity than the easy swing of his prose between two alternative modes of expressing the act of knowledge. And we are not surprised when he tells us that 'the elements of objects entered into his thought and were permeated by it', or when he finds the old Delphic injunction 'Know thyself!' inadequate, because, as he insists, inner and outer, self and world, are so interwoven that man can only know himself by know-

---

[32] JA, XVI, 47.
[33] *Biographia Literaria*, Ch. XII. Cf. JA, XXXIX, 29f., 48.
[34] To Frau v. Stein, 9.VII; 24.XI; 20.XII.1786.
[35] *Dichtung u. Wahrheit*, III, 11; JA, XXIV, 63.
[36] *Kampagne in Frankreich*, XXVIII, 25.
[37] *Bedeutende Fördernis durch ein einziges geistreiches Wort*; JA, XXXIX, 48f.

ing the world and by learning to look upon himself as an object.[37]

It was not, then, by the denial of tension but by his complete acceptance of tension as the very condition of existence that Goethe was able to preserve the unity of his being. It was not always so. Only gradually and with much pain and effort did he learn how to manage the tensions which at one time were dangerously insistent and threatened to destroy him as they destroyed his Werther. We can follow something of this development in his use of the two images, *Wanderer* and *Hütte*, which pursue him throughout his life, and represent the two poles of self-realization and self-limitation. Where at first he is flung helplessly from one extreme to the other he learns eventually to accept these alternations as part of the larger rhythms of universal polarity.[38]

The rich texture of Goethe's thought and the variety of his achievement are undoubtedly due to his willingness to accept polarity as an integral part of his mental processes. He moved freely between the poles of reflection and imagination, analysis and synthesis, and learned to exploit each to the full. It is often maintained that Goethe neglected analysis. But though it is true that as a poet he naturally inclined more to synthesis, to expressing things as wholes, yet he knew very well that outside poetry analysis is inevitable, that language by its very nature imposes it, and he was ready enough to accept analysis as a means to knowledge. Indeed, he claims that he himself had always moved from synthesis to analysis and back again, and, in an essay of 1829, *Analyse und Synthese*, he calls them the complementary methods of science, the one being unthinkable without the other. But he felt that, flushed with the success of its analytical technique, science too often tended to neglect synthesis altogether. Hence his insistence that the results of analysis to be valid must constantly be referred back to the living whole; and hence also his belief that it must be possible to perfect an alternative technique which begins with the whole and proceeds to the parts. There must be a way, he told Schiller,[39] of apprehending the form of a living whole and of working from this whole to the parts, 'aus dem Ganzen in die Teile strebend'.

All his life he was concerned with this truth that the whole is more than and different from the sum of its parts, and it is generally accepted that here he was anticipating the findings of *Gestalt*-psy-

[38] Cf. L. A. Willoughby, ' "Wanderer" and "Hut," ' *Études Germaniques*, VI, 219.

[39] *Erste Bekanntschaft mit Schiller. 1794;* JA, XXX, 391.

chology. In the Leipzig poem, *Die Libelle*, the idea is already implicit. In an attempt to catch the secret of the dragon-fly's form in its play of changing colours the hasty youth holds it in his hand, only to find a dull uniform blue. Mephisto gibes at the scientist who reduces everything to its parts, thus losing the vital spirit which holds them together. The *Philosophische Studie* of 1784 expresses the same thought in terms of Spinozian philosophy: 'in every living organism the parts are so inextricably combined with the whole that they can only be grasped in and with the whole.' [40] Goethe then repeats the thought with scientific precision in his *Considerations on Morphology* of 1795, where he shows that we do, in fact, always apprehend things as wholes.[41] It was consequently vain for Professor Wagner to attempt to realize synthetic man by putting the parts together in his laboratory. Homunculus is made, but before he can come into being he must first go through all the forms of creation.

Only the artist can catch form out of flux, create permanence out of change, 'Dauer im Wechsel', as Goethe himself caught the changing forms of human life in the imperishable distichs of the *Römische Elegien* or in the plastic scenes of *Hermann und Dorothea*. But outside of art the only way that man can satisfy the longing of his mind for permanence is to accept change and seek to discover the continuity running through it. This conception of form as a complexity which is constantly changing (he more often uses the word *Gestalt* in a dynamic rather than a static sense), is perhaps Goethe's most valuable contribution to thought, and it is only the nostalgic desire of the human mind for permanence which prevents us from seeking the dynamic form in his own development, which makes us long to hold him fast at one particular stage and regret that he ever passed beyond it. If he had only continued in his early *Sturm und Drang* manner! cries the one. Why did he waste his time and our patience with these dabblings in science? cries the other. What a pity he did not settle down with Friederike or Lili to a life of respectable domesticity! His contemporaries showed similar unwillingness to see that life must go on and that with it a man's style must change. They too found it hard to accept the new where they expected the old and familiar. 'Because my seven brothers did not in the least resemble sister Iphigenie, they were badly received',

[40] JA, XXXIX, 7.
[41] Ibid., 135.

he writes of a novel he had tried out on his friends.[42] And to Eckermann[43] he complained that people had never really been satisfied
with him as he was. 'They always wanted me different from what
it had pleased God to make me. Nor were they really satisfied with
the works I produced.' But, Goethe protests, art, like nature,[44]
must be treated with the respect due to its inevitable and unalterable form. There it stands, 'ein unveränderliches Factum', as much
a hard fact of existence as any actual event—'Das Gedichtete be-
hauptet sein Recht, wie das Geschehene'.[45]

Goethe thought of his own life and works as inevitable, as a
natural growth. And, just as he rejoiced in nature as it is, and in
the unfailing return of the seasons, neither wanting spring to be
red for a change[46] nor to pluck roses in April,[47] so he accepted each
season of his own life as it came with whatever advantages and disadvantages it brought.[47] And when we cling, as so many of us are
tempted to cling, to the young and spontaneous Goethe, captivated
by the poignancy and freshness of his first sensations, we are doing
violence to the form of his being by seeking to arrest his development at a given stage. Surely the way to get the best out of him is
to take him as he is and not as we would have him be.

And are we even sure that the Goethe we cling to and admire is
always as 'spontaneous' as we think he is? Who would not be sorry
to lose this lovely image: 'Wie die Natur sich zum Herbste neigt,
wird es Herbst in mir und um mich her. Meine Blätter werden
gelb, und schon sind die Blätter der benachbarten Bäume abge-
fallen'? And yet it is from the second, carefully revised version of
Werther,[48] completed on the eve of his Italian journey in 1786, a
product of self-criticism both personal and artistic. And the image
itself is obviously inspired by a re-reading of *Macbeth*. The other
great works of his 'spontaneous' youth, *Götz* and *Faust,* he never
thought worth publishing in their first form at all. And who would
recognize from this first quatrain in the *Urfaust* the ballad we know
and love so well?

> Es war ein König in Tule
> Einen goldnen Becher er hett

---

[42] *Kampagne in Frankreich;* JA, XXVIII, 154.
[43] 4.I.1824.
[44] *Kampagne in Frankreich;* JA, XXVIII, 122.
[45] Letter to Reinhard, 31.XII.1809.
[46] *Dichtung u. Wahrheit*, III, 13; JA, XXIV, 158.
[47] In conversation with Eckermann, 27.IV.1825; 12.IV.1829.
[48] Letter of 4.IX.[1772]; JA, XVI, 87.

> Empfangen von seiner Bule
> Auf ihrem Todtesbett.

Who would not agree that the familiar wording is a great improvement? And yet it first appeared in this form in 1790, after Goethe's return from Italy. Many of the poems we associate with Friederike and Lili we quote in a form which is not that of their first inspiration. Thus when we read the young, spontaneous, Goethe we are often in fact reading works produced by a certain measure of reflection.

It would in any case be false to draw a hard and fast distinction between the spontaneous and the reflective Goethe as though they represented rigid opposites. Reflectiveness and spontaneity, conscious and unconscious, are for him like any other pair of opposites, the two poles of a unity between which he is constantly moving. But it is not just a question of oscillation. There is also an upward movement at work, and it can happen that each of the opposites becomes intensified and that they then unite to produce what Goethe called 'ein Drittes, Neues, Höheres, Unerwartetes'.[49] The poem *Um Mitternacht* of 1818 must have come into being by some happy mating of this kind. Here is a poem as spontaneous in effect as one could wish, and as spontaneously composed. Goethe held it specially dear because it came to him 'unexpectedly at the midnight-hour'.[50] Yet how much of conscious reflection has coupled in the creative darkness of the unconscious with ancient and more recent experience to merge at last in images so perfectly articulated that there is no separating sound and sense.

> Um Mitternacht ging ich, nicht eben gerne,
> Klein kleiner Knabe, jenen Kirchhof hin
> Zu Vaters Haus, des Pfarrers; Stern am Sterne,
> Sie leuchteten doch alle gar zu schön;
> Um Mitternacht.

> Wenn ich dann ferner, in des Lebens Weite,
> Zur Liebsten musste, musste, weil sie zog,
> Gestirn und Nordschein über mir im Streite,
> Ich gehend, kommend Seligkeiten sog;
> Um Mitternacht.

> Bis dann zuletzt des vollen Mondes Helle
> So klar und deutlich mir ins Finstere drang,

[49] [*Polarität*]; WA, II, 11, p. 165f.
[50] JA, XXXVII, 221; cf. XXX, 316.

> Auch der Gedanke, willig, sinnig, schnelle
> Sich ums Vergangne wie ums Künftige schlang;
> Um Mitternacht.

If we ask what the poem is 'about', we have to reply that it is not about any or all of these separate experiences of the midnight sky, but about the moment when their symbolic quality is recognized. This illuminating moment of recognition embraces within itself past and future and is therefore eternal. This meaning is not communicated to us in the form of discursive statement. The images speak to us directly, and it is only by brooding on them that the full meaning of the poem emerges. Yet the thought of making the moment eternal by recognizing its significance had long been the subject of Goethe's conscious reflection and, in a later philosophic poem, *Vermächtnis,* he will express this idea in conceptual form:

> Dann ist Vergangenheit beständig,
> Das Künftige voraus lebendig—
> Der Augenblick ist Ewigkeit.

But in the poem *Um Mitternacht,* this reflection is so completely dissolved in images that scarcely a trace of the conceptual remains. Image has become thought, and thought image.

In Goethe the traffic between the conscious and the unconscious is not only in one direction. From early Weimar days he was increasingly interested in his own psychological processes, in the periodic cycle of his creativity, and anxious, through understanding, to obtain some measure of control. The last letter of his life opens up immense vistas of the possibility of integrating elements of the unconscious into consciousness, and elsewhere[51] he speaks in terms of the highest praise of a certain condition of 'bewusste Bewusstlosigkeit', conscious unconsciousness—another of these paradoxes by which he attempts to express the inherent unity of what we experience as opposites.

The advantage of studying Goethe in the way that he himself studied organic nature is that any mental image we may form of him never hardens and becomes static. It can go on growing in our minds as it assimilates new facts and new aspects we may discover about him. They modify, widen, or enrich the picture without overthrowing its fundamental form. And at the risk of sounding paradoxical we may say that the most marked characteristic of this

---

[51] In his review of Fr. Rochlitz' *Für Freunde der Tonkunst* (1824); JA, XXXVII, 282.

fundamental form is his own concern with form. His pursuit of form is the pivot of his being, the unifying principle of all his activities. He sought it constantly in his life as he had found it in nature. His eye was so trained to perceive it that he could catch experience taking shape even as he was still experiencing. He is happy when he can write from Italy that his 'journey is taking on shape'—'meine Reise nimmt eine Gestalt'—[52] that is, he is beginning to see its full significance. It was still easier to see it in retrospect, and *Dichtung und Wahrheit* is an attempt to see his life, not as he had lived it in terms of time and space, but in terms of significance. The motto which he prefixed to the Second Part,[53] 'What one longs for in youth, turns up in old age in plenty', in the recognition of pattern in his life, and of the fulfilment of his destiny in accordance with the laws of organic growth and change.

From Goethe much indeed may be learnt; much of his practical wisdom is still relevant for us today. But the most vital and fruitful things he can teach us are truths concerning forms, forms which each in his own generation must fill with new content. He can teach us that the very forms in which we experience the world are the forms of change and polarity, but that within the change there is continuity, and that, embracing polarity there is unity. In one of the loveliest poems of the *West-Östlicher Divan* Goethe invests his beloved with all the infinite variety, with all the ceaseless change, of nature. As always in his later poetry, she is at once herself and the symbol of everything else. The metrical structure of the ghazel —in which the same rhyme is used throughout, though with slight variation, in the second line of each couplet—brings a sense of continuity into the very form of the poem. It is characteristic of Goethe's unity of being that it should be in a pure love lyric that he gives most perfect expression to his deep sense of the unity and continuity of the universe:

> In tausend Formen magst du dich verstecken,
> Doch, Allerliebste, gleich erkenn' ich dich;
> Du magst mit Zauberschleiern dich bedecken,
> Allgegenwärt'ge, gleich erkenn' ich dich
>
> An der Cypresse reinstem, jungem Streben,
> Allschöngewachs'ne, gleich erkenn' ich dich;

[52] To Frau v. Stein, 18.IV.1787.
[53] Its significance is discussed by Goethe towards the end of II, 9; JA, XXIII, 206f.

In des Kanales reinem Wellenleben,
Allschmeichelhafte, wohl erkenn' ich dich.

Wenn steigend sich der Wasserstrahl entfaltet,
Allspielende, wie froh erkenn' ich dich;
Wenn Wolke sich gestaltend umgestaltet,
Allmannigfalt'ge, dort erkenn' ich dich.

An des geblümten Schleiers Wiesenteppich,
Allbuntbesternte, schön erkenn' ich dich;
Und greift umher ein tausendarm'ger Eppich,
O Allumklammernde, da kenn' ich dich.

Wenn am Gebirg der Morgen sich entzündet,
Gleich, Allerheiternde, begrüss' ich dich;
Dann über mir der Himmel rein sich ründet,
Allherzerweiternde, dann atm' ich dich.

Was ich mit äusserm Sinn, mit innerm kenne,
Du Allbelehrende, kenn' ich durch dich;
Und wenn ich Allahs Namenhundert nenne,
Mit jedem klingt ein Name nach für dich.

Chronology of Important Dates

1749	Johann Wolfgang Goethe born in Frankfurt on August 28.
1765–68	Studies law at Leipzig University; early poetry.
1768–70	Association with pietistic group in Frankfurt.
1770–71	Study at Strasbourg University; friendship with J. G. Herder; receives law degree.
1771–72	Becomes lawyer in Frankfurt; early literary essays ("Shakespeare") and *Goetz von Berlichingen*; serves briefly on Imperial Court of Appeals at Wetzlar.
1774	*The Sorrows of Young Werther* (based on his experiences at Wetzlar); first version of *Faust* (*Urfaust*).
1775	Accepts invitation of Carl August, Duke of Saxe-Weimar to join Court; Goethe remains in Weimar as high-ranking official and celebrated man of letters until his death in 1832.
1776–88	Friendship with Charlotte von Stein.
1777–85	First draft of *Wilhelm Meister* (*Wilhelm Meister's Theatrical Mission*).
1779–80	Travels in Switzerland.
1785	Beginnings of Goethe's scientific studies (botany, optics, anatomy, meteorology, etc.).
1786–88	Travels in Italy; *Egmont*; *Torquato Tasso*; *Iphigenie auf Tauris*.
1788	Meets Christiane Vulpius, later (1806) to be his wife.
1789	Birth of his son August.
1790	*Faust, A Fragment.*
1791–1817	Goethe directs the Weimar Theater.

1792   Participates in campaign in France.

1794   Beginnings of friendship with Schiller (1758–1805); their correspondence (publ. 1828) is one of the most important documents of German literary criticism.

1795–96   Publication of *Wilhelm Meister's Apprenticeship*.

1806   *Faust I* concluded (publ. 1808); Weimar occupied by French troops; Napoleon in Weimar.

1808   Interview with Napoleon in Erfurt.

1809   *Elective Affinities*.

1810   *Science of Color* concluded.

1811   Autobiography, *Poetry and Truth,* begun (4 parts: 1811–1833).

1812   Meeting with Beethoven.

1813   Defeat of Napoleon at Leipzig.

1813–14   Goethe spends several months in the Rhine and Main country and takes a special interest in mediaeval art.

1816   Death of his wife.

1817–19   Publication of studies in morphology.

1819   *West-Easterly Divan* (poems) published.

1823–32   J. P. Eckermann is Goethe's secretary; his *Conversations with Goethe* (1836–48) are a major biographical document.

1825   Work on *Faust II*; completed July 1831.

1829   *Wilhelm Meister's Travels* completed.

1830   Goethe's son dies in Rome.

1832   Goethe dies on March 22.

Notes on the Editor and Contributors

VICTOR LANGE, editor of this volume, is Professor of German Literature at Princeton, and the author of a number of studies on eighteenth and twentieth century German literature.

BARKER FAIRLEY, Emeritus Professor of German at the University of Toronto, has written on Heine (1954) and Raabe (1961), and has contributed significantly to a fresh view of Goethe. (See bibliography.)

WILLY HARTNER is Professor at the University of Frankfurt and Director of the Institute for the History of Science.

ERICH HELLER, Professor of German at Northwestern University, is the author of *The Disinherited Mind* (1952), a book on Thomas Mann, *The Ironic German* (1958), and *Studien zur modernen Literatur* (1963).

GEORG LUKÁCS, the outstanding Marxist critic, has dealt with Goethe in numerous studies on European intellectual history and aesthetics.

RONALD PEACOCK, Professor of German at the University of London, is the author of several volumes of literary criticism, among them *The Poet in the Theatre* (1946), *The Art of the Drama* (1957), and *Goethe's Major Plays* (1959).

KARL REINHARDT (1886–1958), was one of the most eminent German classical scholars; his essays are collected in *Von Werken und Formen* (1948), *Tradition und Geist* (1960), and *Vermaechtnis der Antike* (1960).

OSKAR SEIDLIN is Professor of German at Ohio State University. His most recent critical studies are *Essays in German and Comparative Literature* (1961) and *Von Goethe zu Thomas Mann* (1963).

KARL VIËTOR (1892–1952) was Kuno Francke Professor of German Art and Culture at Harvard. Apart from his authoritative *Goethe the Poet* (1949) and *Goethe the Thinker* (1950), he wrote *Der junge Goethe* (1930) and a number of articles on the German classical tradition, *Geist und Form* (1952).

ELIZABETH MARY WILKINSON, Professor of German at University College, London, is Secretary of the English Goethe Society, the author of important essays on Goethe, and, with L. A. Willoughby, the editor of Schiller's *On the Aesthetic Education of Man* (1967).

LEONARD ASHLEY WILLOUGHBY, Emeritus Professor of German at the University of London, is the author of *The Classical Age of German Literature* (1926) and *The Romantic Movement in German Literature* (1930).

Selected Bibliography

The best and most convenient current editions of Goethe's works are the *Gedenkausgabe der Werke, Briefe und Gespräche*; 24 vols., Zürich, Artemis Verlag 1948–1964, and the well-annotated "Hamburg" edition (1948 ff., 14 vols.; 4 vols. correspondence). There is no comprehensive modern edition of Goethe's work in English. Of the more than 50 English translations of *Faust* only one, by Bayard Taylor (Modern Library) has, despite its Victorian limitations, continuing poetic appeal; other recent versions are by G. M. Priest (1929); Alice Raphael (1955); L. MacNeice (1952); W. Kaufmann (1961).

Comprehensive accounts of Goethe's life and works are: Benedetto Croce, *Goethe*. London: Methuen and Co., 1923; Richard Friedenthal, *Goethe: His Life and Times*. London: Weidenfeld, 1965; Friedrich Gundolf, *Goethe*. Berlin: G. Bondi, 1916; Henry Hatfield, *Goethe: A Critical Introduction*. Cambridge, Mass.: Harvard University Press, 1964; George Henry Lewes, *The Life of Goethe*. (First published in 1855; most recent edition with introduction by Victor Lange.) New York: Frederick Ungar Publishing Co., 1965; Heinrich Meyer, *Goethe. Das Leben im Werk*. Hamburg-Bergedorf: Stromverlag, 1951; Emil Staiger, *Goethe*. 3 vols. Zürich: Artemis Verlag, 1952–1959; Karl Viëtor, *Goethe, the Poet*. Cambridge, Mass.: Harvard University Press, 1949; Karl Viëtor, *Goethe, the Thinker*. Cambridge, Mass.: Harvard University Press, 1950.

The cultural background of Goethe's work is admirably established by W. H. Bruford in *Culture and Society in Classical Weimar*. Cambridge: Cambridge University Press, 1962; August Hermann Korff's *Geist der Goethezeit*. Leipzig: J. J. Weber, 1923, is a classic survey of German intellectual and literary history during the age of Goethe.

An excellent, detailed chronological survey of Goethe's life is provided in Heinz Nicolai, *Zeittafel zu Goethes Leben und Werk*. Frankfurt: Fischer Bücherei (#617), 1964.

Current Goethe scholarship as well as periodic bibliographies are to be found in the publications of the *English Goethe Society* (London) and the *Goethe Gesellschaft* (Weimar).

Among the recent distinguished general studies of Goethe's achievement as man of letters, scientist, and administrator are: Arnold Bergstraesser (ed.), *Goethe and the Modern Age*. Chicago: Henry Regnery Company, 1950; Arnold Bergstraesser, *Goethe's Image of Man and Society*. Chicago: Henry Regnery Company, 1949; Ernst Beutler, *Essays um Goethe*. Bremen: Schünemann (Sammlung Dieterich), sixth edition, 1962; James Boyd, *Goethe's Knowledge of English Literature*. Oxford: Clarendon Press, 1932; Ernst Cassirer, *Goethe und die geschichtliche Welt: Drei Aufsätze*. Berlin: B. Cassirer, 1932; Ernst Robert Curtius, "Goethe als Kritiker" in *Kritische Essays zur Europäischen Literatur*. Bern: Francke, 1950, pp. 28–58; Herbert von Einem, *Beiträge zu Goethes Kunstauffassung*. Hamburg: Schröder, 1956; Barker Fairley, *Goethe as Revealed in His Poetry*. Chicago: Chicago University Press, 1932; Barker Fairley, *A Study of Goethe*. Oxford: Clarendon Press, 1947; Matthijs Jolles, *Goethes Kunstanschauung*. Bern: Francke, 1957; Wolfgang Leppmann, *The German Image of Goethe*. Oxford: Clarendon Press, 1961; Georg Lukács, *Goethe und seine Zeit*. Bern: Francke, 1947; Rudolf Magnus, *Goethe as Scientist*. New York: Henry Schumann, 1949; Roy Pascal, "Goethe und das Tragische. Die Wandlung von Goethes Shakespeare Bild" in *Goethe*. Weimar: 1964, vol. XXV, pp. 38–53; Frederick William Sternfeld, *Goethe and Music*. New York: New York Public Library, 1954; Paul Stöcklein, *Wege zum späten Goethe. Dichtung, Gedanke, Zeichnung*. Hamburg: Schröder, second edition, 1960; Fritz Strich, *Goethe and World Literature*. London: Routledge & Paul, 1949; Hans Joachim Schrimpf, *Das Weltbild des späten Goethe*. Stuttgart: J. B. Metzler, 1956.

Among critical studies dealing with specific works of Goethe, the following will be found useful: Stuart Atkins, *Goethe's "Faust". A Literary Analysis*. Cambridge, Mass.: Harvard University Press, 1958; Stuart Atkins, *The Testament of Werther in Poetry and Drama*. Cambridge, Mass.: Harvard University Press, 1949; James Boyd, *Goethe's "Iphigenie of Tauris": An Interpretation and Critical Analysis*. Oxford: Blackwell, 1942; Wilhelm Emrich, *Die Symbolik von Faust II*. Bonn: Athenäum Verlag, 1957; André François-Poncet, *Les Affinités Électives de Goethe*. Paris: Alcan, 1910; Harold Jantz, *Faust as a Renaissance Man*. Philadelphia: University of Pennsylvania Press, 1951; Ronald Peacock, *Goethe's Major Plays*. Manchester: Manchester University Press, 1959; Wolfdietrich Rasch, *Goethes Torquato Tasso. Die Tragödie des Dichters*. Stuttgart: J. B. Metzler, 1954; Hans Reiss, *Goethes Romane*. Bern: Francke, 1963.

Essays that might have been included in a more comprehensive collection of modern Goethe criticism are:

Auden, Wystan Hugh. "Introduction," *Goethe's Italian Journey*. New York: Random House, Inc., 1963.

Benjamin, Walter. "Goethes Wahlverwandschaften," *Schriften*. Frankfurt: Surkamp Verlag, 1955. Vol. I, pp. 55–140.

Eliot, Thomas Stearns. "Goethe as the Sage," *On Poetry and Poets*. New York: Farrar, Straus & Giroux, Inc., 1947. Pp. 240–64.

Emrich, Wilhelm. "Das Problem der Symbolinterpretation in Hinblick auf Goethes 'Wanderjahre,'" *Euphorion,* XLVII (1952), pp. 331–52.

Fuchs, Albert. "Goethes Spätzeit," *Spätzeiten und Spätzeitlichkeit.* Bern: Francke Verlag, 1962. Pp. 118–32.

Henel, Heinrich. "Type and Proto-Phenomenon in Goethe's Science," *Publications of the Modern Language Association of America,* LXXI (1955), pp. 651–68.

Jaspers, Karl. "Goethes Menschlichkeit." *Rechenschaft und Ausblick.* München: R. Piper Verlag, 1951. Pp. 50–68.

Kayser, Wolfgang. "Goethes Auffassung von der Bedeutung der Kunst," *Kunst und Spiel.* Göttingen: Verlag Vanderhoek und Rupprecht, 1961. Pp. 64–85.

Mann, Thomas. "Goethe's Career as a Man of Letters," *Essays of Three Decades.* New York: Alfred A. Knopf, Inc., 1947. Pp. 43–65.

Mayer, Hans. "Goethes Begriff der Realität," *Von Lessing bis Thomas Mann.* Pfullingen: Neske Verlag, 1959. Pp. 155–79.

Müller, Günther. "Goethes Morphologie in ihrer Bedeutung für die Dichtungskunde," Goethe und die Wissenschaft. Frankfurt: Klostermann, 1953. Pp. 23–24.

Ortega y Gasset, José. "In Search of Goethe from Within," *The Dehumanization of Art.* New York: Doubleday & Company, Inc. (Anchor Books), 1953. Pp. 121–60.

Santayana, George. "Goethe's *Faust," Three Philosophical Poets.* New York: Doubleday & Company, Inc. (Anchor Books), 1953. Pp. 127–78.

Staiger, Emil. "Goethes Lyrik," *Goethes Werke, Gedenkausgabe.* Zürich: Artemis Verlag, 1950. Vol. I, pp. 722–58.

Trunz, Erich. "Goethes Altersstil," *Wirkendes Wort,* V (1954–55), pp. 134–39.

Valéry, Paul. "Discours en l'honneur de Goethe," *Variété IV.* Paris: Librairie Gallimard, 1938. Pp. 93–126.

Wellek, René. "Goethe," *A History of Modern Criticism: 1750–1950.* New Haven, Conn.: Yale University Press, 1955. Vol. I, pp. 201–26.